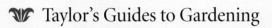 Taylor's Guides to Gardening

Nancy J. Ondra

FRANCES TENENBAUM, Series Editor

Expert Review by MARILYN WELLAN,
Vice President and President-Elect of the American Rose Society

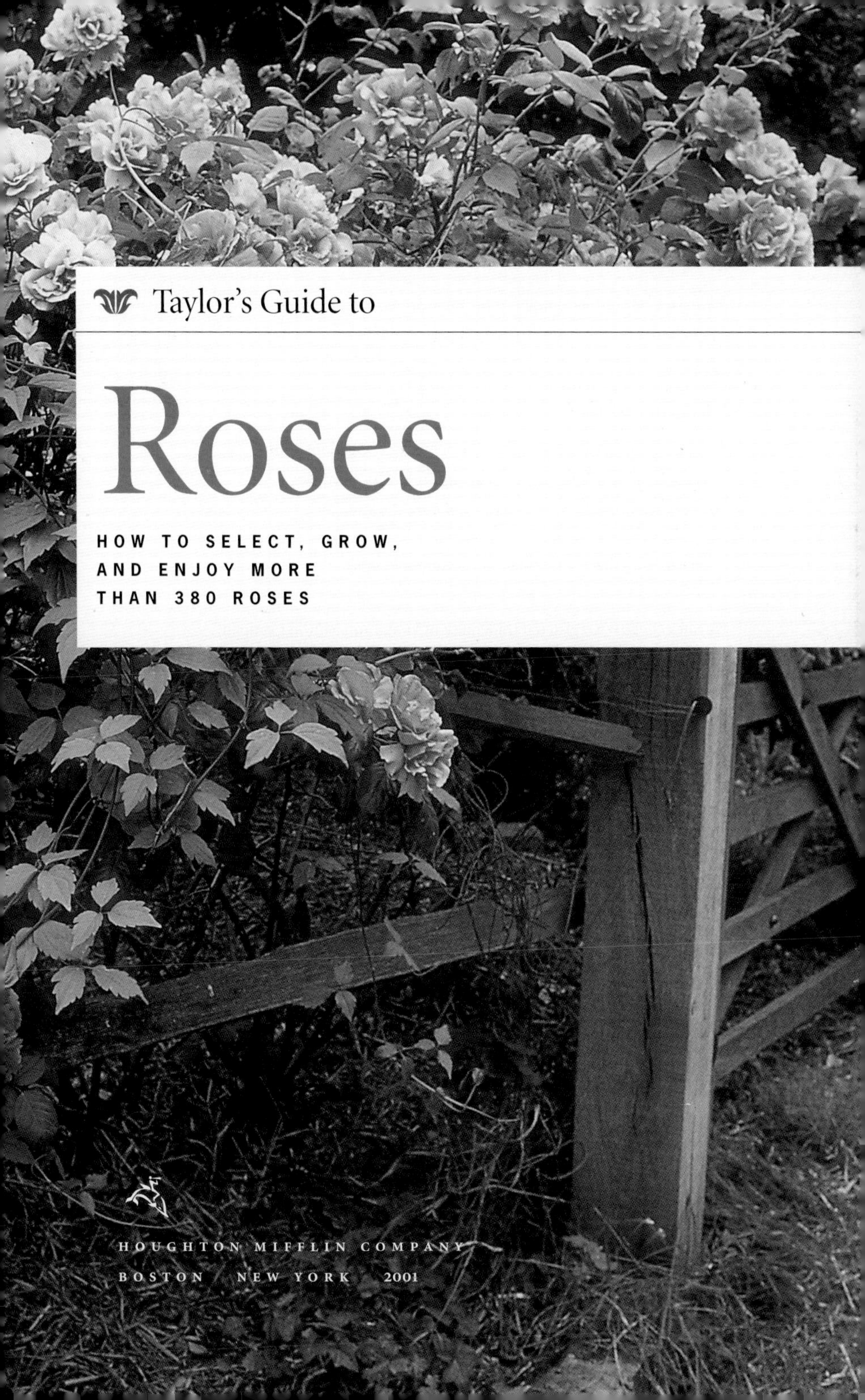

Taylor's Guide to

Roses

HOW TO SELECT, GROW,
AND ENJOY MORE
THAN 380 ROSES

HOUGHTON MIFFLIN COMPANY

BOSTON   NEW YORK   2001

Visit our Web site: www.houghtonmifflinbooks.com.

Taylor's Guide is a registered trademark of Houghton Mifflin Company.

Library of Congress Cataloging-in-Publication Data
Ondra, Nancy J.
   Taylor's guide to roses : how to select, grow and enjoy
more than 380 roses / Nancy J. Ondra.
      p. cm. — (Taylor's guides to gardening)
   ISBN 0-618-06888-0
   1. Roses.   2. Rose culture.   I. Title: Guide to roses.   II. Title. III. Series.
SB311 O53 2001
635.9'33734—dc1   00-068248

Cover photograph by Rich Baer
Book design by Anne Chalmers
Typefaces: Minion, News Gothic

Printed in Singapore
TWP 10 9 8 7 6 5 4 3 2 1

Contents

✿ Introduction

❧ AN INTRODUCTION TO GROWING ROSES

Few plants offer the romance and allure of roses, so it's little wonder that this group has such an appeal for gardeners. For some of us, it's the charm of a lush garden brimming with beautiful flowers and rich fragrance; for others, it's the luxury of a vase filled with just-picked blooms, or the magic of a single perfect rose. There are as many reasons to grow roses as there are gardeners who enjoy them.

Curiously enough, there are also few plant groups that have such an aura of mystery and difficulty about growing them. Over the years, roses have garnered a reputation for being fussy and disease-prone, and it's true that some can be a real challenge to grow to show-quality perfection. But if all you're interested in is growing great garden roses, there are many wonderful selections that can provide months of landscape interest, in the form of flowers, fruits, fall color, and other special features. Best of all, you can enjoy all of these benefits in return for just general good garden care: thorough soil preparation, mulching, fertilizing, watering, and other routine tasks you do to keep your whole landscape looking its best. Yes, pruning is part of it, but it doesn't have to be the mystery many make it out to be. And yes, spraying might be part of it, too, and this book recommends only organic controls. But careful plant selection can help you grow good roses without relying heavily on sprays.

The biggest mistake you can make with roses is not growing them at all. After that, everything else is secondary!

A Bit of Botany

A big part of the fun of growing roses is reading about them in books and catalogs and talking about them with other gardeners. To that end, it's helpful to learn a little of the lingo so that you can understand what you're reading and you're able to follow along in discussions.

Anatomy of a Rose

The labeled illustrations on page 3 point out many of the important structures on a rose shoot and a rose plant, and they give you the terms commonly used for those parts.

Most roses you buy today are grafted (or, more correctly, budded), which means that buds or shoots of a desired rose are attached to the roots of another rose, called the rootstock, so that they grow together to make one plant. The point at which the two parts join is called the bud union. In most cases, it's easy to see this part, because it's usually slightly swollen. If a knobby area is not visible and you know the rose is grafted, you can assume the bud union is at the point where several main stems (canes) join at the base of the plant.

Canes that are attached above or at the bud union, called the top growth, almost always belong to the desired rose. (Occasionally a plant will produce a "sport" — a shoot with traits that differ from the rest of the plant, such as vigor, habit, or flower color.) Canes that emerge from below the bud union are called suckers; they are outgrowths of the rose used as the rootstock. Left to grow, suckers usually crowd out the desired top growth, so you should remove them as soon as you see them. It's best to snap these off where they emerge from the root, rather than just cut them off at ground level; otherwise, the plant is likely to produce another sucker at that point.

Flower Formalities

You'll also run across jargon rose people use to describe the ways the flowers are put together. Some of these terms refer to the number of petals, while others relate to the physical form of the bloom. Here are the terms for petal counts, as currently defined by the American Rose Society.

SINGLE: 4 to 11 petals

SEMIDOUBLE: 12 to 16 petals

DOUBLE: 17 to 25 petals

FULL: 26 to 40 petals

VERY FULL: more than 41 petals

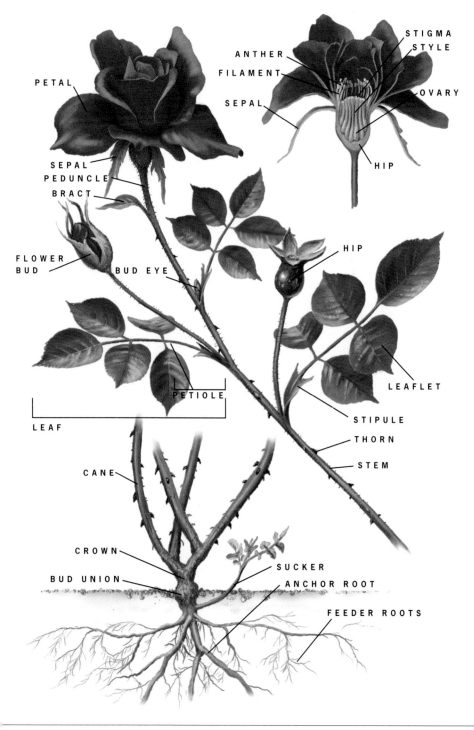

STIGMA
STYLE
ANTHER
FILAMENT
OVARY
SEPAL
HIP

PETAL

SEPAL
PEDUNCLE
BRACT

HIP

FLOWER
BUD
BUD EYE

LEAFLET

PETIOLE

STIPULE

LEAF
THORN
STEM

CANE

CROWN
SUCKER
BUD UNION
ANCHOR ROOT

FEEDER ROOTS

Other sources may use slightly different definitions, such as "very double" as shorthand for "full" or "very full."

Flower form terms generally are self-explanatory, but a few could use some explanation.

CUPPED: The petals have a moderate inward curve, giving the flower a cuplike appearance when viewed from the side.

GLOBULAR: The petals have a strong inward curve, giving the flower a globelike shape when viewed from the side.

HIGH-CENTERED: The inner petals are arranged in a cone that's taller than the outer petals.

POMPON: Many short petals, all of the same length, are arranged to create a domed to rounded appearance when viewed from the side.

REFLEXED: The outer petals curve downward (reflex), giving the flower a ball-like shape when viewed from the side.

ROSETTE: Many short petals are arranged so that they create a flat, low-centered appearance when viewed from the side.

SAUCER-SHAPED: The petals have a slight inward curve, creating a broad, shallow bowl.

A "once-blooming" rose produces all its flowers in one main display, called a flush, each year. This flush usually lasts for several weeks. "Repeat-flowering" roses produce two or more flushes of bloom each year.

The Name of the Rose

Species, or wild, roses generally have two names: a Latin-based scientific (botanical) name with two or more parts — such as *Rosa eglanteria* — and a common name — such as eglantine. When a change occurs naturally in a plant (such as a white-flowering seedling of a normally red-flowered rose), that is called a variety. When a variety results from or is sustained by human intervention, this is correctly called a cultivar (short for *culti*vated *vari*ety). A cultivar may be the result of hybridization (when the pollen from one plant is placed on the female reproductive parts of another plant to produce seedlings with genes from both parents), or it may be the result of people actively reproducing a variety by rooting cuttings (sections of stem growth of the desired plant).

Cultivars usually have at least one "fancy" name, such as 'Rainbow's End' or 'Knock Out', which is chosen by the breeder or by the company that sells it. (This name is written within single quotation marks.) When a rose is sold in more than one country, it may have more than one fancy name. If the rose is registered with the International Registration Authority for Roses (a function of the American Rose Society), it may also receive a "code name." This code name begins with three capital letters that denote the hybridizer or introducer, followed by additional lowercase letters, as in TANorstar. This code name stays the same regardless of where the rose is sold.

All that being said, you'll see names listed in a number of different ways in books, magazines, and catalogs. In this book, the rose names are primarily treated as they are listed in *Modern Roses XI*, a checklist of over 24,000 roses that is published by the American Rose Society.

In addition to the three types of names just discussed — the scientific (botanical) name; the "fancy" name; and the commercial code name — some roses, especially older varieties, also have common names, which can be thought of as nicknames they have acquired over the years. In this book, you will see all four types of names, though most roses are known by just a few types of names, or just one name. All of the possible names a rose goes by are given to help readers find and recognize specific roses in catalogs and other reference books. Each entry name is the registered or most commonly recognized name for that rose. Then, synonyms (abbreviated "syn." or "syns."), or alternate names for that rose, are given. They are listed in a specific order: fancy names; scientific names; common names; and code names. Thus, an entry for a rose with fancy, species, and common names looks like this:

'Alba Maxima'

Syns. 'Great Double White', 'Maxima'; *Rosa alba maxima;* Jacobite Rose

An entry for a rose with two alternate fancy names and a code name looks like this:

'Alba Meidiland'

Syns. 'Alba Meilandécor', 'Meidiland Alba'; MEIflopan

Roses by Class

With many thousands of roses available, it's convenient to group them in various ways. One way is to divide them by their date of introduction.

SPECIES ROSES: These roses have been growing in the wild for hundreds or thousands of years.

OLD GARDEN ROSES: These roses were introduced before 1867, the year when the hybrid tea rose 'La France' was introduced.

MODERN ROSES: These roses were introduced in 1867 or afterward.

Within these three divisions, roses are subdivided by their physical characteristics, such as their growth habits, foliage traits, and flower forms. The main subdivisions of old garden roses include the following.

ALBA: Their flowers are generally white or pale pink against gray-green leaves; once-flowering.

BOURBON: The first repeat-flowering roses, they originated on the Indian Ocean island called the Isle of Bourbon, now known as Reunion Island. They are very fragrant.

CENTIFOLIA: Also referred to as "cabbage roses," these full flowers often have more than 100 petals; once-blooming.

DAMASK: Intensely fragrant flowers that are usually white, pink, or red; some bloom once while others repeat.

HYBRID CHINA: These open plants are rather tender, needing winter protection north of Zone 7. They are usually repeat-flowering.

HYBRID GALLICA: These flowers are usually pink, red, or purple and have intense fragrance. The plants generally have few thorns and are once-flowering.

HYBRID PERPETUAL: These repeat-flowering roses have fragrant flowers that are usually pink or red (sometimes white).

MOSS: Centifolia roses that produce a slightly sticky green or brown mosslike growth on their flower stems and buds; fragrant and mostly once-blooming.

NOISETTE: Large, rather sprawling plants with clustered, fragrant flowers; somewhat cold-tender.

PORTLAND: Very fragrant, usually pink blooms; sometimes called damask perpetuals; repeat-flowering.

TEA: The flowers are in the light yellow, pink, or white range and are borne on canes that have few thorns; are best in Zone 7 and south; repeat-flowering.

The class known as Modern Roses is also divided into a number of subdivisions. Here are some of the main ones (most of which are repeat-flowering).

HYBRID TEA: High-centered, long-stemmed flowers, generally one per stem, bloom on rather upright, narrow plants, usually in flushes every six weeks or so. This is the classic rose used for cut flowers.

FLORIBUNDA: High-centered flowers are produced in clusters, usually with nearly continuous bloom. These plants tend to be hardier than hybrid teas.

GRANDIFLORA: These plants have high-centered flowers held singly or in clusters on rather tall plants; otherwise they are very similar to hybrid teas.

POLYANTHA: Small blooms appear in large clusters on relatively compact, free-flowering plants.

SHRUB: This large group actually contains several classes, including the hybrid kordesii, hybrid moyesii, hybrid musk, hybrid rugosa, and shrub classes. These plants vary widely in height and habit. This also includes the popular group known as English or Austin roses, which were hybridized in England by the rose breeder David Austin.

MINIATURE AND MINI-FLORA: Scaled-down versions of larger modern roses, these plants can range in size from 6 inches to 6 feet tall, though they normally are in the 1- to 2-foot range. Their leaves and flowers are proportionately diminutive. Mini-floras have flowers and leaves that are in between those of miniatures and floribundas in size.

CLIMBERS: This is a mixed group of roses with long, arching canes that need some kind of support. This group includes the climbing hybrid tea, climbing floribunda, climbing grandiflora, hybrid wichurana, large-flowered climber, and climbing miniature classes.

❦ CHOOSING THE RIGHT ROSE

With thousands of roses to choose from, how on earth do you decide which ones to grow? It's easy to be enticed by glossy catalog pictures or by already-flowering plants at your local nursery, and even the most experienced rose growers are occasionally tempted into impulse purchases. But if you want to get the best results for your time and money, it's worth doing some research to discover which roses will best meet your needs and conditions.

It's helpful to start with a list of what you're looking for in a rose. Here are some points to consider.

- What do you want the rose for — a bed or border, a container, an arbor, a hedge, or some other use? Do you plan to cut the flowers for arrangements?
- How much space do you have? If your garden is fairly small, look for compact roses that are in scale with your other plants. Large properties, obviously, can support larger roses.

If you want multiseason interest, look for roses that have attractive leaves or showy fruits as well as beautiful flowers. Red-leaved rose (R. glauca), for instance, offers pink flowers in spring, orange-red hips in fall, and purple-flushed foliage all through the growing season.

- What colors do you like best? Are you looking for bright reds, oranges, golds, or stripes, or do you prefer more pastel shades?

- Is fragrance important to you?

- How much maintenance are you willing to do? Hybrid tea roses, for instance, can require careful attention to disease control and pruning, while many shrub roses can perform respectably with minimal care.

- What growing conditions do you have to offer? Keep in mind the hardiness zone you live in (refer to the USDA Plant Hardiness Zone Map on page 460 if you're not sure).

Do Your Homework

Once you have your wish list, it's time to do some research. Books are a great place to start, but you can't beat getting firsthand advice from gardeners who are already growing roses in your area. They can tell you which roses perform best in your local conditions, and they'll be happy to share invaluable growing tips to get the best out of the roses you choose. If you can't find anyone in your area to talk to, contact the American Rose Society (P.O. Box 30,000, Shreveport, LA 71130; 318-938-5402; www.ars.org) to see if there is a rose group to join in your area. The ARS also has a Consulting Rosarian program, which lists experienced ARS members who are willing to answer rose-related questions. These volunteers are a great source of information on all aspects of rose growing. There are many sources of rose-growing information on the Web, too, including forums where novice and experienced rose growers can post and answer questions. Two super on-line resources are the rose-related forums at Garden-Web (http://forums.gardenweb.com/forums) and the roses site at Help-MeFind (www.helpmefind.com/roses).

Seeing roses in person is another way to identify those that would best suit your needs, especially if you're looking for a specific color or fragrance. Rose displays in public gardens are usually labeled, so you can see the names of those that appeal to you. Look for tours of local private gardens, too; they're a great opportunity to see roses used in a home landscape.

You'll often see lists of "best" roses for particular uses, such as the best climbing roses, or the most fragrant roses. These can be helpful as a starting point for your wish list, but don't let them limit you, and don't assume that a rose that's rated highly by one person or group will perform well in your particular conditions.

GRAFTED VERSUS OWN-ROOT ROSES

Once you've decided on the roses you want, you may have a choice of buying grafted or "own-root" plants. Each has advantages and disadvantages.

Grafted plants are top growth of a desired rose attached to the roots of another rose (called the rootstock). This propagation technique enables producers to quickly create a garden-ready plant, and it allows the choice of different rootstocks to suit particular growing conditions. Three of the most commonly used rootstocks in the United States are

- 'Dr. Huey': Tolerates average to dry, alkaline soil.

- 'Fortuniana': Well adapted to hot climates and tolerates nematodes (soil-borne pests); needs regular and generous fertilization and may take an extra year or two to settle in and produce good top growth.

- *Rosa multiflora:* Well adapted to cold climates; tolerates acidic soil and nematodes.

The same top growth grafted onto different rootstocks can perform differently; that's why two roses of the same name purchased from different sources may not grow equally well in your garden. In most cases, you won't know which rootstock a plant is grafted to, but if you want the best results, look for suppliers who can tell you which rootstock they use and whether it is suitable for your area. (Even better, buy from suppliers who use virus-free rootstock to minimize the chance of your rose developing this incurable disease.)

In recent years, a growing number of nurseries have begun offering "own-root" roses: roses propagated by cuttings and allowed to form their

'Dr. Huey' is used as a rootstock for grafted roses in many areas. It often survives long after the original top growth of a grafted rose has died back.

own roots. Reported benefits of this approach include better winter survival, longer life, and minimal chance of rose mosaic virus, a common rose malady. If cold weather kills the top growth of an own-root rose, chances are good that new growth will sprout from the roots, and this new growth will be the same rose you started with. When the top growth of a grafted rose dies back, the new growth will be whatever rose was used as the rootstock; sometimes it's pretty, but it's rarely what you wanted for your garden.

Some rose growers swear by own-root roses, while others feel the benefits of selecting the rootstock make grafted plants a better choice for them. There is no one right answer as to which is best; if you have the room, why not try both and see which works best for you?

ROSE GROWING BASICS

Whole volumes have been written about caring for roses, so it's easy to see that we can cover only the highlights of good rose growing here. For more information, check out the wide variety of books and Internet sites available, and seek out fellow rose appreciators in your area to learn what works best in your particular conditions.

Selecting the Site

Before you grab your checkbook or credit card to order all the roses on your wish list, do a reality check to make sure you have the right conditions to grow them.

Roses need at least 6 hours of sun per day to perform their best. It doesn't have to be six or more continuous hours; in fact, many roses appreciate morning sun, a little midday shade, and then afternoon sun. It is possible to grow roses with less than 6 hours of sun, but you'll need to be willing to experiment with many different roses to see which work for your conditions, and be prepared to keep trying despite some disappointments. It helps to start out with roses that are noted for tolerating some shade, such as alba and hybrid musk roses. Also, look for roses that have a reputation for excellent disease resistance, because roses growing in shade are less vigorous and are more susceptible to disease development.

Well-drained soil is a necessity for virtually all garden roses. Roses grow best with a steady supply of moisture, but they don't like soggy soil. If you want to plant in an area where water stands after a rain, or where

Most roses need full sun for healthy growth and abundant bloom, but hybrid musk roses, such as 'Moonlight', can tolerate a bit of shade.

the soil tends to stay squishy underfoot for more than a few hours, you'll need to lift the soil level by building raised beds.

It's smart to test the soil in any site you've chosen for planting. Your local Cooperative Extension Service can help you get your soil tested and give you recommendations for adjusting the pH (the relative acidity or alkalinity) and the nutrient levels, if necessary. Many gardeners overlook this step, assuming that if other plants on their property are doing well, the soil must be suitable for roses as well. Sometimes that is true. But if there *is* some kind of imbalance, it's much easier to correct the problem *before* you plant, or else choose another site that's better suited for roses. It may also save you months or years of wondering why your roses just aren't performing up to your expectations.

Rose Buying Basics

You've done your research, and you know which roses you want; now it's time to shop! There are two main ways roses are sold: bareroot (plants that aren't actively growing, with only packing material around their roots) and container-grown or potted (actively growing roses).

Bareroot roses are mainly available from late fall through early spring. The stems should be straight and sturdy, with an even, green color, and the roots should be brown and slightly damp. They may look unpromising at planting time, but they usually settle into their new home quickly and catch up to container-grown roses by the end of their first growing season.

Container-grown roses are enticing, because you can mostly see what you're getting, and there's more of an instant result when you plant them. Look for a plant that has at least three sturdy canes — ideally at least ½ inch in diameter — coming from the bud union (the knobby area near the soil line). Look for a metal label on the plant, and check that against any other label on the plant to make sure the names match. Be aware that the containerized roses sold at nurseries are often the same bareroot plants that were available earlier in the season, but these have had their roots trimmed to fit the pot. Even though the top growth looks good, the plant may actually have a poor root system. A few root tips peeking out of the drainage holes on the bottom of the pot are a clue that there are at least some roots.

Some retail outlets sell "boxed" roses, which are essentially bareroot plants with their roots enclosed in a soil-filled cardboard box. These roses can be a good buy early in the season, before they begin active growth, but be careful if you see shoot growth on boxed roses. The roots are growing at the same time as the shoots, and it's easy to damage those tender roots when you take the rose out of the box at planting time. (Do *not* follow the instructions that tell you to leave the box intact when you plant.) Also, like potted roses, boxed roses have had their roots chopped to fit in their container, so they may have rather small root systems to support their top growth.

Buying roses in person gives you the opportunity to inspect the plants you want to buy, and that's a big advantage. On the downside, the selection is quite limited at most retail outlets. Sale prices can be tempting, but keep in mind that bargain plants may not be a good deal in the long run; they may be lower quality, they may not be suitable for your area, and they may not have been properly cared for. If you're a beginner, you're better off buying a few good-quality roses than many inexpensive but possibly unhealthy plants. As you gain more experience growing roses, you'll learn how to spot a true bargain and avoid a cheap, sickly plant.

Purchasing roses from mail-order nurseries tremendously increases your selection, although customer service varies widely. Reputable nurseries can provide lots of helpful advice, they'll ship your roses (usually bareroot but sometimes in pots) at the right planting time for your area, and they'll guarantee the health and proper naming of their roses. Other companies may have customer service representatives that know nothing about roses, and they may send mislabeled or unhealthy plants. Don't assume that the companies with the prettiest catalogs sell the best plants. Before placing any orders, talk to other gardeners or search the Internet for nursery reviews to find out the positive and negative experiences others have had with the nurseries you are considering. (The Plants by Mail FAQ at http://pbmfaq.dvol.com is a great place to start on-line.)

Preparing the Planting Area

Creating a good planting site is one of the most important steps to growing healthy, beautiful roses. Fertile, free-draining but evenly moist soil is the Holy Grail of the rose gardener — a standard of perfection most of us have to work for, since very few of us are lucky enough to start with ideal soil. Fortunately, it's possible to improve just about any soil, if you're willing to invest some time and energy.

First, you need to remove any existing vegetation on your chosen planting site. If grass is growing there, don't just dig or till it into the soil; that's a good way to create a future weed problem! The chopped-up bits of grass are likely to take root and grow again, requiring major weeding around your newly planted roses. It's better to strip off the turf with a spade or sod cutter and use it to fill bare spots in the remaining lawn, or else pile it in an out-of-the-way spot to decompose.

Preparing a good planting site for your roses provides ideal growing conditions for companion plants, too. Some rose lovers choose to grow miniature roses around the base of full-sized bushes; others enjoy pairing their roses with annuals, perennials, and bulbs.

If you're stuck with rocky or hard-to-dig clay soil, it's tempting to dig a small hole that's just large enough to hold the roots of one rose plant. But it's worth putting in a few minutes or hours of work at this stage to prepare a proper hole; your rose will thank you with years of healthy, vigorous growth. For individual rose plants, it's best to dig a hole that's at least 2 feet across and 2 feet deep. But if you have several rose bushes to plant, consider preparing a whole bed for them, instead of individual holes; in the long run, it will be much easier to prepare and maintain. Either way, place the soil you remove in a wheelbarrow or on a tarp and remove any large rocks. Mix in any soil amendments that were indicated by the soil test you had done when you selected the site. This is also a good time to improve your soil's nutrient- and water-holding capacity, as well as its drainage, by mixing in a generous amount of organic matter, such as compost or decomposed farm animal manure. For best results, add about one part organic material for every two to four parts of soil you removed from the planting area. (If you have three buckets of soil, for example, mix them with one of the same-size buckets filled with your chosen organic matter.)

If you plan to buy bareroot roses, you'll most likely be planting during the cold, damp days of late fall (around Thanksgiving in most areas) or in early spring. In that case, consider preparing the planting site earlier in the fall, while the weather is pleasant for working outside; then the actual planting stage will go quickly.

Planting Roses

Once the soil is prepared, it's time to get your roses growing! Here are some tips for getting them off to a good start.

One word of advice here: It's smart to always wear sturdy, gauntlet-type gloves when working around your roses. Most thorn pricks are mild, but in a few cases, they can cause serious injuries. It's worth the little bit of bother to protect your hands from getting hurt.

BAREROOT ROSES: As soon as you receive bareroot roses, remove the packing material, trim off any damaged or broken parts, and set the roots to soak in a tub or bucket of water overnight. The next day, take some of the soil you removed from the planting hole and create a mound at the base of the hole. The height of the mound will depend on where you live and on the individual plant you're working with. In mild-winter areas, you'll want the bud union to be about even with or slightly above the soil surface; in cold-winter areas (roughly north of Zone 6), it should be 2 to 4 inches below the surface. If you're starting with an own-root (nongrafted) plant, set the plant so the crown (the point where the canes emerge from the roots) is just below the soil surface.

To judge the planting depth — how high the mound must be — set the bareroot plant on top of the soil mound in the hole and lay a stick across the hole. Adjust the plant so the bud union or crown is at the right level relative to the soil surface, as indicated by the stick, then add or remove soil from the mound so the rose will be sitting at the right level. Spread the roots as evenly as possible over the mound, fill in around the roots with more soil to hold the plant in place, then add some water to settle the soil around the roots. Add some more soil and then more water, alternating until the hole is full. Use some of the remaining soil to create a mounded ring about a foot or two wide around the plant, to collect rainwater and direct it toward the developing root system. Lastly, mound mulch or more of the remaining soil over the exposed canes, leaving only the tips exposed, to keep them from drying out. Leave this mound on until warmer weather returns in spring, causing the buds to swell, then remove it gradually (over a week or so).

CONTAINER-GROWN ROSES: If you are planting a container-grown rose, you don't need to make a mound of soil. Place the pot in the hole to judge the depth of the plant as you would for a bareroot rose. Add or remove soil as needed so the rose will sit at the right level. Now, remove the potted plant from the hole. If possible, use a sharp knife to carefully cut around and remove the bottom of the pot, then cut several slits up the sides almost to the upper rim. Carefully grasp the entire rootball and pot, slipping your fingers under the base to hold the bottom of the rootball. Place it into the hole, turn the plant if necessary so it looks good to you, then finish cutting the side slits so you can remove the sides of the pot. If you can't cut the pot, tip the container on its side and slide the rootball as carefully as possible out of the pot, then place it in the hole. Add some soil to steady the rootball, then pour in some water to settle the soil around the roots. Continue adding more soil, then more water, until the hole is filled. Use some of the remaining soil to create a mounded ring about a foot or two wide around the plant, to collect rainwater and direct it toward the developing root system. After planting, water every few days, especially during warm weather, to keep the roots from drying out.

Maintaining Your Roses

Rose maintenance can be as simple or as complicated as you want to make it. Of course, the more careful you are to meet their needs, the better they will perform. But be careful not to fuss too much over your roses; overzealous fertilizing or spraying can actually cause more harm than good!

MULCHING: Mulching generously is one of the most important things you can do to encourage healthy rose growth. Mulch insulates the soil, protecting roots from the stress of rapid temperature changes, and it cuts down on evaporation, so roots are more likely to stay evenly moist. There are many options for mulch materials, depending on what is readily available in your area. Some gardeners swear by homemade mulches of chopped leaves or grass clippings, while others prefer the convenience of purchased mulches, such as shredded bark. Gardeners in your area can tell you which mulches are easily available locally, and which work best for roses in your growing conditions. For most mulches, you'll want to apply a 2- to 4-inch-deep layer in spring. Check the depth of the layer every two to three months (or at least once a year), and add more mulch to keep the layer at the proper thickness.

WATERING: There's no doubt about it — roses appreciate a regular supply of water! If Mother Nature doesn't supply at least an inch of rain per week while your roses are actively growing, you'll need to supply supplemental water if you want your roses to thrive. (In hot, dry climates, of course, your roses will need more water, while they can get by with less in cooler, more humid areas.) As a general rule of thumb, that translates into 4 to 5 gallons of water per plant per week. It's better to apply supplemental water in one or two deep soakings per week than to give daily spritzes.

Drip-irrigation systems and soaker hoses are two ways to deliver water right to the soil and minimize water loss to evaporation. This approach also helps to keep the leaves dry, which discourages the development of some diseases. Overhead sprinkling can work fine too, but it's generally best to do this in the morning so the foliage can dry quickly.

FERTILIZING: Producing all those fabulous flowers takes lots of energy, so your roses need a steady supply of nutrients to bloom their best. Wait until newly planted roses have flowered once before fertilizing them, then apply more fertilizer every four to six weeks until late summer. Fertilize established roses in early spring, then again every four to six weeks until late summer.

There's an amazing array of both chemical and organic fertilizers to choose from. At your local garden center, you'll find a variety of granular (dry) and liquid-based fertilizers that are fine for roses. Experiment with one or a few, applying them according to package directions, to see which work best for you, or talk to other rose gardeners in your area to find out which fertilizers they like best. Experienced rose growers can tell you how to find some of their favorite commercial fertilizers (Mills Magic Rose Mix is one that many swear by), and they can give you the recipes for making and using their favorite homemade fertilizers. One such organic growth enhancer is alfalfa tea, basically made by soaking chopped alfalfa or salt-free alfalfa pellets in water to create a nutrient-rich liquid fertilizer.

DEADHEADING: With all this good care, your roses should soon produce many beautiful blooms. Once those flowers start to fade, it's time to consider deadheading — removing the spent flowers to prevent the plant from wasting energy on producing hips, the fruits of the rose plant. Roses that bloom only once a year generally don't need deadheading; in fact, the hips are often quite ornamental. But on repeat-flowering roses, deadheading can greatly increase the production of more flowers in the later bloom cycles.

Removing individual spent blooms in cluster-flowering roses can be time-consuming, so consider waiting until the entire cluster is finished before cutting it off.

You'll often see advice that says to cut off spent flowers just above the uppermost five-leaflet leaf on that stem, which is fine if you have a vigorous, well-branched bush. But if your plant is young or has few stems, it's best to remove as few leaves as possible; if that means cutting just above a three-leaflet leaf, or even just below the flower, that's okay! The important thing to remember is that the shoot that emerges from the bud below that cut won't be any thicker than the cane it arises from. So whenever you can, try to make your cut where the cane is fairly sturdy.

If you're growing roses that produce many clusters of flowers, or many small blooms, it can be a real chore to snip off each one individually. In that case, consider shearing them off with hedge clippers. Your plants will look a little rough, but they'll grow out again, and they'll be better off than if you hadn't deadheaded at all.

Stop deadheading your plants about a month before the first fall frost in your area. You don't want to encourage your roses to produce new growth at this time; tender new shoots are quite prone to cold damage.

WINTERIZING: Mild-climate gardeners don't have much to worry about here, but if you grow roses in cooler climates (Zone 5 and colder), you'll need to take a few extra steps to help your roses survive the winter. The easiest approach, of course, is to grow only roses that are fully hardy in your area. Use published hardiness guidelines as a starting point: if you live in Zone 5, for instance, look for roses that are rated for at least Zone 5 (and ideally for a colder zone). Many factors can affect winter hardiness, though, so a rose that can survive a Zone 5 winter in one area or in one year may not make it in another area or another year. It may take several years of trial and error to find out which roses will overwinter successfully in your particular conditions. If you can, talk to other rose gardeners in your area to find out which roses survive for them with little or no winter protection; benefiting from their experience will save you time and money.

If you do need to winterize, local gardeners can also advise you on the winter-protection techniques that work best in your area. Generally, this involves mounding 6 or more inches of soil or mulch over the base of the plant, to insulate the bud union and the base of the canes from cold. Some gardeners also cover their roses with commercial rose cones, which are sold at many garden centers. Others actually dig up their plants partway and tip them over to the ground, then cover them with soil or mulch. The techniques you'll use depend on which roses you want to grow, and on how much effort you're willing to expend.

🌹 PRUNING ROSES

The whole topic of rose pruning is enough to send normally confident gardeners running the other way. It doesn't have to be intimidating, though; if you follow a few basic steps, your roses should survive just fine. Once you gain experience, you can fine-tune your techniques to encourage optimum growth from your plants.

The Fundamentals of Pruning

You'll do most of your pruning chores while your rose plants are dormant (not actively growing). In mild-winter areas, this can be as early as December and January; in very cold climates, as late as March into April. When the bud eyes (the growth buds along the canes) turn red and start to swell, that's a good sign that it's time to do some pruning.

Start with a sharp, clean pair of hand-held pruning shears with curved bypass-type (scissors-like) blades. Most brands can cut stems up to ½ inch in diameter. For thicker canes, you'll need a pair of long-handled lopping shears, and possibly a fine-toothed pruning saw. Most important, you need a sturdy pair of thorn-proof gloves. If you can find them, gauntlet-style gloves are a great choice; they'll protect your forearms and wrists as well as your hands.

There are two main types of pruning cuts: thinning cuts and heading cuts. A thinning cut removes a stem where it emerges from a main cane or from the base of the plant. You use this type of cut to remove old, spindly, or twiggy growth, and thus open up the center of the plant. A heading cut is a cut made above a bud to encourage bushier, branching growth. It is made about ¼ inch above a bud, at a slight angle sloping away from the bud. Pruning to a bud that points away from the center of the plant will encourage outward growth, which is desirable on most roses. If you want to encourage more upright growth on a sprawling rose, try pruning to an inward-facing bud instead.

Some gardeners recommend sealing pruning cuts — at least those on canes that are ⅛ inch in diameter or larger — with glue or fingernail polish, to prevent pests called cane borers from entering the canes and causing dieback. Whether you do this or not is up to you, but be aware that if cane borers do strike, they can seriously damage a cane before you notice the damage, and you may have to remove a foot or more of that cane to reach a point where the pith (the cane center) is white and undamaged.

Every pruning session starts the same way: cut out any dead, damaged, or diseased growth. If two canes are rubbing against each other, remove one. Beyond that, the pruning you do depends on the type of rose you're working on (see next section). When you are finished pruning dormant plants, pick or trim off any remaining foliage, and clean up any dropped trimmings.

There's another pruning term you'll often hear rose gardeners use in a joking tone: shovel pruning. No, they're not suggesting you whack off canes with a swinging shovel; they're talking about just digging out an unwanted or unhealthy bush — usually to make room for another rose. Unless you have a special reason to try to save a sickly or disappointing plant, consider shovel-pruning that loser and replacing it with a new rose from your wish list.

Pruning Basics by Class

Different types of roses have different pruning needs. Here are some very simplified guidelines that will provide respectable results in most conditions. As you observe how your roses respond and you gain confidence in your pruning skills, you will learn modifications to get the best out of your particular plants.

HYBRID TEAS AND GRANDIFLORAS: On an established plant, your goal is four to six sturdy canes emerging from the bud union or crown. If your plant has more than that, cut out the oldest of the extra canes. Prune the remaining canes back by about half, to a point where the

Don't worry if your climbing roses don't bloom for a few years after planting; they need some time to build up flowering growth. After that, you'll be rewarded with an abundance of bloom year after year.

cane is at least pencil-thick and the pith in the center of the cane is white. In cold-winter areas, you may be left with 6 inches of top growth; in mild areas, you may keep a 2- to 3-foot structure. You are aiming for an open-centered, vase-shaped plant.

FLORIBUNDAS: On these roses, you want to leave more main canes (roughly 6 to 10) on each plant, and you'll prune those canes back by only about a third.

MINIATURES AND MINI-FLORAS: Most of these selections do fine if you just trim all the canes back to 8 to 15 inches in height. Prune tall-growing minis as you would floribundas.

SHRUBS: The members of this diverse group vary in their pruning needs, but most of them benefit from having a few of their oldest stems removed each year, as long as the plant is still producing vigorous new growth from its base. Overall, trim the plant to create a pleasing, natural outline. Prune once-blooming shrubs right after they flower. If you prune them during the dormant season, you'll remove all the flower buds, which form soon after the plant has bloomed.

CLIMBERS: Most climbers need at least two or three years to build up enough top growth to produce flowers; during that time, they need little or no pruning. Established climbers generally do fine with just light pruning: trim the main canes only if they overgrow their space, then cut back the side shoots from these main canes back to 4 to 6 inches. If you have a once-blooming climber, prune right after flowering; prune repeat-flowering roses during the dormant season.

KEEPING ROSES HEALTHY

Roses have a reputation for being susceptible to disease and pest problems, and that reputation is not completely unearned. Some roses are quite prone to these problems, and they need special care—usually in the form of regular spraying with fungicides and pesticides—to stay healthy. Happily, there are others that are much less enticing to pests and diseases, so you can still enjoy growing roses without worrying too much about keeping bugs and fungi at bay.

Pest and Disease Control Basics

Problem prevention starts when you select the roses you want to grow. If you're willing to follow a regular spray program, you have the widest range of roses to choose from; if you'd rather spray seldom or not at all, you need to look for selections that are described as disease-resistant. When you find one, research further to find out *which* diseases it's resistant to: black spot, powdery mildew, and rust are three big ones. Some problems are more common in one area than another, so you need to find out which ones are most likely to occur in your area, and look for the roses that are most resistant to those particular problems. Keep in mind that "resistant" does not mean that the rose won't ever be infected by disease; it's just less likely to be seriously affected than a susceptible rose growing in the same conditions.

It's also helpful to learn which pests are most common in your area so that you can choose your roses with that in mind. If Japanese beetles are a major problem in your garden, for instance, you might want to choose roses with little or no fragrance; these pests seem to prefer highly perfumed blooms. Thrips — tiny pests that cause discolored petals — are mostly a problem on white and light-colored blooms; darker flowers generally show much less damage.

Once your roses are in the ground, careful attention to regular watering, fertilizing, mulching, and pruning will help keep them vigorous, and vigorous plants are much more likely to shrug off pests and diseases. Keeping dropped leaves and flowers picked up, and removing any discolored leaves as soon as you see them, will go a long way to preventing diseases from getting started. Take frequent opportunities to admire your roses, so if a pest or disease problem does crop up, you'll spot it quickly and can take appropriate control measures before it gets out of hand. You need to identify the problem correctly before you can choose the right control, so if you're unsure, take a sample of the damaged growth — enclosed in a plastic bag — to your local nursery, your county's Cooperative Extension Service office, or your rose-growing mentor to get a correct identification and control suggestions.

Common Rose Pests and Diseases

Here's a very brief overview of a few common problems you're likely to encounter.

NAME / DESCRIPTION	DAMAGE	CONTROLS
APHIDS Small green, red, gray, or brown, soft-bodied insects that cluster on buds, shoots, and leaf undersides.	Stunted growth and deformed flowers and shoots.	Squash them with your fingers; knock them off with a strong spray of water; try an insecticidal soap spray.
BEETLES Hard-shelled, oval to oblong insects on leaves, shoots, and flowers.	Small to large holes in leaves or petals; the larvae of some feed on roots, reducing plant vigor.	Handpick and drop into soapy water; use an organic spray.
CATERPILLARS Soft-bodied, wormlike insects in a range of colors and sizes; the larvae of moths and butterflies.	Holes in leaves and buds.	Handpick and drop into soapy water; spray with BT (*Bacillus thuringiensis*).
SPIDER MITES Tiny, red, yellowish, or brown, spiderlike pests on undersides of leaves; small, fine webs may be visible.	Stippled or pale leaves; stunted growth.	Spray with a strong blast of water, or with an insecticidal soap. Make sure to get leaf undersides.
THRIPS Tiny, brown, thin-bodied insects visible on petals or leaves.	Brown streaks in leaves and petals; deformed buds and flowers.	Remove infested flowers and buds; spray new buds with insecticidal soap.
BLACK SPOT Fungal disease common during humid or wet weather.	Brown or black spots with fringed margins; infected leaves turn yellowish around the spot and drop prematurely, weakening growth.	Avoid wetting foliage. Pick off and destroy infected leaves, and clean up dropped leaves. Spray with a fungicide to prevent further infection.
POWDERY MILDEW Fungal disease common when humidity is high with warm days and cool nights.	White or gray patches with a powdery appearance on leaves, shoots, buds, and flowers; premature leaf drop.	Pick off and destroy infected leaves, and clean up dropped leaves. Spray with a fungicide to prevent further infection.
ROSE MOSAIC VIRUS Transmitted when infected buds or rootstocks are used to produce grafted plants.	Yellowish mottling or banding on leaves; stunted growth.	Buy only certified virus-free roses; remove and destroy severely infected plants.
ROSE ROSETTE Virus thought to be spread by mites.	Fast-growing canes with many thorns and deformed, reddish shoots; plant dies within a year or two.	Immediately remove and destroy infected plants.
RUST Fungal disease most common in damp, cool areas of the western U.S.	Reddish orange bumps on leaf undersides, with corresponding yellow spots on upper leaf surface; premature leaf drop.	Pick off and destroy infected leaves, and clean up dropped leaves. Spray with a fungicide to prevent further infection.

Gallery of Roses

▲ *Rosa banksiae*
Species
SIZE: 20 to 30 feet
Single or double flowers 1 inch across
Fragrant
Zones 8 to 10
P. 405

◀ *Rosa eglanteria*
Species
SIZE: 6 to 10 feet as a shrub; 10 to 15 feet with
support
Single flowers 1 to 2 inches across
Moderate fragrance
Zones 4 to 9
P. 406

▲ *Rosa gallica officinalis*
 (inset, *R. g. versicolor*)

Species

SIZE: 3 to 4 feet
Semidouble flowers to 4 inches across
Moderate fragrance
Zones 3 to 10
P. 406

▼ *Rosa glauca*

Species

SIZE: 6 to 15 feet
Single flowers about 1 inch across
Zones 2 to 8
P. 407

◄ *Rosa hugonis*
Species
SIZE: 4 to 9 feet
Single flowers about 2 inches across
Zones 4 to 8
P. 408

▼ *Rosa roxburghii*
Species
SIZE: 3 to 10 feet
Double flowers 2 to 4 inches across
Variable fragrance
Zones 6 to 9
P. 409

▲ *Rosa rugosa*
  (inset, *R. r. alba*)
Species
SIZE: 4 to 12 feet
Single flowers 3 to 4 inches across
Fragrant
Zones 2 to 9
P. 410

▼ *Rosa sericea pteracantha*
Species
SIZE: 8 to 12 feet
Single flowers about 2 inches across
Bright red thorns on new growth
Zones 5 to 9
P. 410

▲ *Rosa setigera*

Species

SIZE: 5 to 20 feet as a shrub; 15 to 30 feet with support

Single flowers 2 to 3 inches across

Variable fragrance

Zones 4 to 9

P. 411

▼ *Rosa spinosissima*

Species

SIZE: 2 to 6 feet

Single flowers 1 to 2 inches across

Light fragrance

Zones 3 to 8

P. 412

► *Rosa virginiana*

Species

SIZE: 5 to 7 feet
Single flowers 2 inches across
Variable fragrance
Zones 3 to 8
P. 412

▼ *Rosa wichurana*

Species

SIZE: To 6 feet as a shrub; 10 to 20 feet with
support
Single flowers to 2 inches across
Fragrant
Zones 5 to 9
P. 413

▲ 'Alba Maxima'

Alba

SIZE: 6 to 8 feet
Double flowers 3 to 4 inches across
Fragrant
Zones 4 to 8
P. 222

◄ 'Alba Semi-plena'

Alba

SIZE: About 6 feet
Semidouble flowers up to 2 inches across
Fragrant
Zones 4 to 9
P. 223

▲ 'Belle Amour'

Alba

SIZE: 5 to 6 feet
Semidouble flowers 3 to 4 inches across
Fragrant
Zones 5 to 8
P. 238

▼ 'Celestial'

Alba

SIZE: 5 to 6 feet
Double flowers 2 to 3 inches across
Fragrant
Zones 5 to 8
P. 255

▲ 'Félicité Parmentier'

Alba

SIZE: 4 to 5 feet

Very double flowers 2 inches across

Very fragrant

Zones 4 to 8

P. 296

▼ 'Great Maiden's Blush'

Alba

SIZE: 6 to 8 feet

Very double flowers 3 inches across

Fragrant

Zones 3 to 8

P. 316

▶ 'Königin von Dänemark'

Alba

SIZE: 4 to 6 feet
Very double flowers 2½ to 3½ inches across
Zones 4 to 8
P. 340

▼ 'Mme. Legras de St. Germain'

Alba

SIZE: 6 to 8 feet as a shrub; 12 to 15 feet with support
Very double flowers 2 to 4 inches across
Fragrant
Zones 3 to 8
P. 366

▲ 'Boule de Neige'

Bourbon

SIZE: 4 to 5 feet as a shrub; 8 to 10 feet with support
Very double flowers about 3 inches across
Very fragrant
Zones 6 to 10
P. 245

▼ 'Grüss an Teplitz'

Bourbon

SIZE: 5 to 6 feet
Double flowers 3 to 3½ inches across
Fragrant
Zones 5 to 10
P. 318

▲ 'Honorine de Brabant'
Bourbon
SIZE: 6 to 8 feet
Double flowers 2 to 3 inches across
Fragrant
Zones 6 to 9
P. 326

▼ 'La Reine Victoria'
Bourbon
SIZE: 4 to 6 feet
Double flowers 3 to 3½ inches across
Zones 5 to 9
P. 343

▲ 'Louise Odier'

Bourbon

SIZE: 4 to 8 feet
Double flowers 2½ to 3½ inches across
Very fragrant
Zones 5 to 10
P. 352

▼ 'Mme. Ernest Calvat'

Bourbon

SIZE: 5 to 6 feet
Double flowers 3 to 4 inches across
Very fragrant
Zones 5 to 9
P. 364

▲ 'Mme. Isaac Pereire'

Bourbon

SIZE: 6 to 8 feet as a shrub; 8 to 10 feet with
support

Very double flowers 4 to 5 inches across

Very fragrant

Zones 6 to 9

P. 365

▼ 'Mme. Pierre Oger'

Bourbon

SIZE: 4 to 6 feet

Double flowers 2 to 3 inches across

Very fragrant

Zones 6 to 10

P. 366

▲ 'Souvenir de la Malmaison'
Bourbon
SIZE: 2 to 6 feet
Very double flowers 4 to 5 inches across
Very fragrant
Zones 6 to 9
P. 431

◄ 'Variegata di Bologna'
Bourbon
SIZE: 5 to 8 feet as a shrub; 8 to 10 feet with
support
Very double flowers 3 to 4 inches across
Fragrant
Zones 5 to 9
P. 450

▲ 'Zéphirine Drouhin'

Bourbon

SIZE: 8 to 15 feet with support

Semidouble or double flowers 3 to 4 inches across

Fragrant

Zones 6 to 9

P. 458

▼ 'Cabbage Rose'

Centifolia

SIZE: 5 to 7 feet

Very double flowers to 3 inches across

Very fragrant

Zones 4 to 8

P. 248

▲ 'Fantin-Latour'
Centifolia
SIZE: 3 to 8 feet
Very double flowers 3 to 4 inches across
Very fragrant
Zones 5 to 8
P. 294

▼ 'Louis Philippe'
China
SIZE: 2 to 3 feet
Double flowers 3 inches across
Variable fragrance
Zones 7 to 10
P. 352

▲ 'Old Blush'
China
SIZE: 2 to 6 feet
Semidouble flowers about 3 inches across
Light fragrance
Zones 6 to 10
P. 378

▶ 'Autumn Damask'
Damask
SIZE: 3 to 5 feet
Double blooms about 3½ inches across
Very fragrant
Zones 4 to 7
P. 231

▲ 'Celsiana'

Damask

SIZE: 4 to 5 feet
Semidouble flowers about 4 inches across
Very fragrant
Zones 4 to 8
P. 256

▼ 'Ispahan'

Damask

SIZE: 4 to 6 feet
Double flowers 2 to 3 inches across
Very fragrant
Zones 5 to 9
P. 331

▲ 'La Ville de Bruxelles'
Damask
SIZE: 3 to 5 feet
Very double flowers 3 to 5 inches across
Very fragrant
Zones 5 to 9
P. 346

▼ 'Léda'
Damask
SIZE: 3 to 4 feet
Double flowers 3 inches across
Fragrant
Zones 4 to 9
P. 348

◄ 'Marie Louise'
Damask
SIZE: 3 to 6 feet
Very double flowers 4 to 5 inches across
Very fragrant
Zones 4 to 9
P. 355

▼ 'Mme. Hardy'
Damask
SIZE: 4 to 6 feet as a shrub; 7 to 10 feet with support
Very double flowers 2½ to 3½ inches across
Fragrant
Zones 5 to 8
P. 364

▲ 'Mme. Zöetmans'
Damask
SIZE: About 4 feet
Very double flowers 3 inches across
Very fragrant
Zones 5 to 9
P. 367

▼ 'Mme. Plantier'
Hybrid alba
SIZE: 4 to 8 feet as a shrub; 10 to 20 feet with
support
Very double flowers 2 to 4 inches across
Very fragrant
Zones 4 to 8
P. 367

▲ 'Mermaid'
Hybrid bracteata
SIZE: 6 to 30 feet
Single flowers to 6 inches across
Fragrant
Zones 7 to 10
P. 358

▼ 'Archduke Charles'
Hybrid China
SIZE: 3 to 5 feet
Double blooms 3 inches across
Fragrant
Zones 7 to 10
P. 230

▲ 'Cramoisi Supérieur'
Hybrid China
SIZE: 3 to 6 feet
Double flowers 2 to 3 inches across
Variable fragrance
Zones 7 to 10
P. 270

▶ 'Hermosa'
Hybrid China
SIZE: 2 to 4 feet
Double flowers 2 to 3 inches across
Variable fragrance
Zones 6 to 10
P. 325

▲ 'Mutabilis'
Hybrid China
SIZE: 3 to 5 feet
Single flowers 2 to 3 inches across
Zones 7 to 10
P. 372

◄ 'Harison's Yellow'
Hybrid foetida
SIZE: 4 to 10 feet
Semidouble flowers 2 to 2½ inches across
Fragrant
Zones 3 to 9
P. 322

▲ 'Alain Blanchard'
Hybrid gallica
SIZE: About 4 feet
Semidouble flowers about 3 inches across
Fragrant
Zones 5 to 9
P. 221

▼ 'Alika'
Hybrid gallica
SIZE: 6 to 8 feet
Single or semidouble flowers to 4 inches across
Moderate fragrance
Zones 4 to 8
P. 224

▲ 'Belle de Crécy'
Hybrid gallica
SIZE: 3 to 5 feet
Very double flowers 3 inches across
Very fragrant
Zones 4 to 8
P. 238

▲ 'Camaieux'
Hybrid gallica
SIZE: 3 to 4 feet
Double flowers about 3 inches across
Fragrant
Zones 4 to 8
P. 249

◄ 'Cardinal de Richelieu'
Hybrid gallica
SIZE: 3 to 6 feet
Double flowers about 3 inches across
Very fragrant
Zones 4 to 8
P. 252

▲ 'Charles de Mills'
Hybrid gallica
SIZE: 3 to 6 feet
Very double flowers to 5 inches across
Fragrant
Zones 4 to 8
P. 258

▼ 'Complicata'
Hybrid gallica
SIZE: 5 to 8 feet as a shrub; to 10 feet with support
Single flowers to 5 inches across
Variable fragrance
Zones 5 to 8
P. 267

▲ 'Hippolyte'

Hybrid gallica

SIZE: 4 to 6 feet

Double flowers 3 inches across

Fragrant

Zones 4 to 9

P. 326

▼ 'La Belle Sultane'

Hybrid gallica

SIZE: 4 to 6 feet

Semidouble flowers $3\frac{1}{2}$ to 5 inches across

Variable fragrance

Zones 4 to 8

P. 341

▲ 'Tuscany'

Hybrid gallica

SIZE: 3 to 5 feet
Semidouble flowers about 3½ inches across
Fragrant
Zones 4 to 8
P. 448

▶ 'Chevy Chase'

Hybrid multiflora

SIZE: 12 to 15 feet with support
Double flowers about 1½ inches across
Zones 5 to 9
P. 260

▲ 'Russelliana'
Hybrid multiflora
SIZE: 6 to 12 feet as a shrub; 10 to 20 feet with support
Very double flowers about 3 inches across
Fragrant
Zones 5 to 9
P. 416

▼ 'Tausendschön'
Hybrid multiflora
SIZE: 8 to 12 feet with support
Double flowers about 3 inches across
Zones 4 to 9
P. 440

▲ 'Veilchenblau'

Hybrid multiflora

SIZE: 10 to 20 feet with support
Semidouble flowers 1 to 2 inches across
Fragrant
Zones 5 to 9
P. 451

▼ 'Baronne Prévost'

Hybrid perpetual

SIZE: 4 to 5 feet
Very double flowers about 4 inches across
Very fragrant
Zones 5 to 8
P. 235

▲ 'Enfant de France'
Hybrid perpetual

SIZE: 4 to 5 feet
Very double flowers about 5 inches across
Very fragrant
Zones 5 to 9
P. 287

▼ 'Frau Karl Druschki'
Hybrid perpetual

SIZE: 4 to 6 feet as a shrub; 8 to 10 feet as a climber
Very double flowers 3 to 5 inches across
Zones 5 to 9
P. 304

▲ 'Marchesa Boccella'
Hybrid perpetual
SIZE: 3 to 6 feet
Very double flowers 3 to 4 inches across
Very fragrant
Zones 5 to 9
P. 354

▼ 'Paul Neyron'
Hybrid perpetual
SIZE: 4 to 6 feet
Very double flowers 5 to 6 inches across
Variable fragrance
Zones 5 to 8
P. 384

▲ 'Reine des Violettes'

Hybrid perpetual

SIZE: 5 to 8 feet as a shrub; 8 to 12 feet with support

Very double flowers 3 to 5 inches across

Very fragrant

Zones 5 to 9

P. 401

▼ 'Frühlingsgold'

Hybrid spinosissima

SIZE: 6 to 8 feet

Single flowers 3 to 4 inches across

Fragrant

Zones 4 to 9

P. 306

▶ 'Frühlingsmorgen'

Hybrid spinosissima

SIZE: 5 to 7 feet
Single flowers 3 to 4 inches across
Moderate fragrance
Zones 5 to 9
P. 307

▼ 'Stanwell Perpetual'

Hybrid spinosissima

SIZE: 3 to 8 feet
Double flowers 3 to 4 inches across
Fragrant
Zones 4 to 8
P. 433

◄ 'Empress Josephine'

Miscellaneous old garden rose

SIZE: 4 to 5 feet
Double flowers 3 to 4 inches across
Light fragrance
Zones 3 to 9
P. 287

◄ 'Crested Moss'

Moss

SIZE: 3 to 6 feet
Double flowers 2 to 3 inches across
Fragrant
Zones 5 to 9
P. 271

▸ 'Henri Martin'

Moss

SIZE: 5 to 6 feet
Double flowers 3 inches across
Very fragrant
Zones 4 to 9
P. 323

▾ 'Salet'

Moss

SIZE: 4 to 5 feet
Very double flowers 2½ to 3½ inches across
Very fragrant
Zones 5 to 8
P. 417

▲ 'William Lobb'

Moss

SIZE: 6 to 8 feet as a shrub; 8 to 12 feet with support
Double flowers 3 to 4 inches across
Fragrant
Zones 4 to 9
P. 454

◄ 'Aimée Vibert'

Noisette

SIZE: 4 to 5 feet
Double flowers about 2 inches across
Fragrant
Zones 8 to 10
P. 221

▲ 'Alister Stella Gray'

Noisette

SIZE: 5 to 7 feet as a shrub; to 15 feet with
support
Semidouble flowers to 3 inches across
Fragrant
Zones 7 to 10
P. 225

▶ 'Blush Noisette'

Noisette

SIZE: 4 to 5 feet as a shrub; 8 to 12 feet with
support
Double flowers up to 2½ inches across
Very fragrant
Zones 7 to 10
P. 244

▲ 'Céline Forestier'

Noisette

SIZE: 8 to 20 feet with support
Double flowers about 5 inches across
Fragrant
Zones 7 to 10
P. 256

▼ 'Champneys' Pink Cluster'

Noisette

SIZE: 6 to 8 feet
Double flowers to 2 inches across
Fragrant
Zones 7 to 10
P. 258

▲ 'Lamarque'

Noisette

SIZE: 10 to 30 feet with support

Double flowers 3 to 4 inches across

Fragrant

Zones 7 to 10

P. 343

▼ 'Mme. Alfred Carrière'

Noisette

SIZE: 6 to 10 feet as a shrub; 10 to 20 feet with support

Double flowers about 4 inches across

Very fragrant

Zones 6 to 10

P. 363

▲ 'Nastarana'

Noisette

SIZE: 3 to 8 feet as a shrub; 10 to 15 feet with support

Single or semidouble flowers about 2 inches across

Fragrant

Zones 6 to 9

P. 373

▼ 'Rêve d'Or'

Noisette

SIZE: 8 to 10 feet as a shrub; 10 to 18 feet with support

Semidouble to double flowers 3 to 4 inches across

Fragrant

Zones 7 to 10

P. 402

▲ 'Comte de Chambord'
Portland
SIZE: 3 to 5 feet
Double flowers 3 to 4 inches across
Very fragrant
Zones 5 to 9
P. 267

▼ 'Rose de Rescht'
Portland
SIZE: 3 to 4 feet
Very double flowers 2 to 3 inches across
Very fragrant
Zones 5 to 8
P. 414

◄ 'Rose du Roi'
Portland
SIZE: 3 to 4 feet
Double flowers 3 to 4 inches across
Very fragrant
Zones 6 to 9
P. 414

◄ 'Yolande d'Aragon'
Portland
SIZE: 4 to 6 feet
Very double flowers about 3½ inches across
Very fragrant
Zones 5 to 9
P. 457

▲ 'Duchesse de Brabant'

Tea

SIZE: 3 to 5 feet
Very double flowers to 5 inches across
Very fragrant
Zones 7 to 10
P. 282

▼ 'Mons. Tillier'

Tea

SIZE: 3 to 6 feet
Very double flowers 3 inches across
Variable fragrance
Zones 7 to 10
P. 368

▲ 'Mrs. B. R. Cant'

Tea

SIZE: 3 to 8 feet
Very double flowers about 4 inches across
Variable fragrance
Zones 7 to 10
P. 370

▼ 'Mrs. Dudley Cross'

Tea

SIZE: 4 to 8 feet
Very double flowers 3 to 4 inches across
Light to moderate fragrance
Zones 7 to 10
P. 370

▲ 'Abbaye de Cluny'
Hybrid tea
SIZE: 3 to 4 feet
Double flowers 3 to 5 inches across
Fragrant
Zones 5 to 9
P. 219

▼ 'Alpine Sunset'
Hybrid tea
SIZE: 2 to 4 feet
Double flowers to 6 inches across
Fragrant
Zones 5 to 9
P. 226

◄ 'Baronne Edmond de Rothschild'

Hybrid tea

SIZE: 3 to 4 feet
Double flowers 4 to 5 inches across
Fragrant
Zones 5 to 9
P. 235

▼ 'Chicago Peace'

Hybrid tea
SIZE: 4½ to 6 feet
Double flowers 5 to 6 inches across
Zones 5 to 9
P. 261

▶ 'Chrysler Imperial'

Hybrid tea

SIZE: 3 to 6 feet
Double flowers to 5 inches across
Very fragrant
Zones 6 to 9
P. 263

▼ 'Crystalline'

Hybrid tea

SIZE: 4 to 5 feet
Double flowers to 5 inches across
Fragrant
Zones 5 to 10
P. 272

▲ 'Dainty Bess'

Hybrid tea

SIZE: 3 to 8 feet
Single flowers 4 to 5 inches across
Light scent
Zones 5 to 9
P. 272

▼ 'Dolly Parton'

Hybrid tea

SIZE: 3½ to 5 feet
Double flowers 5 to 6 inches across
Very fragrant
Zones 5 to 9
P. 276

▲ 'Double Delight'
Hybrid tea
SIZE: 3 to 5 feet
Double flowers about 5 inches across
Fragrant
Zones 6 to 10
P. 279

▼ 'Dublin'
Hybrid tea
SIZE: 4 to 5 feet
Double flowers about 4½ inches across
Fragrant
Zones 6 to 10
P. 281

◄ 'Duet'

Hybrid tea

SIZE: 3 to 6 feet
Double flowers to 4 inches across
Zones 5 to 10
P. 282

▼ 'Elegant Beauty'

Hybrid tea

SIZE: 3 to 5 feet
Double flowers about 4 inches across
Zones 5 to 9
P. 284

▲ 'Elina'
Hybrid tea
SIZE: 3 to 5 feet
Double flowers to 6 inches across
Zones 5 to 10
P. 285

▼ 'Elizabeth Taylor'
Hybrid tea
SIZE: 4 to 5 feet
Double flowers 4 to 5 inches across
Zones 5 to 9
P. 285

▲ 'Étoile de Hollande'

Hybrid tea

SIZE: 2 to 3 feet
Double flowers about 3 inches across
Very fragrant
Zones 5 to 9
P. 290

▼ 'First Prize'

Hybrid tea

SIZE: 3 to 5 feet
Double flowers 4 to 6 inches across
Zones 6 to 9
P. 298

▲ 'Folklore'
Hybrid tea
SIZE: 6 to 10 feet
Very double flowers 4½ to 5 inches across
Very fragrant
Zones 5 to 9
P. 301

▼ 'Fragrant Cloud'
Hybrid tea
SIZE: 3 to 5 feet
Double flowers to 5 inches across
Very fragrant
Zones 5 to 9
P. 302

▲ 'Gemini'
Hybrid tea
SIZE: 3 to 6 feet
Double flowers to 4½ inches across
Light fragrance
Zones 5 to 9
P. 308

▼ 'Helmut Schmidt'
Hybrid tea
SIZE: 2 to 5 feet
Double flowers 4 to 5 inches across
Light fragrance
Zones 5 to 9
P. 323

▲ 'Ingrid Bergman'
Hybrid tea
SIZE: 2 to 4 feet
Double flowers 4 to 6 inches across
Variable fragrance
Zones 5 to 9
P. 329

▼ 'Just Joey'
Hybrid tea
SIZE: 2 to 5 feet
Double flowers 4 to 6 inches across
Fragrant
Zones 5 to 9
P. 336

▲ 'Kardinal'
Hybrid tea
SIZE: 4 to 5 feet
Double flowers 3 to 4½ inches across
Light fragrance
Zones 5 to 8
P. 337

▼ 'Keepsake'
Hybrid tea
SIZE: 2½ to 6 feet
Double flowers 3 to 4 inches across
Fragrant
Zones 5 to 10
P. 338

▲ 'Marijke Koopman'
Hybrid tea
SIZE: 4 to 6 feet
Double flowers 4 to 5 inches across
Variable fragrance
Zones 5 to 9
P. 357

▼ 'Midas Touch'
Hybrid tea
SIZE: 4 to 5 feet
Double flowers about 4 inches across
Moderate fragrance
Zones 5 to 10
P. 359

▲ 'Mirandy'
Hybrid tea
SIZE: 4 to 5 feet
Double flowers 5 to 6 inches across
Very fragrant
Zones 5 to 9
P. 361

▼ 'Mister Lincoln'
Hybrid tea
SIZE: 4 to 6 feet
Double flowers 4 to 6 inches across
Very fragrant
Zones 5 to 9
P. 362

▲ 'Mrs. Oakley Fisher'

Hybrid tea

SIZE: 3 to 5 feet
Single flowers about 3 inches across
Variable fragrance
Zones 6 to 10
P. 371

▼ 'Olympiad'

Hybrid tea

SIZE: 4 to 6 feet
Double flowers 4 to 5 inches across
Zones 5 to 9
P. 379

▲ 'Pascali'
Hybrid tea
SIZE: 3 to 6 feet
Double flowers 3 to 4 inches across
Light fragrance
Zones 6 to 9
P. 383

◄ 'Peace'
Hybrid tea
SIZE: 4 to 5 feet
Double flowers 5 to 6 inches across
Light fragrance
Zones 5 to 9
P. 385

▲ 'Peter Frankenfeld'

Hybrid tea

SIZE: 4 to 5 feet
Double flowers 4 to 5 inches across
Zones 5 to 9
P. 388

▼ 'Pristine'

Hybrid tea

SIZE: 4 to 7 feet
Double flowers to 6 inches across
Light fragrance
Zones 5 to 9
P. 396

▲ 'Rio Samba'
Hybrid tea
SIZE: 5 to 8 feet
Double flowers 3 to 5 inches across
Zones 5 to 10
P. 402

▼ 'Secret'
Hybrid tea
SIZE: 3 to 5 feet
Double flowers 4 to 6 inches across
Very fragrant
Zones 5 to 9
P. 423

▲ 'Silver Jubilee'
Hybrid tea
SIZE: 3 to 4 feet
Double flowers 3 to 4 inches across
Zones 5 to 9
P. 426

▼ 'Spice Twice'
Hybrid tea
SIZE: 4 to 7 feet
Double flowers 5 to 6 inches across
Light fragrance
Zones 5 to 10
P. 432

▲ 'St. Patrick'

Hybrid tea

SIZE: 3 to 5 feet
Double flowers 4 to 5 inches across
Zones 6 to 10

P. 434

▼ 'Taboo'

Hybrid tea

SIZE: 4 to 6 feet
Double flowers 3 to 4 inches across
Variable fragrance
Zones 5 to 9

P. 438

▲ 'Tiffany'
Hybrid tea
SIZE: 3 to 5 feet
Double flowers 4 to 5 inches across
Fragrant
Zones 4 to 9
P. 444

▼ 'Touch of Class'
Hybrid tea
SIZE: 4 to 6 feet
Double flowers 4 to 5½ inches across
Zones 5 to 10
P. 444

▲ 'Toulouse Lautrec'

Hybrid tea

SIZE: 3 to 6 feet
Very double flowers 3 to 4 inches across
Fragrant
Zones 4 to 9
P. 445

▼ 'Tropicana'

Hybrid tea

SIZE: 4 to 6 feet
Double flowers 4 to 5 inches across
Variable fragrance
Zones 5 to 9
P. 447

▲ 'Veterans' Honor'

Hybrid tea

SIZE: 4 to 5 feet
Double flowers 5 to 6 inches across
Moderate fragrance
Zones 5 to 9
P. 452

▼ 'Voodoo'

Hybrid tea

SIZE: 4 to 6 feet
Double flowers 4 to 6 inches across
Fragrant
Zones 5 to 10
P. 452

▲ 'Yves Piaget'
Hybrid tea
SIZE: 3 to 5 feet
Very double flowers to 6 inches across
Fragrant
Zones 5 to 9
P. 458

▼ 'Angel Face'
Floribunda
SIZE: 2½ to 4 feet
Double flowers 4 inches across
Fragrant
Zones 5 to 9
P. 229

▲ 'Apricot Nectar'
Floribunda
SIZE: 2 to 4 feet
Double blooms 4 to 5 inches across
Fragrant
Zones 5 to 9
P. 230

▼ 'Betty Boop'
Floribunda
SIZE: 3 to 5 feet
Single or semidouble flowers about 4 inches
    across
Variable fragrance
Zones 5 to 10
P. 240

▲ 'Betty Prior'
Floribunda
SIZE: 3 to 4 feet
Single flowers about 3½ inches across
Zones 5 to 9
P. 241

▼ 'Bill Warriner'
Floribunda
SIZE: 2 to 3 feet
Double flowers about 4 inches across
Light fragrance
Zones 5 to 9
P. 241

▲ 'Bridal Pink'
Floribunda
SIZE: 3 to 4 feet
Very double flowers to 4 inches across
Moderate fragrance
Zones 6 to 10
P. 246

▼ 'Class Act'
Floribunda
SIZE: 2 to 4 feet
Semidouble flowers to 4 inches across
Zones 5 to 9
P. 265

▲ 'Dicky'
Floribunda
SIZE: 3 to 4 feet
Double flowers to 3½ inches across
Zones 5 to 10
P. 275

▼ 'English Miss'
Floribunda
SIZE: 2 to 3 feet
Very double flowers 2 to 3 inches across
Very fragrant
Zones 5 to 9
P. 288

▲ 'Escapade'
Floribunda
SIZE: 2½ to 4 feet
Semidouble flowers 3 inches across
Light fragrance
Zones 5 to 9
P. 290

▼ 'Europeana'
Floribunda
SIZE: 2 to 3 feet
Semidouble to double flowers about 3 inches across
Zones 5 to 9
P. 291

◄ 'Eyepaint'
Floribunda
SIZE: 3 to 4 feet
Single flowers 2 to 3 inches across
Zones 5 to 9
P. 292

▼ 'First Edition'
Floribunda
SIZE: 3½ to 5 feet
Double flowers 2 to 3 inches across
Zones 5 to 9
P. 297

▲ 'First Kiss'

Floribunda
SIZE: 2 to 4 feet
Double flowers to 4 inches across
Zones 5 to 9
P. 298

▼ 'Fragrant Delight'

Floribunda
SIZE: 3 to 4 feet
Double flowers 3 inches across
Very fragrant
Zones 5 to 9
P. 303

▲ 'French Lace'

Floribunda

SIZE: 2½ to 4 feet
Double flowers 3 to 4 inches across
Zones 7 to 10
P. 104

▼ 'Gene Boerner'

Floribunda

SIZE: 4 to 5 feet
Double flowers 3 to 3½ inches across
Zones 5 to 9
P. 309

▲ 'Grüss an Aachen'
Floribunda
SIZE: 1½ to 3 feet
Very double flowers 3 inches across
Variable fragrance
Zones 4 to 9
P. 318

▼ 'Guy de Maupassant'
Floribunda
SIZE: 3 to 8 feet
Very double flowers 2½ to 3 inches across
Fragrant
Zones 5 to 9
P. 319

▲ 'Iceberg'
Floribunda
SIZE: 3 to 8 feet
Double flowers 3 inches across
Light fragrance
Zones 4 to 9
P. 328

◄ 'Intrigue'
Floribunda
SIZE: 3 to 4 feet
Double flowers 3½ inches across
Very fragrant
Zones 5 to 9
P. 330

▲ 'Ivory Fashion'

Floribunda

SIZE: 2 to 4 feet

Semidouble to double flowers 3½ to 4½ inches
across

Variable fragrance

Zones 5 to 9

P. 332

▼ 'La Sévillana'

Floribunda

SIZE: 3 to 4 feet

Semidouble flowers 2 to 3 inches across

Zones 6 to 9

P. 344

▲ 'Lavaglut'

Floribunda

SIZE: 3 to 4 feet
Double flowers 2½ inches across
Zones 4 to 9
P. 344

▼ 'Little Darling'

Floribunda

SIZE: 4 to 6 feet
Double flowers 3 inches across
Moderate fragrance
Zones 5 to 10
P. 350

▲ 'Livin' Easy'
Floribunda
SIZE: 3 to 5 feet
Double flowers 3 inches across
Moderate fragrance
Zones 5 to 9
P. 351

▼ 'Margaret Merril'
Floribunda
SIZE: 3 to 5 feet
Double flowers 4 inches across
Fragrant
Zones 5 to 9
P. 355

◄ 'Nearly Wild'
Floribunda
SIZE: 2 to 4 feet
Single flowers about 2 inches across
Light fragrance
Zones 4 to 9
P. 374

◄ 'Nicole'
Floribunda
SIZE: 5 to 7 feet
Double flowers 4 inches across
Zones 5 to 9
P. 376

▸ 'Playboy'
Floribunda

SIZE: 3 to 6 feet
Single flowers about 3½ inches across
Light fragrance
Zones 5 to 9
P. 392

▾ 'Playgirl'
Floribunda

SIZE: 3 to 4 feet
Single flowers 3 inches across
Zones 5 to 9
P. 393

▲ 'Playtime'
Floribunda
SIZE: 2 to 3 feet
Single flowers about 3 inches across
Zones 5 to 9
P. 393

▼ 'Poulsen's Pearl'
Floribunda
SIZE: 2½ to 3½ feet
Single flowers 2½ to 3 inches across
Light fragrance
Zones 5 to 9
P. 394

▲ 'Priscilla Burton'

Floribunda

SIZE: 2 to 6 feet

Semidouble flowers about 3 inches across

Variable fragrance

Zones 5 to 9

P. 395

▼ 'Regensberg'

Floribunda

SIZE: 18 to 30 inches

Semidouble or double flowers about 4½ inches across

Variable fragrance

Zones 5 to 8

P. 401

▲ 'Scentimental'
Floribunda
SIZE: 3 to 6 feet
Double flowers about 4½ inches across
Fragrant
Zones 5 to 9
P. 420

▼ 'Sexy Rexy'
Floribunda
SIZE: 3 to 5 feet
Very double flowers about 3 inches across
Light fragrance
Zones 5 to 9
P. 423

▲ 'Sheila's Perfume'

Floribunda

SIZE: 2 to 4 feet

Semidouble or double flowers about 3½ inches across

Fragrant

Zones 5 to 10

P. 425

▼ 'Showbiz'

Floribunda

SIZE: 2 to 4 feet

Semidouble or double flowers 3 inches across

Zones 5 to 9

P. 425

▲ 'Simplicity'
Floribunda
SIZE: 4 to 6 feet
Semidouble flowers 3 to 4 inches across
Zones 5 to 9
P. 427

▼ 'Singin' in the Rain'
Floribunda
SIZE: 3 to 6 feet
Double flowers 2 to 3 inches across
Moderate fragrance
Zones 5 to 10
P. 428

▲ 'Sun Flare'

Floribunda
SIZE: 2 to 4 feet
Double flowers 4 inches across
Fragrant
Zones 5 to 10
P. 435

▶ 'Sunsprite'

Floribunda
SIZE: 2 to 5 feet
Double flowers about 3 inches across
Very fragrant
Zones 5 to 10
P. 436

▲ 'Trumpeter'
Floribunda
SIZE: 2 to 4 feet
Double flowers 2½ to 3½ inches across
Zones 5 to 10
P. 448

◀ 'Crimson Bouquet'
Grandiflora
SIZE: 3½ to 4½ feet
Double flowers about 4 inches across
Zones 5 to 9
P. 271

▲ 'Earth Song'
Grandiflora
SIZE: 3 to 5 feet
Double flowers up to 4½ inches across
Light fragrance
Zones 4 to 9
P. 284

▶ 'Fame!'
Grandiflora
SIZE: 4 to 6 feet
Double flowers up to 5 inches across
Variable fragrance
Zones 5 to 9
P. 294

▲ 'Gold Medal'

Grandiflora
SIZE: 4 to 6 feet
Double flowers 4 to 5 inches across
Zones 5 to 9
P. 314

▼ 'Pink Parfait'

Grandiflora
SIZE: 3 to 4 feet
Double flowers 3½ to 4 inches across
Light fragrance
Zones 5 to 9
P. 391

▲ 'Queen Elizabeth'
Grandiflora
SIZE: 5 to 8 feet
Double flowers about 4 inches across
Zones 5 to 9
P. 398

▼ 'Tournament of Roses'
Grandiflora
SIZE: 2 to 6 feet
Double flowers about 4 inches across
Zones 5 to 9
P. 446

▲ 'Champlain'
Hybrid kordesii
SIZE: 3 to 4 feet
Double flowers about 3 inches across
Light fragrance
Zones 3 to 9
P. 257

◄ 'Dortmund'
Hybrid kordesii
SIZE: 5 to 8 feet as a shrub; 8 to 30 feet with
support
Single flowers about 3½ inches across
Zones 4 to 9
P. 278

▲ 'Heidelberg'
Hybrid kordesii
SIZE: To 6 feet as a shrub; 6 to 8 feet with support
Doubles flowers 4 inches across
Light fragrance
Zones 5 to 9
P. 322

▶ 'John Cabot'
Hybrid kordesii
SIZE: 4 to 8 feet as a shrub; 6 to 10 feet with support
Double flowers 2 to 3 inches across
Variable fragrance
Zones 3 to 9
P. 334

◄ 'John Davis'

Hybrid kordesii

SIZE: 4 to 7 feet as a shrub; 8 to 10 feet with
support

Double flowers 3 to 4 inches across

Variable fragrance

Zones 3 to 9

P. 335

◄ 'William Baffin'

Hybrid kordesii

SIZE: 5 to 8 feet as a shrub; 8 to 12 feet with
support

Semidouble or double flowers 3 to 4 inches
across

Zones 3 to 9

P. 453

▲ 'Geranium'
Hybrid moyesii
SIZE: 6 to 10 feet
Single flowers 2 inches across
Zones 5 to 8
P. 310

▶ 'Nevada'
Hybrid moyesii
SIZE: 6 to 8 feet
Single or semidouble flowers 3 to 5 inches across
Zones 5 to 9
P. 375

▲ 'Ballerina'

Hybrid musk

SIZE: 4 to 5 feet
Single flowers 1 to 2 inches across
Zones 5 to 10

P. 234

▼ 'Belinda'

Hybrid musk

SIZE: 4 to 6 feet
Semidouble flowers about ¾ inch across
Light fragrance
Zones 6 to 10

P. 236

▲ 'Buff Beauty'
Hybrid musk
SIZE: 5 to 6 feet as a shrub; 8 to 12 feet with
    support
Very double flowers to 4 inches across
Fragrant
Zones 5 to 9
P. 247

▼ 'Cornelia'
Hybrid musk
SIZE: 4 to 6 feet as a shrub; 8 to 12 feet with
    support
Double flowers to 1 inch across
Variable fragrance
Zones 6 to 9
P. 269

◄ 'Erfurt'
Hybrid musk
SIZE: 4 to 5 feet
Semidouble flowers 4 to 5 inches across
Very fragrant
Zones 6 to 9
P. 289

▼ 'Felicia'
Hybrid musk
SIZE: 3 to 8 feet
Double flowers 3 inches across
Fragrant
Zones 6 to 10
P. 295

▲ 'Kathleen'

Hybrid musk

SIZE: 4 to 8 feet as a shrub; 8 to 15 feet with
support

Single flowers 1 to 1½ inches across

Variable fragrance

Zones 6 to 9

P. 338

▼ 'Lavender Lassie'

Hybrid musk

SIZE: 5 to 8 feet as a shrub; 10 to 15 feet with
support

Double flowers 3 inches across

Fragrant

Zones 6 to 9

P. 346

▲ 'Moonlight'
Hybrid musk

SIZE: 4 to 8 feet as a shrub; 10 to 12 feet with support

Single or semidouble flowers 2 inches across

Fragrant

Zones 6 to 9

P. 369

▼ 'Nymphenburg'
Hybrid musk

SIZE: 6 to 8 feet as a shrub; 12 to 18 feet with support

Semidouble flowers about 3 inches across

Fragrant

Zones 6 to 10

P. 378

▲ 'Paul's Himalayan Musk Rambler'

Hybrid musk
SIZE: 20 to 30 feet with support
Double flowers 1½ inches across
Fragrant
Zones 4 to 9
P. 385

▼ 'Penelope'

Hybrid musk
SIZE: 5 to 8 feet
Semidouble flowers 2 to 3 inches across
Fragrant
Zones 6 to 10
P. 387

▲ 'Prosperity'
Hybrid musk
SIZE: 4 to 5 feet as a shrub; 8 to 10 feet
Semidouble to double flowers 2 inches across
Moderate fragrance
Zones 6 to 9
P. 397

◄ 'Robin Hood'
Hybrid musk
SIZE: 4 to 7 feet
Semidouble flowers ½ to 1 inch across
Zones 6 to 10
P. 404

▲ 'Vanity'

Hybrid musk

SIZE: 4 to 8 feet

Single or semidouble flowers 3 to 3½ inches across

Fragrant

Zones 5 to 9

P. 450

▼ 'Will Scarlet'

Hybrid musk

SIZE: 5 to 8 feet as a shrub; 10 to 12 feet with support

Semidouble flowers 2 to 3 inches across

Zones 6 to 9

P. 455

▲ 'Agnes'
Hybrid rugosa
SIZE: 4 to 6 feet
Double flowers to 3 inches across
Fragrant
Zones 4 to 8
P. 220

▼ 'Belle Poitevine'
Hybrid rugosa
SIZE: 3 to 4 feet
Semidouble flowers to 4 inches across
Fragrant
Zones 4 to 8
P. 239

▲ 'Blanc Double de Coubert'
Hybrid rugosa
SIZE: 4 to 6 feet
Double flowers up to 3 inches across
Very fragrant
Zones 3 to 8
P. 243

▼ 'Buffalo Gal'
Hybrid rugosa
SIZE: 3 to 4 feet
Semidouble flowers 3 to 4 inches across
Fragrant
Zones 3 to 8
P. 247

▲ 'David Thompson'
Hybrid rugosa
SIZE: 3 to 5 feet
Semidouble or double flowers 2½ inches across
Fragrant
Zones 3 to 9
P. 274

▼ 'Delicata'
Hybrid rugosa
SIZE: 3 to 4 feet
Semidouble flowers to 3½ inches across
Variable fragrance
Zones 3 to 9
P. 274

▲ 'Fimbriata'

Hybrid rugosa

SIZE: 4 to 5 feet
Semidouble flowers about 3 inches across
Very fragrant
Zones 4 to 8
P. 297

▼ 'Frau Dagmar Hartopp'

Hybrid rugosa

SIZE: 3 to 5 feet
Single flowers 3 to 4 inches across
Moderate fragrance
Zones 3 to 8
P. 303

◀ 'Hansa'
Hybrid rugosa
SIZE: 4 to 10 feet
Double flowers 3 to 4 inches across
Very fragrant
Zones 3 to 8
P. 320

▼ 'Henry Hudson'
Hybrid rugosa
SIZE: 2 to 3 feet
Double flowers 2½ to 3 inches across
Fragrant
Zones 2 to 8
P. 324

▲ 'Jens Munk'
Hybrid rugosa
SIZE: 4 to 6 feet
Semidouble flowers 3 inches across
Variable fragrance
Zones 2 to 8
P. 333

▼ 'Linda Campbell'
Hybrid rugosa
SIZE: 3 to 6 feet as a shrub; 8 to 10 feet with
support
Double flowers 3 inches across
Zones 4 to 9
P. 349

▲ 'Max Graf'

Hybrid rugosa

SIZE: 1 to 2 feet
Single flowers 2 to 3 inches across
Moderate fragrance
Zones 3 to 8
P. 358

◄ 'Roseraie de l'Hay'

Hybrid rugosa

SIZE: 5 to 8 feet
Double flowers 3 to 4 inches across
Very fragrant
Zones 3 to 8
P. 415

▶ 'Rugosa Magnifica'
Hybrid rugosa
SIZE: 4 to 5 feet
Double flowers 3 to 4 inches across
Fragrant
Zones 4 to 8
P. 416

▼ 'Sarah Van Fleet'
Hybrid rugosa
SIZE: 5 to 8 feet
Semidouble or double flowers 3½ inches across
Very fragrant
Zones 5 to 9
P. 418

▲ 'Scabrosa'
Hybrid rugosa
SIZE: 3 to 7 feet
Single flowers about 5 inches across
Variable fragrance
Zones 3 to 8
P. 419

▼ 'Schneekoppe'
Hybrid rugosa
SIZE: 3 to 4 feet
Semidouble flowers 3½ inches across
Fragrant
Zones 3 to 8
P. 421

▲ 'Sir Thomas Lipton'
Hybrid rugosa
SIZE: 4 to 8 feet
Semidouble or double flowers about 3½ inches across
Very fragrant
Zones 4 to 8
P. 428

▼ 'Thérèse Bugnet'
Hybrid rugosa
SIZE: 5 to 7 feet
Double flowers about 4 inches across
Fragrant
Zones 2 to 8
P. 443

▲ 'Cécile Brünner'
Polyantha
SIZE: About 3 feet
Double flowers up to 2 inches across
Light fragrance
Zones 5 to 10
P. 255

▼ 'China Doll'
Polyantha
SIZE: 1 to 2 feet
Double flowers about 2 inches across
Zones 5 to 10
P. 262

▲ 'La Marne'
Polyantha
SIZE: 3 to 6 feet
Single or semidouble flowers 2 inches across
Zones 6 to 9
P. 342

▼ 'Marie Pavié'
Polyantha
SIZE: 2 to 4 feet
Semidouble or double flowers 2 inches across
Fragrant
Zones 5 to 9
P. 356

▲ 'Mrs. R. M. Finch'
Polyantha
SIZE: 2 to 4 feet
Semidouble or double flowers about 2 inches
   across
Light fragrance
Zones 6 to 9
P. 372

▼ 'Orange Mothersday'
Polyantha
SIZE: 2 to 4 feet
Double flowers 1½ inches across
Zones 5 to 9
P. 380

▲ 'Perle d'Or'
Polyantha
SIZE: 3 to 8 feet
Double flowers 1 to 1½ inches across
Fragrant
Zones 6 to 10
P. 387

▶ 'The Fairy'
Polyantha
SIZE: 2 to 3 feet
Double flowers 1 to 1½ inches across
Zones 4 to 9
P. 441

▲ 'White Pet'

Polyantha
SIZE: 1 to 3 feet
Double flowers 1 inch across
Fragrant
Zones 5 to 9
P. 453

▼ 'Abraham Darby'

Shrub
SIZE: About 5 feet as a shrub; 8 to 10 feet with
   support
Double flowers to 6 inches across
Fragrant
Zones 5 to 10
P. 220

▲ 'Alba Meidiland'
Shrub
SIZE: 2 to 3 feet
Double flowers about 2 inches across
Zones 4 to 9
P. 222

▼ 'Alchymist'
Shrub
SIZE: About 6 feet as a shrub; to about 8 feet
with support
Very double flowers up to 4 inches across
Fragrant
Zones 5 to 9
P. 234

▲ 'Ambridge Rose'
Shrub
SIZE: 2½ to 3½ feet
Very double flowers about 3 inches across
Fragrant
Zones 5 to 10
P. 227

▼ 'Applejack'
Shrub
SIZE: 6 to 8 feet
Single or semidouble flowers 3 inches across
Fragrant
Zones 4 to 9
P. 229

▲ 'Autumn Sunset'

Shrub

SIZE: 6 to 8 feet as a shrub; 8 to 12 feet with support

Semidouble or double flowers about 3 inches across

Fragrant

Zones 5 to 9

P. 232

▼ 'Baby Blanket'

Shrub

SIZE: 2 to 3 feet

Double flowers up to 2½ inches across

Zones 5 to 9

P. 233

▲ 'Belinda's Dream'
Shrub
SIZE: 3 to 6 feet
Double flowers about 4 inches across
Fragrant
Zones 5 to 9
P. 237

▼ 'Belle Story'
Shrub
SIZE: 3 to 5 feet
Semidouble flowers to 4 inches across
Fragrant
Zones 5 to 9
P. 240

▶ 'Bonica'
Shrub
SIZE: 3 to 5 feet
Double flowers 1 to 2 inches across
Zones 5 to 9
P. 245

▶ 'Carefree Beauty'
Shrub
SIZE: 4 to 5 feet
Semidouble flowers to 4½ inches across
Moderate fragrance
Zones 4 to 9
P. 253

▲ 'Carefree Delight'

Shrub

SIZE: 3 to 5 feet
Single flowers to 2 inches across
Zones 4 to 10
P. 253

▼ 'Carefree Wonder'

Shrub

SIZE: 3 to 4 feet
Double flowers about 3 inches across
Light fragrance
Zones 4 to 9
P. 254

▲ 'Charlotte'
Shrub
SIZE: 3 to 6 feet
Double flowers about 3½ inches across
Fragrant
Zones 5 to 10
P. 259

▼ 'Charmian'
Shrub
SIZE: 4 to 8 feet
Double flowers about 3 inches across
Fragrant
Zones 5 to 10
P. 260

▲ 'Cocktail'

Shrub

SIZE: 5 to 6 feet
Single flowers 2 to 3 inches across
Light fragrance
Zones 5 to 9
P. 266

▼ 'Constance Spry'

Shrub

SIZE: 5 to 7 feet as a shrub; 10 to 20 feet with
support
Double flowers to 5 inches across
Very fragrant
Zones 5 to 9
P. 268

▲ 'Country Dancer'
Shrub

SIZE: 3 to 5 feet
Double flowers about 3 inches across
Moderate fragrance
Zones 4 to 9
P. 269

▼ 'Dapple Dawn'
Shrub

SIZE: 4 to 6 feet
Single flowers 4 to 5 inches across
Zones 5 to 9
P. 273

▲ 'Distant Drums'
Shrub
SIZE: 3 to 5 feet
Double flowers 4 to 5 inches across
Fragrant
Zones 5 to 9
P. 276

▼ 'Dornröschen'
Shrub
SIZE: 4 to 8 feet
Double flowers 3 to 4 inches across
Fragrant
Zones 4 to 9
P. 277

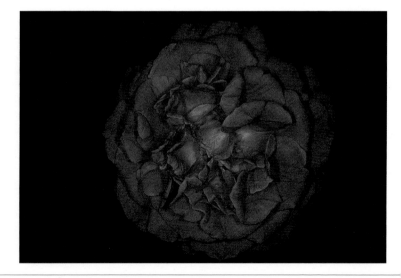

▶ 'Elmshorn'

Shrub

SIZE: 4 to 6 feet

Double flowers 1 to 2 inches across

Light fragrance

Zones 5 to 9

P. 286

▼ 'English Garden'

Shrub

SIZE: 3 to 4 feet

Very double flowers 3 to 4 inches across

Variable fragrance

Zones 5 to 9

P. 288

▲ 'Evelyn'

Shrub

SIZE: 3 to 6 feet as a shrub; 6 to 9 feet as a
climber

Very double flowers 3 to 5 inches across

Variable fragrance

Zones 5 to 9

P. 292

▼ 'Fair Bianca'

Shrub

SIZE: 3 to 5 feet

Very double flowers 3 to 3½ inches across

Very fragrant

Zones 5 to 9

P. 293

▲ 'Fisherman's Friend'
Shrub
SIZE: 3 to 4 feet
Very double flowers 4 to 7 inches across
Very fragrant
Zones 5 to 9
P. 299

▼ 'Flower Carpet'
Shrub
SIZE: 2 to 3 feet
Semidouble flowers about 1½ inches across
Zones 5 to 10
P. 300

▲ 'Fred Loads'

Shrub

SIZE: 4 to 8 feet
Single flowers 3 to 3½ inches across
Zones 5 to 10
P. 305

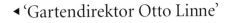

◀ 'Gartendirektor Otto Linne'

Shrub

SIZE: 4 to 6 feet as a shrub; to 10 feet with support
Double flowers 2 inches across
Zones 5 to 9
P. 308

▲ 'Gertrude Jekyll'
Shrub
SIZE: 4 to 10 feet
Very double flowers 4 to 5 inches across
Very fragrant
Zones 5 to 9
P. 310

▼ 'Golden Celebration'
Shrub
SIZE: 4 to 7 feet
Very double flowers 3 to 6 inches across
Fragrant
Zones 5 to 9
P. 312

▲ 'Golden Wings'

Shrub

SIZE: 4 to 6 feet

Single flowers 3 to 5 inches across

Light fragrance

Zones 4 to 8

P. 314

◄ 'Graham Thomas'

Shrub

SIZE: 5 to 12 feet

Double flowers 3 to 4 inches across

Fragrant

Zones 5 to 9

P. 316

▲ 'Happy Child'

Shrub
SIZE: 3 to 4 feet
Very double flowers 3 to 4 inches across
Fragrant
Zones 5 to 9
P. 321

▶ 'Heritage'

Shrub
SIZE: 4 to 5 feet
Double flowers 3 to 5 inches across
Very fragrant
Zones 5 to 9
P. 324

▲ 'Kaleidoscope'
Shrub
SIZE: 2 to 4 feet
Very double flowers 2 to 3 inches across
Zones 5 to 10
P. 336

▼ 'Knock Out'
Shrub
SIZE: To 3 feet
Semidouble flowers 2½ to 3½ inches across
Zones 4 to 9
P. 339

▲ 'Lavender Dream'

Shrub
SIZE: 3 to 5 feet
Semidouble flowers 2 to 3 inches across
Zones 4 to 9
P. 345

▶ 'L. D. Braithwaite'

Shrub
SIZE: 3 to 6 feet
Very double flowers 3 to 4 inches across
Variable fragrance
Zones 5 to 9
P. 347

▲ 'Leander'
Shrub
SIZE: 5 to 7 feet as a shrub; 12 to 14 feet with support
Very double flowers 3 inches across
Fragrant
Zones 5 to 9
P. 347

▼ 'Lilian Austin'
Shrub
SIZE: 3 to 4 feet
Semidouble to double flowers 4 to 5 inches across
Light fragrance
Zones 5 to 9
P. 349

▲ 'Mary Rose'
Shrub
SIZE: 4 to 6 feet
Very double flowers 3 to 5 inches across
Fragrant
Zones 5 to 9
P. 357

▼ 'Morden Centennial'
Shrub
SIZE: 2 to 5 feet
Double flowers about 3 to 4 inches across
Zones 3 to 9
P. 369

◄ 'Oranges 'n' Lemons'
Shrub
SIZE: 4 to 10 feet
Double flowers 3 inches across
Light fragrance
Zones 5 to 9
P. 380

 'Pat Austin'
Shrub
SIZE: 3 to 5 feet
Double flowers 3 to 5 inches across
Fragrant
Zones 5 to 9
P. 383

▶ 'Pearl Meidiland'
Shrub
SIZE: 2 to 3 feet
Double flowers 2½ inches across
Zones 4 to 9
P. 386

▼ 'Petite Pink Scotch'
Shrub
SIZE: 2 to 4 feet
Double flowers ½ to 1 inch across
Zones 5 to 9
P. 388

▲ 'Pink Meidiland'

Shrub

SIZE: 2 to 4 feet
Single flowers 2 to 2½ inches across
Zones 5 to 9
P. 391

◄ 'Prairie Princess'

Shrub

SIZE: 5 to 6 feet as a shrub; 6 feet with support
Semidouble flowers 3 inches across
Zones 3 to 9
P. 395

▲ 'Prospero'
Shrub
SIZE: 2 to 4 feet
Very double flowers 3 to 4 inches across
Fragrant
Zones 5 to 10
P. 397

▼ 'Red Ribbons'
Shrub
SIZE: 2 to 2½ feet
Semidouble flowers 2 to 3 inches across
Zones 5 to 9
P. 400

▲ 'Robusta'

Shrub

SIZE: 5 to 8 feet
Single flowers about 2½ inches across
Zones 4 to 8
P. 404

▼ 'Sally Holmes'

Shrub

SIZE: 4 to 10 feet as a shrub; 10 to 15 feet with
support
Single flowers 4 inches across
Light fragrance
Zones 5 to 9
P. 418

▶ 'Scarlet Meidiland'

Shrub

SIZE: 2 to 4 feet
Double flowers 1 to 2 inches across
Zones 4 to 9
P. 420

▶ 'Sea Foam'

Shrub

SIZE: 2 to 4 feet as a shrub; 8 to 12 feet with
support
Double flowers 2½ inches across
Zones 4 to 9
P. 422

▲ 'Sharifa Asma'

Shrub

SIZE: 3 to 5 feet
Very double flowers 3 to 4 inches across
Very fragrant
Zones 5 to 9
P. 424

▼ 'Sparrieshoop'

Shrub

SIZE: 4 to 10 feet as a shrub; 6 to 10 feet with
support
Single flowers about 4 inches across
Fragrant
Zones 5 to 9
P. 432

▲ 'Tamora'
Shrub
SIZE: 2 to 4 feet
Very double flowers 3 to 4 inches across
Fragrant
Zones 5 to 10
P. 439

▼ 'The Dark Lady'
Shrub
SIZE: 3 to 5 feet
Very double flowers 3 to 5 inches across
Fragrant
Zones 5 to 10
P. 440

◄ 'The Herbalist'
Shrub
SIZE: 3 to 4 feet
Semidouble flowers 2 to 2½ inches across
Zones 5 to 9
P. 442

▼ 'The Prince'
Shrub
SIZE: 2 to 4 feet
Very double flowers 3 inches across
Fragrant
Zones 5 to 9
P. 442

▲ 'Tradescant'
Shrub
SIZE: 3 to 8 feet as a shrub; 8 to 10 feet with support
Very double flowers 2½ to 3½ inches across
Fragrant
Zones 5 to 9
P. 446

▼ 'Baby Grand'
Miniature
SIZE: 12 to 18 inches
Double flowers up to 2 inches across
Light fragrance
Zones 5 to 10
P. 233

▲ 'Beauty Secret'
Miniature
SIZE: 12 to 18 inches
Double flowers about 1½ inches across
Fragrant
Zones 5 to 10
P. 236

▼ 'Black Jade'
Miniature
SIZE: 18 to 24 inches
Double flowers to ¾ inch across
Zones 5 to 10
P. 242

▸'Cal Poly'
Miniature
SIZE: 15 to 30 inches
Double flowers 1½ to 2½ inches across
Zones 5 to 10
P. 249

▸'Candy Sunblaze'
Miniature
SIZE: 18 to 24 inches
Double flowers about 2 inches across
Zones 5 to 10
P. 251

▲ 'Child's Play'

Miniature

SIZE: 15 to 24 inches

Semidouble or double flowers 1 to 2 inches
across

Zones 4 to 10

P. 261

▼ 'Cinderella'

Miniature

SIZE: 8 to 10 inches

Double flowers up to 1 inch across

Variable fragrance

Zones 5 to 9

P. 263

▲ 'Earthquake'
Miniature
SIZE: 15 to 18 inches
Double flowers about 1½ inches across
Zones 6 to 10
P. 283

▼ 'Giggles'
Miniature
SIZE: 18 to 24 inches
Double flowers 1½ inches across
Zones 5 to 9
P. 311

▲ 'Glowing Amber'

Miniature

SIZE: 15 to 30 inches
Double flowers about 2 inches across
Lightly fragrant
Zones 5 to 10
P. 312

▼ 'Gourmet Popcorn'

Miniature

SIZE: 18 to 30 inches
Semidouble flowers 1 inch across
Variable fragrance
Zones 4 to 9
P. 315

▲ 'Green Ice'

Miniature

SIZE: 1 to 2 feet
Double flowers 1 inch across
Zones 5 to 10
P. 317

▶ 'Hoot Owl'

Miniature

SIZE: 1 to 2 feet
Single flowers 1½ inches across
Zones 6 to 10
P. 327

▲ 'Hot Tamale'

Miniature
SIZE: 18 to 30 inches
Double flowers 1 to 2 inches across
Zones 6 to 10
P. 328

▼ 'Irresistible'

Miniature
SIZE: 2 to 3 feet
Double flowers 1½ inches across
Moderate fragrance
Zones 5 to 10
P. 330

▶ 'Jean Kenneally'
Miniature

SIZE: 2 to 3 feet
Double flowers 1½ inches across
Light fragrance
Zones 5 to 10
P. 332

▼ 'Kristin'
Miniature

SIZE: 18 to 30 inches
Double flowers 1 to 2 inches across
Zones 5 to 10
P. 340

▲ 'Little Artist'
Miniature
SIZE: 12 to 18 inches
Semidouble flowers 1 inch across
Zones 5 to 10
P. 350

▼ 'Loving Touch'
Miniature
SIZE: 12 to 30 inches
Double flowers 1½ inches across
Light fragrance
Zones 5 to 10
P. 353

▲ 'Magic Carrousel'

Miniature

SIZE: 12 to 30 inches

Semidouble or double flowers 2 to 2½ inches across

Zones 5 to 10

P. 353

▼ 'Millie Walters'

Miniature

SIZE: 1 to 2 feet

Very double flowers 1½ inches across

Zones 5 to 10

P. 360

▲ 'Minnie Pearl'

Miniature

SIZE: 1 to 2 feet
Double flowers 1½ inches across
Zones 5 to 9
P. 360

▼ 'Miss Flippins'

Miniature

SIZE: 2 to 3 feet
Double flowers about 1 ½ inches across
Zones 5 to 10
P. 362

▲ 'My Sunshine'
Miniature
SIZE: 18 to 22 inches
Single flowers 1 inch across
Light fragrance
Zones 5 to 10
P. 373

▼ 'Pacesetter'
Miniature
SIZE: 18 to 24 inches
Double flowers 1½ inches across
Fragrant
Zones 5 to 9
P. 381

▲ 'Party Girl'

Miniature
SIZE: 12 to 18 inches
Double flowers 1 to 1½ inches across
Moderate fragrance
Zones 6 to 10
P. 382

▼ 'Pierrine'

Miniature
SIZE: 1 to 2 feet
Double flowers 1½ inches across
Zones 6 to 9
P. 390

▲ 'Rainbow's End'
Miniature

SIZE: 1 to 2 feet
Double flowers to 2 inches across
Zones 5 to 9
P. 399

▶ 'Rise 'n' Shine'
Miniature

SIZE: 1 to 2 feet
Double flowers 1½ inches across
Zones 5 to 10
P. 403

▲ 'Scentsational'
Miniature
SIZE: 18 to 30 inches
Double flowers about 2 inches across
Very fragrant
Zones 6 to 10
P. 421

▼ 'Simplex'
Miniature
SIZE: 12 to 18 inches
Single flowers 1 to 1½ inches across
Zones 6 to 10
P. 426

▲ 'Snow Bride'
Miniature

SIZE: 1 to 2 feet
Double flowers 1½ to 2½ inches across
Zones 5 to 10
P. 429

▼ 'Snow Carpet'
Miniature

SIZE: 6 to 12 inches
Very double flowers ¾ inch across
Zones 5 to 10
P. 430

▲ 'Starina'

Miniature

SIZE: 1 to 2 feet
Double flowers 2 inches across
Zones 5 to 9
P. 434

◄ 'Sun Sprinkles'

Miniature

SIZE: 18 to 36 inches
Double flowers 2 to 3 inches across
Variable fragrance
Zones 5 to 10
P. 436

▲ 'Sweet Chariot'
Miniature
SIZE: Double flowers 1 inch across
Very fragrant
Zones 5 to 10
P. 437

▼ 'Sweet Revenge'
Miniature
SIZE: 2 to 3 feet
Double flowers 1½ inches across
Light fragrance
Zones 6 to 10
P. 438

◄ 'Ultimate Pleasure'

Miniature

SIZE: 2 to 3 feet
Double flowers 1 inch across
Light fragrance
Zones 5 to 10
P. 449

▼ 'Winsome'

Miniature

SIZE: 18 to 36 inches
Double flowers 1 to 1½ inches across
Light fragrance
Zones 5 to 9
P. 455

▶ 'X-Rated'
Miniature
SIZE: 18 to 24 inches
Double flowers about 1½ inches across
Variable fragrance
Zones 5 to 10

P. 456

▶ 'Yantai'
Mini-flora
SIZE: 18 to 30 inches
Double flowers about 2 inches across
Light fragrance
Zones 5 to 10

P. 456

▲ 'Aloha'

Climbing hybrid tea

SIZE: 8 to 12 feet with support
Very double flowers to 4 inches across
Fragrant
Zones 5 to 9
P. 225

◄ 'Captain Thomas'

Climbing hybrid tea

SIZE: About 6 feet as a shrub; about 10 feet
with support
Single flowers about 3½ inches across
Light fragrance
Zones 5 to 9
P. 251

▲ 'Candy Cane'

Climbing miniature

SIZE: 4 to 10 feet with support

Single or semidouble flowers 1½ to 2 inches across

Zones 5 to 10

P. 250

▶ 'Jeanne Lajoie'

Climbing miniature

SIZE: 6 to 8 feet with support

Double flowers 1 to 2 inches across

Zones 5 to 10

P. 333

◄ 'Nozomi'

Climbing miniature

SIZE: 1 to 2 feet as a shrub; 3 to 5 feet with support

Single flowers 1½ inches across

Zones 5 to 9

P. 377

▼ 'Red Cascade'

Climbing miniature

SIZE: About 3 feet as a shrub; 6 to 18 feet with support

Semidouble or double flowers ½ to 1 inch across

Zones 5 to 9

P. 399

▲ 'Phyllis Bide'
Climbing polyantha

SIZE: To 6 feet as a shrub; 6 to 10 feet with support
Semidouble flowers about 2 inches across
Light fragrance
Zones 6 to 9
P. 389

▼ 'Sombreuil'
Climbing tea

SIZE: To 8 feet as a shrub; 8 to 15 feet with support
Very double flowers about $3\frac{1}{2}$ to $4\frac{1}{2}$ inches across
Fragrant
Zones 6 to 10
P. 430

◄ 'American Pillar'
Hybrid wichurana
SIZE: 15 to 20 feet with support
Single flowers 2 to 3 inches across
Zones 5 to 9
P. 228

▼ 'Newport Fairy'
Hybrid wichurana
SIZE: 15 to 20 feet with support
Single flowers 2 inches across
Light fragrance
Zones 5 to 10
P. 376

▶ 'Altissimo'

Large-flowered climber

SIZE: 8 to 10 feet with support
Single flowers to 5 inches across
Zones 5 to 9

P. 226

▼ 'America'

Large-flowered climber

SIZE: 8 to 12 feet with support
Very double flowers about 4 inches across
Fragrant
Zones 5 to 9

P. 227

▲ 'Awakening'
Large-flowered climber
SIZE: 8 to 12 feet with support
Very double flowers 1½ to 2½ inches across
Fragrant
Zones 5 to 10
P. 232

▼ 'Bantry Bay'
Large-flowered climber
SIZE: 10 to 15 feet with support
Double flowers to 4 inches across
Light fragrance
Zones 5 to 9
P. 234

▲ 'Blaze Improved'

Large-flowered climber

SIZE: 9 to 12 feet with support
Semidouble flowers about 3 inches across
Zones 5 to 10
P. 243

▼ 'City of York'

Large-flowered climber

SIZE: 8 to 20 feet with support
Semidouble flowers 3 to 4 inches across
Fragrant
Zones 5 to 9
P. 264

▲ 'Clair Matin'

Large-flowered climber

SIZE: To 6 feet as a shrub; 8 to 12 feet with support

Semidouble flowers 2 to 3 inches across

Variable fragrance

Zones 5 to 10

P. 264

▼ 'Compassion'

Large-flowered climber

SIZE: 5 to 7 feet as a shrub; 10 to 15 feet with support

Double flowers up to 5 inches across

Fragrant

Zones 5 to 9

P. 266

▲ 'Don Juan'

Large-flowered climber

SIZE: 8 to 15 feet with support
Double flowers to 5 inches across
Fragrant
Zones 6 to 10
P. 277

▼ 'Dr. Huey'

Large-flowered climber

SIZE: 8 to 10 feet as a shrub; 12 to 18 feet with support
Semidouble flowers 2 to 3 inches across
Zones 4 to 9
P. 280

▲ 'Dr. W. Van Fleet'

Large-flowered climber

SIZE: 15 to 20 feet with support

Double flowers about 3 inches across

Moderate fragrance

Zones 4 to 10

P. 280

▼ 'Dublin Bay'

Large-flowered climber

SIZE: 6 to 8 feet as a shrub; 8 to 12 feet with support

Double flowers 3 to 4 inches across

Variable fragrance

Zones 4 to 10

P. 281

▲ 'Fourth of July'
Large-flowered climber
SIZE: 10 to 15 feet with support
Semidouble flowers 2 to 4 inches across
Light fragrance
Zones 5 to 10
P. 301

▼ 'Galway Bay'
Large-flowered climber
SIZE: 8 to 12 feet with support
Double flowers 3½ inches across
Zones 5 to 9
P. 307

▲ 'Golden Showers'

Large-flowered climber

SIZE: 6 to 14 feet with support
Double flowers 3½ to 4½ inches across
Variable fragrance
Zones 6 to 9

P. 313

▼ 'Handel'

Large-flowered climber

SIZE: 10 to 15 feet with support
Double flowers 3½ inches across
Zones 5 to 9

P. 320

▶ 'Joseph's Coat'

Large-flowered climber

SIZE: To 7 feet as a shrub; 8 to 10 feet with support

Double flowers 3 to 4 inches across

Zones 5 to 9

P. 335

▼ 'Lace Cascade'

Large-flowered climber

SIZE: 5 to 7 feet as a shrub; 10 to 12 feet with support

Double flowers 3 to 4 inches across

Zones 5 to 9

P. 342

◄ 'New Dawn'

Large-flowered climber

SIZE: 8 to 10 feet as a shrub; 10 to 20 feet with support

Double flowers 3 inches across

Fragrant

Zones 5 to 10

P. 375

▼ 'Parade'

Large-flowered climber

SIZE: 6 to 8 feet as a shrub; 8 to 10 feet with support

Double flowers 3½ to 4½ inches across

Fragrant

Zones 5 to 9

P. 381

▲ 'Pierre de Ronsard'
Large-flowered climber
SIZE: 8 to 10 feet with support
Double flowers 3 inches across
Zones 5 to 9
P. 390

▼ 'Polka'
Large-flowered climber
SIZE: 4 to 6 feet as a shrub; 6 to 12 feet with support
Very double flowers about 3½ inches across
Fragrant
Zones 5 to 9
P. 394

▲ 'Rosarium Uetersen'

Large-flowered climber

SIZE: 6 to 8 feet as a shrub; 8 to 12 feet with support

Very double flowers 3 to 4 inches across

Light fragrance

Zone 4 to 9

P. 408

▼ 'Royal Sunset'

Large-flowered climber

SIZE: 6 to 8 feet as a shrub; 8 to 15 feet with support

Double flowers 4 to 5 inches across

Variable fragrance

Zones 6 to 10

P. 415

Encyclopedia
of Roses

❧Encyclopedia of Roses

❦ 'Abbaye de Cluny'

Syns. 'Romantic Serenade'; MEIbrinpay
Hybrid tea. Meilland, 1996.

Looking at the deeply cupped, old-fashioned flowers of this lovely rose in the Romantica Series, you'd probably never guess it's officially classified as a hybrid tea. Large, pointed, orange buds open into nearly globe-shaped, double blooms that are 3 to 5 inches across, with slightly ruffled, rounded petals in various shades of peachy orange. (The color is generally richest in cool weather.) Expect a mild to moderate, somewhat spicy scent. 'Abbaye de Cluny' begins blooming in late spring to early summer, followed by moderate to good repeat bloom through the rest of the growing season. Moderately thorny stems bear semiglossy leaves that are red tinged when young and dark green when mature. Zones 5 to 9.

HOW TO USE

'Abbaye de Cluny' forms an upright bush that's usually 3 to 4 feet tall and 2 to 3 feet wide. Enjoy its beautiful blooms in beds and borders, where it blends beautifully with both soft and bright yellows, pink, purples, and blues. Rainy or very humid weather can cause the outer petals of the buds to shrink, preventing the flowers from opening properly; otherwise, 'Abbaye de Cluny' doesn't seem to have any serious problems.

✨ 'Abraham Darby'

Syn. AUScot
Shrub. Austin, 1985.

This popular English rose offers double, cupped, petal-packed flowers up
to 6 inches wide, held singly or in clusters. In cooler climates, the color is
a rich peachy pink touched with yellow; in warmer areas, the color is a
lighter apricot-pink. Look for good repeat bloom from early summer
into fall. The sweet to fruity fragrance is a plus. The long, arching stems
are quite thorny and bear glossy, leathery, medium to dark green leaves.
Zones 5 to 10.

HOW TO USE

Though officially classified as a shrub rose, 'Abraham Darby' can also be
vigorous enough to grow as a climber (8 to 10 feet tall), especially in
warm climates. The heavy blooms tend to nod a bit, so training it as a
climber is a good way to show off its flowers. As a shrub (growing about 5
feet high and 4 feet wide), 'Abraham Darby' looks great in groups and
makes a handsome addition to the back of a mixed border. Minimal fertilizing can help control its size. This easygoing rose has good overall disease
resistance, but it's smart to take preventive measures against black spot.

✨ 'Agnes'

Hybrid rugosa. Saunders, 1900.

One of the few yellow-flowered hybrid rugosas, 'Agnes' offers fully double, ruffled blooms to 3 inches across, with a rich sweet to fruity scent.
The flowers start as pale yellow with a medium yellow heart and age to
ivory as the petals open. The main flush of bloom, in late spring to early
summer, is prolific; in some areas, 'Agnes' will produce occasional blooms
later in the season as well. The thorny, rather arching stems bear small,
wrinkled, light to medium green leaves. Zones 4 to 8.

HOW TO USE

This shrubby rose grows 4 to 6 feet high and 4 to 5 feet wide. By late summer, its foliage can develop a brownish cast, so it's not a great choice for a
specimen plant or a highly visible area. Instead, try it in a mixed border,
combined with later-blooming perennials and shrubs to draw attention
away from the bronzed rose leaves. In an out-of-the-way spot, a cluster of

'Agnes' plants can make a nice informal hedge. 'Agnes' occasionally develops black spot or rust in some regions.

✻ 'Aimée Vibert'

Syns. 'Bouquet de la Mariée', 'Nivea'
Noisette. Vibert, 1828.

This lovely Noisette rose produces rounded, red-tinted buds that open to musk-scented, fully double, pure white flowers about 2 inches across. They bloom in small clusters against shiny, medium green, finely toothed leaflets on nearly thornless canes. There appears to be some confusion about the height and habit of this rose. The original 'Aimée Vibert' is a shrubby bush with sturdy, spreading canes; it starts blooming in midsummer and offers good rebloom through summer. The form commonly sold as 'Aimée Vibert', however, is usually described as growing much larger, with long, arching canes and minimal rebloom; this may actually be 'Aimée Vibert Scandens' (also known as 'Climbing Aimée Vibert'). Check the catalog description or ask your supplier before you buy to see what to expect from a plant carrying this name. Zones 8 to 10.

HOW TO USE
'Aimée Vibert', in its regular form, grows as shrub 4 to 5 feet tall and wide. Enjoy its later-season bloom in a mixed border, or plant it in groups as a hedge. Disease resistance is generally good.

'Aimée Vibert Scandens' is a medium-sized climber (about 12 feet high and 10 feet wide); you could also prune it into a large shrub.

✻ 'Alain Blanchard'

Hybrid gallica. Vibert, 1839.

'Alain Blanchard' shares the summer-blooming habit and richly colored, petal-packed, fragrant blooms common to the members of the hybrid gallica class. The semidouble, 3-inch-wide, cupped blooms have deep purple-red petals that are mottled with deep pink as they age. The fully open flowers reveal a cluster of bright gold stamens. This lovely old-time rose begins flowering in early summer, with sporadic rebloom for about a month. Vigorous, thorny stems bear medium green leaves. Zones 5 to 9.

HOW TO USE

'Alain Blanchard' produces a wide, low-growing shrub to about 4 feet tall and 4 to 5 feet wide. Established bushes may spread by suckers, making this rose a good choice for an informal hedge. It also contributes seasonal fragrance and color to a shrub planting or mixed border. Disease resistance is generally good.

'Alba Maxima'

Syns. 'Great Double White', 'Maxima'; *Rosa alba maxima;* Jacobite Rose Alba. Introduced before 1500.

It blooms only once, but with its handsome foliage and ornamental hips, this alba is certainly a multiseason rose. The show starts in late spring to early summer, when the rounded, pink-blushed buds open to flattened, double, 3- to 4-inch-wide flowers containing 200 or more petals. The blooms may also have a pale pink blush as they open but are mostly a creamy white color, and they have a heady, sweet scent. In some areas 'Alba Maxima' may rebloom in late summer, but don't depend on it; either way, you can enjoy the generous display of orange-red hips in fall. Throughout the season, the somewhat prickly canes, clad in handsome gray-green leaves, arch out from a narrow base to form a tall shrub. Zones 4 to 8.

HOW TO USE

'Alba Maxima' needs plenty of room; it usually grows 6 to 8 feet tall and about 4 feet wide. Enjoy it planted by itself as a landscape accent, or plant several bushes to create an informal hedge. 'Alba Maxima' also combines well with companions — other roses, shrubs, and/or perennials — for multiseason interest at the back of a border or in a cottage garden setting. If space is limited, try growing it on a pillar or training it to grow on a wall or fence. 'Alba Maxima' is hardy and disease resistant; it can also tolerate light shade.

'Alba Meidiland'

Syns. 'Alba Meillandécor', 'Meidiland Alba'; MEIflopan
Shrub. Meilland, 1987.

Looking for a low-growing, low-maintenance shrub rose? 'Alba Meidiland' might be just the rose for you! The pure white, double, cupped flowers are on the small side (about 2 inches across), but they bloom in large clusters. The first flush of bloom in early to midsummer is profuse; flowers continue to appear into fall. Glossy, dark green leaves make a handsome backdrop for the white blooms and offer yellow fall color. 'Alba Meidiland' forms a vigorous, spreading bush. Zones 4 to 9.

HOW TO USE

'Alba Meidiland' produces a low-spreading bush reaching 2 to 3 feet tall and 4 to 6 feet wide. It is an excellent choice for use as a mounding groundcover. Hardy and disease resistant, it also makes a great space-filler in a border, and it grows well in containers too. Its lack of scent is a small drawback, but it makes up for that with its generous display of blooms that drop off cleanly when they are finished, essentially eliminating the need for deadheading to keep the bush looking great all season.

❀'Alba Semi-plena'

Syn. *Rosa alba semi-plena*
Alba. Cultivated before 1867.

Like its other alba relatives, 'Alba Semi-plena' offers good looks from spring to frost, with beautiful flowers, lovely leaves, and showy fruits. In late spring to early summer, its rounded buds open into semi-double, sweetly scented, milky white blooms accented with clusters of showy yellow stamens. There is no repeat bloom, but that doesn't mean the show is over; 'Alba Semi-plena' produces an abundant crop of oblong red hips in late summer to fall. Both the flowers and fruits show up handsomely against the gray-green foliage. Thorny canes emerge from a narrow base to form an upright-arching shrub. Zones 4 to 9.

HOW TO USE

'Alba Semi-plena' generally grows about 6 feet tall and 5 feet wide, so it needs a fair amount of room to look its best. Plant it in masses to create a great-looking informal hedge, or just admire it planted alone. 'Alba Semi-plena' is also a super addition to a shrub border. Combine it with annuals and perennials in a mixed border, either as a free-standing background plant or trained to a pillar as a vertical accent. This versatile rose even adapts to training on a wall or fence. 'Alba Semi-plena' offers excellent disease resistance and can tolerate light shade.

❦ 'Alchymist'

Syns. 'Alchemist', 'Alchymiste'
Shrub. Kordes, 1956.

Though formally classified as a shrub rose, 'Alchymist' works equally well as either a shrub or a climber. This versatile rose produces rounded buds that open into large, cupped to almost flat flowers up to 4 inches across. Packed with 65 to 75 petals, the fragrant blooms are a lovely blend of peach and yellow. 'Alchymist' flowers generously for several weeks in early summer, with little or no repeat later in the season. The dense foliage is a glossy, deep green tinged with bronze, carried on stout, thorny, arching canes. Zones 5 to 9.

HOW TO USE

'Alchymist' produces tall, somewhat rangy growth. As an upright, vigorous shrub, it grows about 6 feet tall and wide, making a great early-summer accent for a shrub planting or the back of a mixed border. If you don't want to give that much garden space to a once-blooming rose, train it onto a pillar for a vertical border accent, or train it to grow against a wall or fence (it will reach to about 8 feet as a climber). The blooms are held on long stems, making them excellent for cutting. 'Alchymist' is generally disease resistant but may develop some black spot during periods of rainy or very humid weather if you don't take preventive measures.

❦ 'Alika'

Syns. 'Gallica Grandiflora'; *Rosa gallica grandiflora*
Hybrid gallica. Hansen, 1906.

'Alika' blooms just once a season, but what a show! This hybrid gallica produces large, single to semidouble, saucer-shaped blooms up to 4 inches across, with a moderate fragrance. The petals are a bright crimson, contrasting beautifully with the prominent cluster of golden yellow stamens in the center of each flower. The bloom season begins in late spring or early summer and usually lasts 4 to 5 weeks. In fall, 'Alika' puts on another show with a generous crop of oblong, orange hips. Its sturdy, arching canes are clad in medium green leaves that may show reddish fall color, complementing the fall hip display. Zones 4 to 8.

HOW TO USE

Hardy and vigorous, 'Alika' grows as a large, arching shrub. It's larger in stature than many hybrid gallicas, growing 6 to 8 feet tall and about 6 feet wide. Grow it in groups as an informal hedge, or site it at the back of a shrub or mixed border for its seasonal interest. 'Alika' also looks great trained on a tall post or pillar. Disease resistance is generally good.

❦'Alister Stella Gray'

Syn. 'Golden Rambler'
Noisette. Gray, 1894.

If you prefer richly hued roses, this Noisette may not be to your taste, but if you enjoy soft colors and you garden in a warm climate, give this one a look. 'Alister Stella Gray' is a lovely Noisette rose with clusters of long, pointed, orange-yellow buds opening to ruffled, semi-double blooms up to 3 inches wide. The richly fragrant flowers are light yellow with an or-ange-yellow center, eventually aging to ivory white. Blooming usually starts in early summer, with relatively small flower clusters; the display continues moderately through summer to finish with an excellent show of large bloom clusters in fall. The lightly thorny canes carry semiglossy, dark green leaves and have an upright, branching habit. Zones 7 to 10.

HOW TO USE

'Alister Stella Gray' is commonly grown as a climber, reaching up to 15 feet tall. The vigorous, flexible canes adapt well to wrapping around a pil-lar; they also work well trained up an arbor or pergola post. Left unsup-ported, 'Alister Stella Gray' will form a large, somewhat open, arching shrub that is 5 to 7 feet tall and wide. It's a handsome addition to a warm-climate garden, as a hedge, shrub border, or informal area. This rose has moderate to good disease resistance.

❦'Aloha'

Climbing hybrid tea. Boerner, 1949.

This climbing hybrid tea rose is popular with gardeners throughout the country, and with good reason: It's hard to beat for beautiful blooms, strong fragrance, and a long flowering season. Starting in late spring, the large, rounded buds open to very full, cupped flowers up to 4 inches across. The petals are a medium rosy pink (with a touch of salmon) on top and a deeper shade of rose-pink on the underside. 'Aloha' flowers heavily in late spring to early summer, followed by excellent repeat bloom through summer and fall. The sturdy, upright canes bear glossy, dark green leaves. Zones 5 to 9.

HOW TO USE

This is a rose with a bit of an identity crisis: it's classified as a climber, but it makes a great shrub too. Given the support of a post, pillar, arbor, fence, or trellis, 'Aloha' climbs 8 to 12 feet tall. With pruning, it can make a long-blooming shrub for a mixed border. 'Aloha' is generally disease resistant but may show some mildew if not given a site with good air circulation.

❦ 'Alpine Sunset'

Hybrid tea. Cants of Colchester, 1973.

If compact growth, huge blooms, great fragrance, and sunset shades are on your list of must-haves, 'Alpine Sunset' may be just what you're looking for. This handsome hybrid tea rose is known for its very large flowers: they're up to 6 inches across, with 30 petals in each sweetly scented bloom. The individual petals are a soft blend of gold and peachy pink on top with a paler hue on the undersides, and the colors soften as the blooms age. 'Alpine Sunset' produces its main floral display in early summer; after that, it offers smaller bloom displays in separate flushes into fall. Glossy, light to medium green leaves held on vigorous, upright canes make a handsome backdrop for the richly colored flowers. Zones 5 to 9.

HOW TO USE

'Alpine Sunset' forms a bushy plant reaching 2 to 4 feet tall and 2 to 3 feet wide. This rose's compact growth habit makes it a good choice for smaller gardens, or for planting near the front of a flower bed. In Zones 5 and 6, give it a site protected from strong winds to help minimize winter dieback. 'Alpine Sunset' generally has good disease resistance.

❦ 'Altissimo'

Syns. 'Altus'; DELmur
Large-flowered climber. Delbard-Chabert, 1966.

There aren't too many single-flowered climbing roses to choose from, so 'Altissimo' belongs to an elite group. It's not just a novelty rose, though: this large-flowered climber earns its popularity with a long season of blood-red blooms, each crowned with a cluster of showy golden stamens. What they lack in fragrance, they make up for in size: individual blossoms can be up to 5 inches across. Usually produced in small clusters, the flowers first appear in early summer and return in regular flushes through the rest of the growing season. The glowing red petals make a stunning contrast to the large, deep green leaves held on vigorous, upright canes. Zones 5 to 9.

HOW TO USE

Generally reaching 8 to 10 feet in height, the sturdy, branching stems of this vigorous climber make it a perfect choice for training on a wall, fence, trellis, arch, pergola, or pillar. It is usually disease resistant but may develop a bit of black spot during cool, damp weather if you don't take preventive measures.

❀ 'Ambridge Rose'

Syn. AUSwonder
Shrub. Austin, 1994.

Officially classified as a shrub rose, 'Ambridge Rose' also belongs to the group known as English roses. It offers small clusters of very full, medium-size blooms about 3 inches wide, which start out with a cupped form and open into somewhat flattened rosettes. Produced from early summer into fall, the flowers have a peachy pink center with softer pink, somewhat ruffled outer petals, and they offer excellent fragrance. The somewhat prickly canes carry abundant, medium to dark green, semiglossy foliage. Zones 5 to 10.

HOW TO USE

'Ambridge Rose' grows 2½ to 3½ feet tall and 2 to 3 feet wide. The compact, bushy plants blend beautifully with perennials and shrubs in mixed borders. The old-fashioned form of the flowers makes this rose an excellent choice for a cottage garden setting, too — especially if space is at a premium. Disease resistance is generally good, but consider taking preventive measures against powdery mildew and black spot if either of these problems are common in your area.

❀ 'America'

Syn. JACclam
Large-flowered climber. Warriner, 1976.

This popular large-flowered climber is a handsome addition to any garden. 'America' produces pointed buds, held singly or in clusters and opening into fully double, cup-shaped, medium-size blooms about 4 inches across. The petals are a warm coral-pink on top, somewhat lighter below, aging to a paler salmon pink. 'America' usually starts flowering in early to midsummer, a bit later than most roses, but it reblooms well through the rest of the season. The flowers have a strong, somewhat spicy scent. Upright, free-branching stems carry medium-size, medium green, semiglossy foliage. Zones 5 to 9.

HOW TO USE

'America' has vigorous canes that climb 8 to 12 feet tall. It's an excellent choice for covering arbors or training on a trellis, wall, or fence. Wrap it around a pillar near the back of a mixed border, where its coral blooms complement rich purples and blues as well as pastel-flowered perennials and annuals. 'America' is generally disease-resistant but may have some black spot during rainy or very humid conditions unless you've applied preventive sprays.

All-America Rose Selection 1976

✿ 'American Pillar'

Hybrid wichurana. Van Fleet, 1902.

'American Pillar' has declined somewhat in popularity, owing to the introduction of longer-blooming, disease-resistant climbers in easier-to-use colors. If you see an established plant of this rose in full bloom, though, you'll understand why some gardeners still find it enticing. Classified as a hybrid wichurana but commonly referred to as a rambler, 'American Pillar' produces large clusters of single flowers, each 2 to 3 inches across, with little or no scent. The bright reddish pink blooms have a distinct white eye accented with a cluster of golden yellow stamens. It has a single flush of bloom for six to eight weeks in June and July, followed by red hips in fall. Thick, thorny canes bear glossy, leathery, deep green leaves. Zones 5 to 9.

HOW TO USE

'American Pillar' is quite vigorous, growing 15 to 20 feet tall. That makes it too big for trellises and fences, but it could do well on a large arbor or pergola. Alternately, you could train it to grow over a shed or other outbuilding. Disease resistance is good in most areas, but powdery mildew can be a problem in some areas.

❦ 'Angel Face'

Floribunda. Swim & Weeks, 1968.

This floribunda's main claims to fame are its intriguing color and its delightful fragrance. Pointed, reddish buds open to double, ruffled-edged, 4-inch flowers that have a strong, lemony scent. The American Rose Society describes its color as mauve; others see it as lavender-pink or as varying shades of red-violet. Held singly or in small clusters, the blossoms start out with high centers but gradually become cupped, revealing yellow stamens. Flowering begins in early summer and continues into fall. The shiny, deep green leaves are carried on thorny canes. Zones 5 to 9.

HOW TO USE

'Angel Face' forms a low, rounded bush growing 2½ to 4 feet tall and 2 to 3 feet wide. Its compact habit makes it a good choice for planting near the front of a bed, and a group of three or more bushes is certainly a pretty sight. 'Angel Face' can get some black spot, though, so make sure you give it a location with good air circulation. If black spot is a common problem in your area but you really want to enjoy the blooms, use preventive sprays or consider planting a bush of 'Angel Face' in an out-of-the-way place as a source of cut flowers.

All-America Rose Selection 1969

❦ Apothecary's Rose See *Rosa gallica officinalis*

❦ 'Applejack'

Shrub. Buck, 1973.

'Applejack' is one of a number of remarkable roses resulting from a breeding program by Dr. Griffith Buck at Iowa State University. Like its relatives, this shrub rose offers excellent hardiness as well as good repeat bloom and disease resistance. 'Applejack' produces small clusters of pointed, reddish buds that open to large, almost flat, single to semidouble flowers with crinkled petals. The 3-inch blooms are a soft rose-pink lightly stippled with crimson and have a spicy-sweet scent. Bushes bloom generously in early summer, with some rebloom later in the season. The long, arching canes are covered with leathery, medium green leaves that have a light fruity fragrance. Zones 4 to 9.

HOW TO USE

'Applejack' needs plenty of room: Its rambling stems generally grow 6 to 8 feet tall and 6 to 7 feet wide. Enjoy it as a large shrub in an informal area, or use it in masses as a tall hedge. Its long stems also adapt to training as a climber. 'Applejack' has excellent hardiness and disease resistance.

❦ 'Apricot Nectar'

Floribunda. Boerner, 1965.

This pretty floribunda is a favorite with gardeners who enjoy great fragrance. Egg-shaped, yellow buds blushed with pink open to display double blooms that are 4 to 5 inches across, with a loose high-centered form that becomes broadly cupped. The petals are mostly creamy yellow, shading to deeper yellow at the base and blushed with peach or pink near the tips. The long-lasting flowers are graced with a wonderful, moderate to strong, fruity fragrance. Usually produced in tight clusters, the flowers first appear in late spring to early summer, with good repeat bloom into fall. Moderately thorny canes carry shiny, deep green leaves. Zones 5 to 9.

HOW TO USE

'Apricot Nectar' forms an upright, somewhat open bush, generally growing 2 to 4 feet tall and about as wide. Try it in a bed or border near a bench, deck, or patio so you can sit and enjoy the fragrance. Or use it in a foundation planting near a window, so the scent can drift indoors. Add a few bushes to the cutting garden, too. 'Apricot Nectar' seems to perform best in warm, dry conditions. It usually offers moderate disease resistance, but black spot can be a problem if you don't take preventive measures.

All-America Rose Selection 1966

❦ 'Archduke Charles'

Hybrid China. Laffay, before 1837.

Most rose flowers fade as they age, but not those of 'Archduke Charles'. Hybrid Chinas share the unique trait of having blooms that actually get darker as they get older. The loose, double, 3-inch-wide blooms of this selection open a light rosy pink; as they mature, the petals age to red and then deep crimson. A single bush can bear cupped flowers at all different stages at one time, giving a distinctive multicolored effect. The color change happens quickest during the heat of summer. The clustered, fragrant blooms appear first in late spring and repeat well into fall. The somewhat thorny, upright stems carry small, rich green, semiglossy leaves. Zones 7 to 10.

HOW TO USE

'Archduke Charles' is a great old-fashioned rose for warm-climate gardens, especially those with limited space; it forms a somewhat open but compact bush that's 3 to 5 feet tall and about 3 feet wide. Try this rose in masses as a low hedge or plant it alone for a landscape accent. It's also a marvelous addition to mixed borders and foundation plantings. 'Archduke Charles' generally has good disease resistance but may develop a bit of powdery mildew in some areas.

☜ 'Autumn Damask'

Syns. 'Castilian', 'Four Seasons', 'Old Castilian', 'Quatre Saisons', 'Rose des Quatre Saisons'; *Rosa bifera, R. bifera semperflorens, R. damascena bifera, R. damascena semperflorens, R. semperflorens;* Rose of Castille
Damask. Cultivated before 1600.

As you may guess from the large number of names this rose goes by, there is some confusion about its origins, but that doesn't interfere with the garden value of this amazingly fragrant damask. Its rounded, reddish pink buds open to loosely double, ruffled, medium pink blooms about 3½ inches across, with a crown of yellow stamens. 'Autumn Damask' flowers generously in late spring to early summer, and again in fall, with occasional bloom in between. Olive green leaves are borne on rather spreading, thorny canes. Zones 4 to 7.

HOW TO USE

This vigorous rose has a somewhat open habit, growing 3 to 5 feet tall and about 3 feet wide. Planted in a group, it makes an attractive low hedge or background for a perennial border; it also works well in a shrub border or trained along a fence. 'Autumn Damask' has moderate disease resistance. Without preventive sprays, it may get a bit of black spot, causing bronzed foliage by fall, and it may have a touch of mildew in some areas.

❦ 'Autumn Sunset'

Shrub. Lowe, 1986.

Great color, super scent, months of flowers, excellent disease resistance, and better-than-average hardiness — what more could you ask for? This shrub rose produces large, pointed, orange buds that open into semidouble to double, loosely cupped blooms about 3 inches across. As the name implies, they bloom in sunset shades of orange, peach, and yellow, showing their richest hues in cool weather. Held in clusters, the flowers have a wonderful fruity fragrance. They usually first appear in early summer, with good to excellent repeat bloom well into fall, followed by rounded, orange hips. Very thorny canes carry glossy, medium to deep green leaves. Zones 5 to 9.

HOW TO USE

Though 'Autumn Sunset' is officially classified as a shrub rose, you'll most often see it used as an 8- to 12-foot climber. Train it to cover an arch, arbor, wall, fence, or trellis — anywhere you'd enjoy months of color and fragrance. Left unsupported, 'Autumn Sunset' forms a rather mounded shrub that's usually 6 to 8 feet tall and about as wide. It is well suited for use as a landscape accent or screen planting. Diseases seldom seriously bother this rose.

❦ 'Awakening'

Large-flowered climber. Blatna, 1935.

Imagine a rose with all the superb qualities of the climber 'New Dawn' but with fuller, old-fashioned flowers. Too good to be true? Not at all; it's the large-flowered climber called 'Awakening'! This excellent sport of 'New Dawn' offers pointed, medium pink buds that open to reveal fully double, flattened rosettes that are 1½ to 2½ inches across. Each flower is filled with light pink petals that tend to roll under along their edges, creating a quilled effect. Opinions vary regarding the intensity of its scent, but the perfume is most often at least moderate, with sweet or fruity overtones. Flowering usually begins in late spring to early summer, with good repeat continuing through the rest of the growing season. Slender, thorny canes carry medium green, glossy leaves. Zones 5 to 10.

HOW TO USE

'Awakening' makes a superb moderate-sized climber, generally growing 8 to 12 feet in height. Enjoy it on a trellis or let it scramble up into a small tree;

it looks great trained against a fence, too. It also is very pretty against a wall, although the poor air circulation in this type of site can encourage the development of mildew. Otherwise, disease resistance is normally good.

❦ 'Baby Blanket'

Syns. 'Oxfordshire', 'Sommermorgen'; KORfullwind
Shrub. Kordes, 1993.

This free-flowering little shrub rose bears large clusters of cupped, double blooms up to 2½ inches wide. Blooming through summer, 'Baby Blanket' produces crinkle-edged petals in shades of light pink surrounding a cluster of golden yellow stamens. The only thing lacking is great fragrance — the scent is very light. Bushy, spreading stems bear small, dark green, glossy foliage. Zones 5 to 9.

HOW TO USE

Growing 2 to 3 feet tall and 4 to 5 feet wide, 'Baby Blanket' is perfectly suited for use as a groundcover. Its small stature also makes it a good choice for the front of a flower bed or border. 'Baby Blanket' offers excellent disease resistance.

❦ 'Baby Grand'

Syn. POUlit
Miniature. Poulsen, 1994.

This wonderful miniature rose may be small in stature, but it's big on charm! Blooming over a long period — from early summer into fall — 'Baby Grand' produces small clusters of lovely medium pink, long-lasting blooms up to 2 inches across. The full, lightly fragrant flowers open to an almost flattened form, accompanied by small, bright green leaves that cover the low, bushy stems. Zones 5 to 10.

HOW TO USE

'Baby Grand' forms a compact, rounded bush that usually grows 12 to 18 inches tall and about as wide. It looks great planted in masses around a deck or patio, or as an edging for a bed, border, or walkway. It's also well suited for growing in containers. 'Baby Grand' offers excellent disease resistance.

❦ 'Ballerina'

Hybrid musk. Bentall, 1937.

It's hard to think of a way to improve on this remarkable, easy-to-grow hybrid musk rose, except perhaps to add more fragrance. 'Ballerina' produces single, shallow-cupped-to-flat flowers starting in late spring to early summer, followed by moderate summer rebloom and abundant rebloom in fall. Each flower has light pink petals with deeper pink edges; they fade to a near white center accented with a cluster of bright yellow stamens that darken quickly as the blooms open. The individual flowers are small, 1 to 2 inches across, but they're held in large, domed clusters, making an eye-catching display. Look for a generous crop of tiny orange-red hips in fall. Arching, lightly thorny canes are densely covered with medium to light green, semiglossy leaves. Zones 5 to 10.

HOW TO USE

'Ballerina' forms a relatively compact bush that's generally 4 to 5 feet tall and wide. (Hard pruning — cutting back by about half during winter — can encourage the bush to grow about 3 feet tall and wide.) 'Ballerina' is pretty enough to grow by itself, but it also looks great planted with perennials and shrubs in a mixed border or foundation planting, or in groups as a hedge. This versatile, nonfussy rose offers good disease resistance.

❦ 'Bantry Bay'

Large-flowered climber. McGredy, 1967.

If you're looking for a handsome climber with a long bloom season, 'Bantry Bay' belongs on your list of roses to consider. This selection offers clusters of loosely double, slightly fragrant blooms up to 4 inches across. The cupped flowers open to a flattened form, revealing a cluster of golden stamens surrounded by rich rosy pink petals. Flowering usually starts in early summer and repeats through summer into fall. Held on vigorous, branching stems, the shiny, dark green leaves make a lovely background for the beautiful blooms. Zones 5 to 9.

HOW TO USE

'Bantry Bay' is a moderately vigorous climber, usually reaching 10 feet but sometimes stretching to 15 feet in height. Train it up an arbor or try it on a pergola post for a long season of bloom. It also looks handsome trained against a fence or wrapped around a pillar. 'Bantry Bay' offers good disease resistance.

❦ 'Baronne Edmond de Rothschild'

Syns. 'Baronne de Rothschild'; MEIgriso
Hybrid tea. Meilland, 1968.

This handsome hybrid tea rose isn't especially generous with its blooms, but when it does flower, the fragrance is a true delight. The 4- to 5-inch, high-centered double blooms are a rich, deep reddish pink, with pink-streaked white on the backs of the petals. Flowering starts in early summer, with scattered rebloom through the summer. The thorny, upright canes bear glossy, bright green, leathery leaves. Zones 5 to 9.

HOW TO USE

'Baronne Edmond de Rothschild' usually grows 3 to 4 feet tall and 2 to 3 feet across. It's perhaps not the best choice for garden display, since it's show of bloom isn't prolific, but if you enjoy having fragrant, beautiful roses for cut-flower use, consider adding this one to your cutting garden. 'Baronne Edmond de Rothschild' generally has good disease resistance, but you may want to take preventive measures against black spot, especially in warm, humid climates.

❦ 'Baronne Prévost'

Hybrid perpetual. Desprez, 1842.

This classic hybrid perpetual has long been popular with gardeners who enjoy the classic "old rose" look and fragrance. 'Baronne Prévost' has large, plump, reddish buds that open to broad, flattened flowers, each about 4 inches across and packed with over 100 petals. The outer petals are broad and smooth; the inner petals are smaller and crinkled. Held singly or in small clusters, the flowers are a bright rose-pink that turns lighter pink as they age. 'Baronne Prévost' begins with a generous display of blooms in late spring to early summer, followed by scattered rebloom in summer and usually another good show in the fall. The heavily scented flowers and medium green, semiglossy leaves are held on thorny, sturdy, upright stems. Zones 5 to 8.

HOW TO USE

'Baronne Prévost' forms a good-looking, broad shrub that's usually 4 to 5 feet tall and 3 to 4 feet wide. It combines beautifully with a variety of companions. Try it with other old roses and/or shrubs in a shrub border, or with perennials, annuals, herbs, and other plants in a mixed border or cottage garden setting. 'Baronne Prévost' has moderate disease resistance; if black spot is common in your area, be prepared to take preventive measures.

❦ 'Beauty Secret'

Miniature. Moore, 1965.

More than 30 years after its introduction, 'Beauty Secret' is still among the most popular miniature roses. Its tapered buds open to high-centered blooms with pointed petals in a superb shade of cherry red. Held in small to medium-size clusters, the double flowers reach about 1½ inches across and have a pleasant fruity scent. The bloom season starts in early summer, with dependable repeat bloom through the rest of the season. Glossy, leathery, medium green leaves held on upright, well-branched stems make a handsome backdrop for the bright blooms. Zones 5 to 10.

HOW TO USE

'Beauty Secret' produces a vigorous, bushy plant reaching 12 to 18 inches tall and about as wide. This compact habit makes it a natural for edging beds, borders, and walkways. Try it in groups around a deck or patio, or enjoy it up close in containers. Held on strong, straight stems, the long-lasting blooms also make wonderful cut flowers for miniature arrangements. 'Beauty Secret' offers good disease resistance.

ARS Award of Excellence for Miniature Roses 1975; Miniature Rose Hall of Fame 1999

❦ 'Belinda'

Hybrid musk. Bentall, 1936.

If you like the bountiful bloom and dependable repeat flowering of 'Ballerina' but are looking for a bit more color impact, 'Belinda' may be the rose for you! The semidouble, lightly fragrant blooms of this hybrid musk are a rich rosy pink, with a touch of white and a cluster of stamens at the center of each blossom. The individual flowers are fairly small —

just about ¾ inch across — but they're grouped into large, showy clusters. The bushes bloom prolifically in late spring to early summer, followed by scattered rebloom in summer and another flush of bloom in fall. Slightly thorny, arching canes carry rich green, semiglossy foliage. Zones 6 to 10.

HOW TO USE

'Belinda' usually grows as a rather dense, bushy shrub reaching 4 to 6 feet tall and about as wide. Enjoy its long season of bloom at the back of a mixed border with perennials and other flowers, or plant it in groups to form a dense, low hedge. It also makes a handsome accent planted by itself. Let its arching canes spill over a low wall, or use it as a low climber on a pillar. Like other hybrid musk roses, 'Belinda' can tolerate light shade, so it's a good choice for sites with bright light but less than full sun. This rose is generally disease resistant.

✿ 'Belinda's Dream'

Syn. 'Belinda's Rose'
Shrub. Basye, 1992.

This striking shrub rose combines beauty and fragrance with good vigor and disease resistance. Plump, pointed, rose-pink buds held in small clusters open to fully double blooms up to 4 inches across. High-centered when newly opened, the medium pink flowers spread out to a rather flattened form, with outer petals that fold back at the tips. The blooms have a distinct, fruity scent. Flowering starts in late spring or early summer and continues freely through the rest of the growing season. The pink blooms look especially lovely against the dark bluish green leaves held on sturdy, upright canes. Zones 5 to 9.

HOW TO USE

'Belinda's Dream' grows as a bushy shrub that's 3 to 6 feet tall and about as wide. It's magnificent in a mixed border as a background for perennials in white or shades of yellow, peach, purple, or blue. It also looks great planted alone as an accent, or in masses for an informal hedge. 'Belinda's Dream' is generally trouble-free but may develop a bit of black spot in some areas; take preventive measures if needed.

✿ 'Belle Amour'

Alba. Date unknown.

The American Rose Society classifies 'Belle Amour' as an alba, though others often group this selection with the damask roses. Either way, it's an attractive addition to a collection of "old" roses. Produced in small clusters, the semi-double, somewhat cupped blooms are each 3 to 4 inches across, with ruffled, medium pink petals. The center of each bloom is crowned with a cluster of bright yellow stamens that are visible when the flower has opened fully. The blossoms generally have a rich, somewhat spicy fragrance. 'Belle Amour' produces a generous flush of bloom for several weeks in early summer. There's no rebloom later, but you do get to enjoy a display of rounded, orange-red hips in fall. Vigorous, upright, moderately thorny stems carry large, medium green leaves. Zones 5 to 8.

HOW TO USE

'Belle Amour' forms a bushy shrub that usually reaches 5 to 6 feet tall and about 4 feet wide. Combine it with other antique roses for a fragrance-rich early-summer garden, or enjoy its multiseason display in a shrub planting. The flowers and fruit also add interest to the back of a mixed border, combined with perennials and other plants to carry the show in mid- to late summer. 'Belle Amour' generally has good disease resistance.

✿ 'Belle de Crécy'

Hybrid gallica. Date unknown.

If fragrance is high on your list of "must-haves", you definitely need to consider growing 'Belle de Crécy'. This glorious hybrid gallica produces clusters of rounded, reddish buds that open to 3-inch-wide, shallow-cupped blooms. As they age, the flowers become rather flattened in form as the petals fold back to reveal a small greenish center. Packed with over 100 crinkled petals, the richly perfumed blooms open in a rich pink; the petals quickly age to a reddish purple, then to a light lilac-purple. 'Belle de Crécy' blooms only once, but the flowering season lasts for several weeks in early summer. The mostly thornless stems carry deeply toothed, dark gray-green foliage. Zones 4 to 8.

HOW TO USE

'Belle de Crécy' produces a relatively compact bush growing 3 to 5 feet tall and about 3 feet across. The upright-to-arching canes of this beloved old rose are rather flexible, so they tend to sprawl a bit under the weight of the blooms. Planting in groups will allow the stems to support each other and produce a handsome show. Try this rose in a mass as a landscape accent, as an informal hedge, in a mixed border, or in a foundation planting, where its wonderful scent can drift indoors through open windows. To reach its potential, 'Belle de Crécy' really needs ideal growing conditions — full sun, steady soil moisture, and shelter from strong winds — so choose the planting site carefully to get the best bloom display. This rose generally has good disease resistance, although it may develop a bit of powdery mildew, particularly in fall.

❦ 'Belle Poitevine'

Hybrid rugosa. Bruant, 1894.

It's a hybrid rugosa, so you know it has to be tough — but 'Belle Poitevine' is also quite charming. Tapered, deep red buds open to large, loose, semidouble blooms up to 4 inches across. Cupped when newly opened, the fragrant flowers open flat, with crinkled, rosy pink petals surrounding a cluster of yellow stamens. The bush blooms freely in early summer, with good repeat bloom through summer and into fall. In some years, 'Belle Poitevine' will produce large, orange-red hips in fall, but don't depend on it; still, you can appreciate the way the heavily veined, deep green leaves turn bright yellow at the end of the growing season. The prickly canes are vigorous and upright. Zones 4 to 8.

HOW TO USE

In cool climates, 'Belle Poitevine' tends to be fairly compact, normally growing 3 to 4 feet tall and about as wide. In warmer climates, this spreading shrub can reach 6 to 8 feet in height and about 6 feet in width. Adaptable and easy to grow, it makes a marvelous rose for just about any part of the garden. Plant it alone as an eye-catching specimen, or grow it in groups or as a low hedge. The long season of bloom makes it a great addition to mixed borders or cottage gardens, blended with perennials, annuals, bulbs, herbs, and other roses. 'Belle Poitevine' offers excellent disease resistance.

❦ 'Belle Story'

Syn. AUSelle
Shrub. Austin, 1985.

This lovely English rose produces distinctive cupped blooms in a soft shade of clear pink, with a boss of reddish stamens accenting the gold-touched center. Held singly or in clusters, the large, semidouble blooms of 'Belle Story' reach up to 4 inches in diameter and have a pleasant spicy scent. Flowering begins in late spring to early summer, with moderate to good rebloom through the rest of the summer. The slightly thorny, branching stems carry a rather sparse display of small, medium green, semiglossy leaves. Zones 5 to 9.

HOW TO USE

Growing only 3 to 5 feet tall and about as wide, 'Belle Story' is a good choice for accenting a bed or border in smaller garden. Its habit can be a bit sprawling, especially after a heavy flush of blooms, which may weigh down the stems. Planting in groups of three or more, however, can help develop a denser, bushier look, creating an attractive landscape accent or a beautiful addition to a mixed border containing pastel-flowered perennials. 'Belle Story' is generally quite disease resistant.

❦ 'Betty Boop'

Syn. WEKplapic
Floribunda. Carruth, 1999.

If you like your flowers bright and bold, this dazzling floribunda is just the rose for you! Long, pointed, ivory buds tinged with red open into single to semidouble, ruffled to flat flowers about 4 inches across, with a crown of golden orange stamens in the center. The intricately shaded blooms begin with yellowish petals heavily blushed with scarlet on the edges. As they age, the yellow fades to cream and then white, while the edge matures to cherry red. Each flower cluster contains blooms in various stages, creating an intriguing, ever-changing display. Some say they can detect little fragrance, but many describe the scent as moderate to strong and rather fruity. 'Betty Boop' starts the season with a profusion of blooms in late spring or early summer, with generous repeat through the rest of the summer into fall. Moderately thorny canes bear glossy foliage that's reddish when new and dark green when mature. Zones 5 to 10.

HOW TO USE

'Betty Boop' produces a bushy, spreading shrub that's 3 to 5 feet tall and about as wide. A group of three or more bushes used as a hedge or mass creates an attention-getting landscape accent. 'Betty Boop' also looks great against a background of dark evergreens; use it to add zip to an otherwise all-green foundation planting. Disease resistance is generally quite good; take preventive measures against black spot or powdery mildew in areas where these problems are common.

All-America Rose Selection 1999

'Betty Prior'

Floribunda. Prior, 1935.

'Betty Prior' is a rose for people who think they can't grow roses. With a minimum of basic good care, this tough, trouble-free floribunda blooms freely for months, and it's rarely bothered by diseases — a big plus! Reddish, rounded buds open to single, cupped to saucer-shaped blooms about 3½ inches across. The petals are bright reddish pink, fading to nearly white at the base, where they are accented with a cluster of golden stamens. Unfortunately, 'Betty Prior' produces little or no scent, but it makes up for that by producing dazzling clusters of flowers from late spring or early summer well into fall. Vigorous, upright, moderately thorny canes carry medium green, semiglossy foliage. Zones 5 to 9.

HOW TO USE

'Betty Prior' forms a bushy shrub, usually reaching 3 to 4 feet tall and about as wide. Its compact size and long flowering season make it a magnificent partner for perennials, annuals, and shrubs in a mixed border or foundation planting. Plant a single bush by itself as an accent, or enjoy the display of multiple plants in a mass or hedge. 'Betty Prior' usually has excellent disease resistance.

'Bill Warriner'

Syn. JACsur
Floribunda. McGredy, 1977.

The elegant color and exquisitely formed flowers of this compact floribunda have earned it a place in gardens across the country. Pointed, pink buds tinged with red open into double, high-centered blooms about 4 inches across, with a color in the salmon pink to coral pink range. Held in large clusters, the flowers have a light, sweet scent, and they appear almost continually from late spring or early summer into fall. Semiglossy, deep green leaves are carried on moderately thorny, well-branched canes. Zones 5 to 9.

HOW TO USE

'Bill Warriner' has a compact, bushy habit, generally growing 2 to 3 feet tall and about as wide. It's a beauty in beds, border, and foundation plantings, where its gentle color blends easily with many other colors, although it looks particularly pretty with yellow blooms, or with blues and purples, such as those of lavender or catmints (*Nepeta* spp.). 'Bill Warriner' generally offers very good disease resistance.

❦ 'Black Jade'

Syn. BENblack
Miniature. Benardella, 1985.

Black it isn't — but it's close! 'Black Jade' is a splendid miniature rose with tiny, near black buds that open into velvety, deep red, high-centered blooms up to ¾ inch across. When fully open, the double blooms reveal a cluster of bright yellow stamens that contrast handsomely with the dark red petals. The flowers have little or no scent, but they appear in a generous flush in early summer, with good repeat bloom through the rest of the growing season. The glossy, dark green leaves make a lovely backdrop for the richly colored flowers. Zones 5 to 10.

HOW TO USE

'Black Jade' forms a vigorous bush usually growing 18 to 24 inches tall and about as wide. Tuck it into flower beds and borders: it looks superb against silver-leaved plants such as dusty miller *(Senecio cineraria)* and artemisias. 'Black Jade' is also a great addition to low plantings around decks and patios, or along walkways. This marvelous miniature generally has good disease resistance.

ARS Award of Excellence for Miniature Roses 1985

❦'Blanc Double de Coubert'

Hybrid rugosa. Cochet-Cochet, 1892.

The dazzling contrast of delicate, snow-white petals against deeply veined, rich green leaves is enough to send chills up your spine! The clustered buds of this hybrid rugosa have a light pink blush, but they open to pure white, double blooms up to 3 inches across. Fully opened flowers have a flattened form, with the somewhat crinkled petals surrounding a cluster of sunny yellow stamens. The strongly perfumed blooms begin appearing in late spring to early summer and continue through summer into fall. If you're lucky, you might see a few reddish hips develop by fall; fortunately, the yellowish fall leaf color is more dependable. The vigorous, upright-to-arching canes are quite prickly. Zones 3 to 8.

HOW TO USE

'Blanc Double de Coubert' forms a large, somewhat rounded shrub that usually reaches 4 to 6 feet in height and about the same width. Established bushes often spread by suckers, forming a dense, prickly thicket that makes an excellent hedge. This handsome hybrid rugosa is also valuable for adding multiseason interest to shrub borders, and it makes a handsome background for perennials — especially a collection of white-flowered plants. Now for the downside: the thin white petals are soon spotted by rain during wet weather, and even during good weather, the browned petals of spent flowers tend to hang on, detracting from the newly opened blooms. That means deadheading is a must if you want this rose to look its best, so make sure you site it where you can access all parts of the bush without stepping on its companions. Otherwise, 'Blanc Double de Coubert' is generally trouble-free.

❦'Blaze Improved'

Syns. 'Blaze', 'Blaze Superior', 'Improved Blaze', 'New Blaze'
Large-flowered climber. Jackson & Perkins, 1950.

By whatever name you call it (see below), this large-flowered climber is an impressive sight in full bloom. Individually, the cupped, semidouble blooms are about 3 inches across. Grouped into large clusters and blooming from early summer to fall, the scarlet-red flowers provide a splendid show of color. Unfortunately, they don't have much fragrance, but the wealth of bloom certainly makes up for that lack. The shiny, bright green leaves held on fast-growing canes make a handsome contrast to the richly colored flowers. Zones 5 to 10.

HOW TO USE

'Blaze Improved' typically grows 9 to 12 feet in height. It's a classic for accenting arbors, fences, and trellises, and it's vigorous enough to dress up a shed or other small outbuilding. This rose is generally quite disease resistant, but both black spot and mildew have been reported, so be prepared to take preventive measures.

Be aware that 'Blaze Improved' travels under several different names. The original 'Blaze' was introduced in 1932; it was popular but unfortunately flowered only once each season in most areas. In 1950, Jackson & Perkins began marketing 'Blaze Improved'. Apparently properly known as 'Demokracie' or 'Blaze Superior', it's virtually identical to the original 'Blaze' except for its extended blooming season. Over time, the name 'Blaze Improved' or 'Blaze Superior' has generally been shortened to just 'Blaze'. So if you see a 'Blaze' that's described as repeat flowering, it most likely is 'Blaze Improved'.

'Blush Noisette'

Noisette. Noisette, before 1817.

This lovely Noisette rose has long been prized by warm-climate gardeners for its generous, long-lasting display of demurely colored but boldly scented blooms. 'Blush Noisette' produces large, tight clusters of plump, reddish pink buds that open up to double blooms about 2½ inches across. The cupped flowers are a delicate shade of palest pink, revealing a cluster of golden yellow stamens when fully open, and they have a noticeable, somewhat spicy scent. Flowering usually begins in late spring to early summer and repeats dependably through the summer, often winding up with another heavy flush of flowers toward the end of the growing season. Flexible, slightly thorny stems carry semiglossy, medium green leaves. Zones 7 to 10.

HOW TO USE

This versatile rose adapts equally well to life as a shrub or a climber. With light pruning, 'Blush Noisette' grows as a compact shrub, 4 to 5 feet high and 3 to 4 feet wide. Try it alone as a landscape accent, or plant it in masses for a handsome flowering hedge. It also blends beautifully with pastel-flowered perennials and annuals in a mixed border. Another option is to enjoy 'Blush Noisette' as a climber; it can reach 8 to 12 feet in height. Wrap it around a pillar, or train it against a wall or fence. This adaptable rose is durable and generally disease resistant, and it can tolerate light shade.

❧ 'Bonica'

Syns. 'Bonica '82', 'Demon'; MEIdomonac
Shrub. Meilland, 1985.

"Sturdy but stunning" sums up the strong points of this justly popular shrub rose. 'Bonica' produces generous clusters of oval buds that open to double, 1- to 2-inch, cupped blooms. The petals are a rich, warm rosy pink when just opened, gradually aging to a soft pink. They begin flowering in early summer, with moderate summer rebloom and another flush of flowers in fall. The lack of scent is unfortunate, but on the plus side, there is a crop of small orange hips scattered over the bush in fall. Arching canes bear a dense covering of glossy, dark green leaves. Zones 5 to 9.

HOW TO USE
'Bonica' produces a bushy, spreading shrub that's 3 to 5 feet tall and about 4 feet wide. It's hard to think of a place this trouble-free rose *wouldn't* look great! Try it alone or in groups as a landscape accent, or in a row for a fabulous flowering hedge. Tuck it into a foundation planting, or pair it with perennials, annuals, and other shrubs in a mixed border. 'Bonica' is generally touted as being disease-free, but it can develop black spot in humid conditions if you don't use preventive measures.

'Royal Bonica' (MEImodac) is a more recent introduction, with fuller flowers in a deeper shade of pink.

All-America Rose Selection 1987

❧ 'Boule de Neige'

Bourbon. Lacharme, 1867.

The crisp contrast of pure white blooms against deep green leaves adds a cool touch to the hottest summer day. This beautiful Bourbon rose produces rounded, white buds touched with reddish pink, opening to milk-white flowers about 3 inches across and packed with over 100 petals. As the beautifully symmetrical blooms open, the outer petals fold back, gradually giving each flower a rounded shape and revealing a touch of green in the center. The flowers are strongly scented. 'Boule de Neige' blooms for several weeks in early summer, with scattered rebloom through the rest of the growing season. Shiny, dark green, leathery leaves carried on thorny, branching canes perfectly complement the chaste white flowers. Zones 6 to 10.

HOW TO USE

As a shrub, 'Boule de Neige' forms a slender, upright bush that's usually 4 to 5 feet tall and 3 to 4 feet wide. Try it in mixed or shrub borders, or planted close together to form a flowering hedge. The long, arching canes also adapt well to life as an 8- to 10-foot climber, and since the heavy blooms tend to nod slightly, this is a great way to keep them up where you can enjoy them. Wrap the canes around a pillar or pergola post, or train them horizontally along a wall or fence. 'Boule de Neige' generally has good disease resistance, but it may develop some black spot during very humid conditions unless given preventive sprays.

✵ 'Bridal Pink'

Syn. JACbri
Floribunda. Boerner, 1967.

Widely grown for use as a cut flower, 'Bridal Pink' also makes a pretty garden rose. This floribunda offers elegantly tapered pink buds that open to high-centered, very double flowers in a delicate shade of clear medium to light pink. Individual blooms are up to 4 inches across and have a moderate spicy fragrance. Flowers bloom in clusters starting in late spring to early summer, with occasional rebloom in summer and more flowers in fall. The leathery, deep green leaves make a handsome background for the charming flowers. Zones 6 to 10.

HOW TO USE

'Bridal Pink' forms an upright bush that's 3 to 4 feet tall and about as wide. It's perhaps not the best rose for a beginner, since it does appreciate a bit of pampering, and it may develop some mildew or black spot in humid conditions if you don't take preventive measures. Still, if you're willing to give it a warm, sunny spot with regular watering and fertilizing, it can make a lovely rose for a bed or border. If you enjoy flower arranging, consider growing a few bushes of 'Bridal Pink' in your cutting garden for long-lasting cut flowers.

❦ 'Buffalo Gal'

Syns. 'Foxi', 'Foxi Pavement'; UHLater
Hybrid rugosa. Uhl, 1989.

This easy-care hybrid rugosa goes by many names, but whatever you call it, it's a good garden rose, especially for difficult sites. Pointed, deep pink buds open into semidouble, flattened, purplish pink blooms that are 3 to 4 inches in diameter. Moderately to very fragrant flowers appear over a long season, from late spring or early summer to frost. Abundant, plump, orange-red hips ripen among the flowers in fall, and the yellowish fall color helps end the growing season on a bright note. Bristly stems bear deeply veined, dark green leaves. Zones 3 to 8.

HOW TO USE
'Buffalo Gal' forms a dense, compact shrub that's 3 to 4 feet in height and spread. This adaptable selection works well just about anywhere you need a dependable, easy-care shrub that provides garden interest from spring into winter: beds, borders, foundation plantings, low hedges, or containers. Rugosa roses are noted for their salt tolerance, making them ideal for planting along driveways or roadsides that are exposed to winter de-icing salts. Like many other rugosa roses, 'Buffalo Gal' has excellent disease resistance.

❦ 'Buff Beauty'

Hybrid musk. Bentall, 1939.

'Buff Beauty' is one of those classic roses that both beginning and experienced gardeners just adore, for its unusual, changeable color as well as its pleasing fragrance. This handsome hybrid musk produces clusters of pink-and-yellow buds that open to sweetly scented, fully double blooms up to 4 inches across. It's hard to describe the flower color exactly, since it varies depending on the growing conditions, but it's generally a peachy orange with touches of gold. The color is richest in indirect light, quickly fading to a light creamy peach in strong sun. The bloom season begins in late spring to early summer, with reasonable repeat flowering through the rest of the growing season. Moderately thorny stems carry large, leathery leaves that are reddish when young and a semiglossy dark green when mature. Zones 5 to 9.

HOW TO USE

The fully opened flowers of 'Buff Beauty' are quite heavy, so you'll often see this rose trained as an 8- to 12-foot climber to support the stems. Try it against a wall of fence, or grow it on a pillar or pergola post. Like many of the hybrid musks, 'Buff Beauty' takes a bit of shade, so it's a good choice if you need a climber for a spot with plenty of bright but indirect light. As a shrub, it grows 5 to 6 feet tall and about as wide. 'Buff Beauty' is wonderful planted alone or in masses as a landscape accent, or as a hedge. Or try it in a mixed border; it looks exquisite paired with soft purple or blue flowers, such as those of bellflowers (*Campanula* spp.) and catmints (*Nepeta* spp.). 'Buff Beauty' generally has good disease resistance.

❦ 'Cabbage Rose'

Syns. *Rosa centifolia, R. gallica centifolia*; Provence Rose Centifolia. Introduced before 1600.

If you enjoy richly perfumed roses, this splendid centifolia is certainly one that should be on your list. Its plump, rounded, reddish buds open to pretty, rosy pink blooms blessed with luxurious fragrance. Each very double bloom is up to 3 inches wide, with a cupped form that quickly becomes rounded as the outer petals roll back. (That's how this plant gets the name "cabbage rose" — however inelegant it sounds, the overlapping petals *do* make the open blooms look rather like heads of cabbage!) Appearing only in early summer, the flowers may be held singly or in clusters. Long, arching, thorny stems carry abundant, gray-green leaves. Zones 4 to 8.

HOW TO USE

'Cabbage Rose' grows 5 to 7 feet tall and about 5 feet wide, with a somewhat open habit. The heavy flowers can quickly weigh down the stems, so it's best to provide some type of support for the canes; consider training them to grow along a fence or up a pillar. Or grow several bushes together as a hedge or mass so they can support each other. 'Cabbage Rose' is perhaps not the best choice for a small garden — there are many other fragrant, fully double roses in the same color range and with longer bloom seasons — but if you enjoy collecting antique roses, give this one a try. It is generally disease resistant but can develop some powdery mildew if you don't take preventive measures, and its flowers may not open fully during spells of wet weather.

❦ 'Cal Poly'

Syn. MORpoly
Miniature. Moore, 1991.

Yellow roses have a charm all their own, and they're especially appealing when they hold their color as well as this marvelous miniature does. Small, egg-shaped, pointed buds unfurl to reveal double, high-centered flowers that are 1½ to 2½ inches across, with clear, deep yellow to medium yellow petals. Held singly or in small clusters, the long-lasting blooms have little or no fragrance, but they appear in abundance over a long season, from late spring or early summer well into fall. Medium to deep green, semiglossy leaves are carried on canes that bear just a few thorns. Zones 5 to 10.

HOW TO USE
'Cal Poly' forms a rather rounded bush growing anywhere from 15 to 30 inches tall and about as wide. Enjoy its cheerful display in beds, borders, and foundation plantings, where it blends easily into either pastel or hot-color themes. It looks great as a low hedge or an edging along a path, and it's super in containers, too. 'Cal Poly' generally offers good to excellent disease resistance.

ARS Award of Excellence for Miniature Roses 1992

❦ 'Camaieux'

Hybrid gallica. 1830.

Striped roses — it seems that you either love them or dislike them. If you enjoy their cheerful, casual appearance but don't have much room to spare, 'Camaieux' might be just the rose for you. The 3-inch blooms of this hybrid gallica open purplish pink irregularly streaked with white; over time, the pink sections age to a soft lilac-purple. The loosely double flowers show a cluster of bright yellow stamens when fully open and have a spicy-sweet scent. There is one show of bloom, usually late spring to early summer; rounded, red hips appear in fall. The arching stems bear small, medium green leaves that have a light grayish cast. Zones 4 to 8.

HOW TO USE

'Camaieux' forms a compact bush growing 3 to 4 feet tall and about 3 feet wide. Grown on its own roots (not grafted), it may spread by suckers, making for a dense, low hedge. It also adds seasonal interest to a shrub border or a mixed border; try pairing it with white- or pink-flowered perennials. Or try growing it in a large container or half-barrel, so you can admire the intriguing flowers up close. 'Camaieux' is generally disease resistant but may develop some mildew in warm, humid conditions if you don't take preventive measures.

🌹 'Candy Cane'

Climbing miniature. Moore, 1958.

This long-blooming climbing miniature rose is definitely something different! Its single to semidouble, flattened flowers are each only 1½ to 2 inches across, but they are held in loose clusters, making an eye-catching display. The pointed-tipped petals start out reddish pink, with white streaks branching out from the center of the distinctive blooms; they age to a lighter rose-pink with white streaks. Best of all, 'Candy Cane' blooms over an amazingly long season, from mid- or late spring to early fall with regular deadheading. Slender, arching stems carry small, medium green leaves. Zones 5 to 10.

HOW TO USE

'Candy Cane' is a vigorous selection, usually growing 4 to 5 feet tall but stretching up to 10 feet in warm climates. It makes a striking display trained against a wall or fence. Or try it planted atop a low wall or in a large container, where it can trail over the side. 'Candy Cane' generally has good disease resistance, but take preventive measures against black spot in humid conditions.

❧ 'Candy Sunblaze'

Syns. 'Romantique Meillandina'; MEIdanclar
Miniature. Meilland, 1991.

There's nothing demure about this lovely little miniature rose! 'Candy Sunblaze' offers a superb show of 2-inch, double blooms in an intense shade of deep pink. The flowers don't have much fragrance, but on the plus side, they're produced in abundance through most of the growing season. The upright stems carry an abundant crop of shiny, deep green leaves that make a beautiful background for the profuse bloom display. Zones 5 to 10.

HOW TO USE

'Candy Sunblaze' produces a compact bush usually growing around 18 inches tall (sometimes up to 2 feet) and about as wide. It's a handsome addition to the front or middle of a flower bed or border. Try it as an accent around a deck or patio, or plant it in a container so you can admire the flowers without bending over. Combine it with silvery leaved plants, such as annual dusty miller *(Senecio cineraria),* for an elegant partnership, or pair it with bright yellow, blue, or purple blooms for a dazzling display. (Make sure you leave plenty of room around the rose for good air circulation, though.) 'Candy Sunblaze' has good disease resistance.

❧ 'Captain Thomas'

Climbing hybrid tea. Thomas, 1935.

It may take a bit of searching to find this lovely selection, but it's worth the hunt if you're a fan of single roses, or yellow roses—or both! Classified as a climbing hybrid tea but sometimes listed as either a large-flowered climber or a shrub, 'Captain Thomas' bears tapered buds that open to lightly perfumed, single blooms about 3½ inches across, with five slightly wavy petals. The flowers start out a sunny yellow and age to creamy white, with a cluster of showy reddish stamens accenting the center. The bloom season usually begins in early summer, with moderate rebloom through the rest of the summer, especially if you deadhead the spent flowers regularly. Long, thorny, sturdy canes bear glossy, light green leaves. Zones 5 to 9.

HOW TO USE

As you may guess by its multiple classifications, 'Captain Thomas' grows either as a rather loose shrub (to about 6 feet tall and wide) or as a climber (to about 10 feet tall). Combine it with other roses or shrubs in a shrub border, train it to grow on a fence or wall, or wrap it around a pillar or pergola post. 'Captain Thomas' usually has excellent disease resistance.

☙ 'Cardinal de Richelieu'

Syn. 'Cardinal Richelieu'
Hybrid gallica. Laffay, 1840.

There aren't too many outstanding purple roses, but this gorgeous hybrid gallica is definitely one of them. 'Cardinal de Richelieu' produces plump, deep reddish pink buds that open to open-cupped to rounded, double, 3-inch blooms in small clusters. The flowers open a velvety deep red that ages to deep purple, with a lighter shade of rosy purple on the backs of the petals and a touch of white at their base. This exquisite rose only blooms once a season, in late spring or early summer, but while it is flowering, you'll glory in the stunning blossoms and luxurious fragrance. Abundant, medium green, semiglossy leaves are held on thin, arching, almost thornless stems. Zones 4 to 8.

HOW TO USE

'Cardinal de Richelieu' forms a bushy plant that's normally 3 to 6 feet tall and 2 to 4 feet across. It appreciates a bit of pampering in the way of regular watering and feeding, and it needs careful thinning and pruning after flowering to produce a good crop of flowers the following year. If you're willing to provide the extra attention, this rose makes a remarkable hedge; like most gallicas, it spreads by suckers to form a dense thicket. 'Cardinal de Richelieu' also looks wonderful trained on a fence or wall or grown up a post or pillar. In a border, it makes a sumptuous early-season show: try it with spring bulbs, irises, and peonies for additional color, and with silver-leaved herbs such as artemisias and sages (*Salvia* spp.). 'Cardinal de Richelieu' is generally disease resistant but occasionally develops a bit of black spot if you don't take preventive measures.

❦ 'Carefree Beauty'

Syns. 'Audace'; BUCbi
Shrub. Buck, 1977.

Here's a rose that truly lives up to its name! This easy-care shrub produces small clusters of long, pointed buds that open to large, semi-double, cupped blooms up to 4½ inches across. The moderately fragrant flowers are a warm rose-pink, aging to lighter pink. 'Carefree Beauty' blooms abundantly in late spring to early summer, with good repeat bloom through summer and into fall. Rounded, orange-red hips also appear in fall. The upright canes bear large, medium green leaves. Zones 4 to 9.

HOW TO USE

'Carefree Beauty' grows as a bushy, spreading shrub that's 4 to 5 feet tall and about as wide. This versatile rose looks great in just about any part of the landscape. Plant it by itself or in groups as an accent, or use it as a long-blooming hedge. It blends beautifully with annuals, perennials, and herbs in a bed or border. This easy-to-grow rose seldom has any disease problems, making it a good choice for low-maintenance areas.

❦ 'Carefree Delight'

Syns. 'Bingo Meidiland', 'Bingo Meillandecor'; MEIpotal
Shrub. Meilland, 1994.

This dependable garden gem is a great choice for anyone who enjoys the "wild" look of single-flowered roses. The long, pointed, deep pink buds of this first-class shrub rose open into simple but elegant, five-petaled flowers up to 2 inches across. The slightly cupped blooms are a pretty medium pink accented with a small white eye and a cluster of clear yellow stamens in the center. Unfortunately, the flowers have little or no scent, but that hardly seems to matter when you see the generous clusters of blooms that decorate the bush from early summer to frost. The orange-red hips are an additional bonus. Thorny, branching, arching canes carry an abundant covering of glossy, deep green leaves. Zones 4 to 10.

HOW TO USE

'Carefree Delight' is a vigorous, spreading rose that forms a compact bush usually 3 to 4 feet tall (sometimes to 5 feet) and 3 to 5 feet wide. It's an excellent addition to flower beds, foundation plantings, mixed beds, and shrub borders. It also makes a marvelous hedge and is pretty enough to look good planted by itself, either singly or in groups. You can even grow it in a large container, such as a half-barrel. 'Carefree Delight' is truly a delight for gardeners who enjoy roses but don't want to fuss with them too much. It offers excellent disease resistance.

All-America Rose Selection 1996

❦ 'Carefree Wonder'

Syn. MEIpitac
Shrub. Meilland, 1990.

Tough and trouble-free, 'Carefree Wonder' makes a wonderful addition to any garden. This sturdy shrub rose produces pointed buds that open to cupped, double blooms usually 3 inches across. The petals are a vibrant, bright pink on top and creamy pink on the undersides, giving the loosely ruffled blooms a two-toned effect. Held singly or in small clusters, the lightly scented flowers appear in abundance from late spring or early summer until frost. Many sources claim that this rose does not set fruit, but a number of gardeners have reported seeing a good show of reddish orange hips on their bushes. During the growing season, 'Carefree Wonder' blooms so heavily that you can hardly see the semiglossy, medium green and thorny stems. Zones 4 to 9.

HOW TO USE

Even without regular pruning, 'Carefree Wonder' produces a compact bush reaching 3 to 4 feet in height and about 3 feet in width. Use it anywhere you would enjoy its easy-care habits and long-lasting bloom display: in beds, borders, and foundations plantings; grown alone or in groups for a dramatic landscape accent; or set close together to form a dense, colorful hedge. While this rose performs admirably with virtually no attention, it will do even better if you give it the good care you give your other roses, in the form of regular watering, fertilizing, and deadheading during the summer. 'Carefree Wonder' has excellent disease resistance.

All-America Rose Selection 1991

❦ 'Cécile Brünner'

Syns. 'Mignon', 'Mlle. Cécile Brünner'; Sweetheart Rose
Polyantha. Ducher, 1881.

You'll often hear this charming polyantha referred to as the sweetheart rose, and little wonder—that name perfectly describes its pretty, petite blooms! Its tiny, tapered, warm pink buds open to perfectly formed, double blooms in a delicate shade of soft pink. Each exquisite blossom is less than 2 inches across when fully open, with a mild, spicy-sweet scent. The clustered flowers appear over a long season, starting in late spring or early summer and continuing through summer into fall. The reddish purple, virtually thornless canes carry a relatively sparse covering of small, deep green leaves. Zones 5 to 10.

HOW TO USE
'Cécile Brünner' forms a low-growing bush that's usually 3 feet tall and 2 feet wide. (If you see a bush or read a description of a 'Cécile Brünner' that's similar in bloom but grows much larger, it probably is a rose known as 'Bloomfield Abundance'.) The compact size of the true 'Cécile Brünner' makes it ideal for beds and borders. It generally has good disease resistance.

'Climbing Cécile Brünner' (Hosp, 1894) is a vigorous climbing form that blooms in early summer. Reaching 10 to 20 feet in height, it looks great climbing up into a tree or covering a small shed. Zones 6 to 10.

❦ 'Celestial'

Syn. 'Céleste'
Alba. Introduced before 1797.

It may not be as dramatic as some of the newer, long-flowering hybrids, but this lovely alba rose is still prized by gardeners for its beautiful blooms, attractive foliage, and wonderful sweet scent. Its pointed pink buds open to open-cupped, loosely double flowers that are 2 to 3 inches across, with soft pink petals surrounding a cluster of golden yellow stamens. 'Celestial' blooms only once, usually in late spring, but it offers another show, of oval, reddish hips, later in the season. The somewhat thorny, upright-to-arching stems bear gray-green foliage. Zones 5 to 8.

HOW TO USE

'Celestial' forms a large, rather rounded shrub that's 5 to 6 feet tall and 4 to 5 feet wide. Try it at the back of a mixed border, paired with peonies, irises, pinks (*Dianthus* spp.), and other early-blooming perennials. Include some plants with silvery foliage, such as lamb's ears *(Stachys byzantina)*, to complement the gray cast of this rose's handsome foliage. 'Celestial' also looks great as a hedge. Like other alba roses, this selection can tolerate light shade, so it's a good choice if you want to grow roses but don't have the full sun most roses demand. 'Celestial' seldom has any disease problems.

❦ 'Céline Forestier'

Noisette. Leroy, 1858.

This elegant Noisette is a charmer for warm-climate gardens. The show usually begins in spring, with a profusion of plump, pink buds that open to large, double blooms up to 5 inches across. The clustered, flattened flowers are mostly pale yellow, with a deeper yellow at the center; the ruffled petals turn creamy white as they age. They have a moderate to strong scent that's both spicy and sweet. 'Céline Forestier' continues to produce its fragrant blooms through summer, often ending the season with another generous flush of flowers in fall. The sturdy, spiny canes carry glossy, medium green leaves. Zones 7 to 10.

HOW TO USE

You'll most often see 'Céline Forestier' grown as a climber, reaching from 8 to as much as 15 or even 20 feet in height. Train it against a wall, fence, or trellis, or try it on an arbor, pillar, or pergola post, so you can admire the delicately shaded blooms and delightful fragrance up close. 'Céline Forestier' can also grow as a shrub, but make sure you give it plenty of room: it can reach up to 8 feet high by 6 feet wide. This vigorous rose generally has good disease resistance, although it will occasionally develop a bit of powdery mildew.

❦ 'Celsiana'

Damask. Introduced before 1750.

Fans of fragrance particularly prize damask roses, and this lovely selection certainly lives up to the reputation of its relatives. 'Celsiana' produces rounded, deep pink buds that unfurl into exquisite, semidouble, 4-inch blooms held in small, nodding clusters. The broad, crinkled and tissue-like petals are pale pink at first, aging quickly to near white. This means a bush in full bloom creates the effect of producing pink and white flowers at the same time. The delicately colored but strongly scented blooms appear over a period of several weeks in late spring to early summer, perfectly complemented by the light bluish green leaves held on arching, thorny canes. Zones 4 to 8.

HOW TO USE

'Celsiana' produces an upright, relatively dense shrub growing 4 to 5 feet tall and about as wide. It's handsome enough to stand alone as a landscape accent, planted singly or in groups, but it also looks great in a mixed border with other pastel colors. Try it with the pale blue flowers of Arkansas blue star *(Amsonia hubrichtii),* and perhaps some white, pink, or blue bellflowers (*Campanula* spp.). 'Celsiana' is generally quite disease resistant, but it may develop powdery mildew in some conditions.

❧ 'Champlain'

Hybrid kordesii. Svejda, 1982.

Here's a knock-your-socks-off red rose tailor-made for you cold-climate gardeners! This hybrid kordesii is part of the Canadian Explorer Series, a group of roses bred at the Agriculture Canada research station in Ottawa and selected for their hardiness, repeat flowering, and disease resistance. 'Champlain' produces tapered buds that open into rich red, velvety-petaled blooms accented with a cluster of golden stamens in the center. The lightly fragrant, double flowers are individually of moderate size (about 3 inches across), but they're held in large clusters that appear reliably from early summer well into fall. Lustrous, medium green leaves are held on prickly canes. Zones 3 to 9.

HOW TO USE

'Champlain' is a fairly compact grower, making a bush that's 3 to 4 feet tall and about as wide. In a bed or border, it looks stunning planted with silvery-leaved plants, such as artemisias and lamb's ears *(Stachys byzantina).* It also makes an outstanding rose for a long-flowering, low hedge. The only drawback to 'Champlain' is that it's a bit slow to put on much size, perhaps because it puts so much energy into flower production. But if you're willing to give it a little extra time, you'll certainly enjoy this remarkable rose. 'Champlain' generally has good disease resistance, although it may develop powdery mildew in some areas.

'Champneys' Pink Cluster'

Syn. 'Champneys' Rose'
Noisette. Champneys, 1811.

The development of this lovely rose by John Champneys in South Carolina ushered in the group of roses later known as Noisettes, named for the French nurserymen who used its offspring to breed other vigorous, fragrant, free-flowering roses. 'Champneys' Pink Cluster' produces large clusters of dark pink buds that open to small, double, cupped flowers up to 2 inches across. The clustered blooms are pale pink and have a pleasing scent. Flowering begins with a generous show in spring, with moderate rebloom in summer and another flush in fall. The almost-thornless canes carry glossy, light green leaves. Zones 7 to 10.

HOW TO USE

This charming rose generally grows as an upright shrub reaching 6 to 8 feet tall and about as wide. It makes a good hedge but also looks great in shrub borders or mixed borders. If your space is limited, try training the flexible stems to grow on a fence or up a post or pillar; it can reach 10 to 12 feet this way. 'Champneys' Pink Cluster' usually is quite disease resistant, but it may develop a touch of mildew or black spot by the end of the growing season in some areas.

'Charles de Mills'

Syn. 'Bizarre Triomphant'
Hybrid gallica. Hardy, before 1746.

The gorgeous blooms of this hybrid gallica make it a favorite with many fans of old roses. 'Charles de Mills' produces plump, rounded buds that expand into large, perfectly formed, flattened, full flowers up to 5 inches across. The color is difficult to describe: it's basically a rich red to reddish purple with a deep pink tinge toward the edges of the outer petals, aging to a lighter pinkish purple. Held in small clusters, the flowers appear over a period of several weeks, usually starting in late spring to early summer. 'Charles de Mills' is generally said to have exceptional fragrance, although some gardeners claim their bushes have little or no scent. The rough, deep green leaves are carried on mostly upright stems that are bristly but not very thorny. Zones 4 to 8.

HOW TO USE

'Charles de Mills' is a vigorous rose with somewhat open habit, growing anywhere from 3 to 6 feet tall and 3 to 5 feet wide. It looks great planted in groups as a landscape accent, or at the back of a mixed border. Grown on its own roots (not grafted, or with the graft union planted deeply), it tends to sucker, making a handsome, dense hedge. The heavy flowers tend to weigh down the canes, so training this rose on an arbor, trellis, pillar, or post is a super way to support the canes and show off the nodding blooms. 'Charles de Mills' is generally disease resistant, although it occasionally develops a bit of black spot or mildew if you don't take preventive measures.

✿ 'Charlotte'

Syns. 'Elgin Festival'; AUSpoly
Shrub. Austin, 1994.

Yellow roses hold a special place in the heart of many a gardener, so this English rose could be cherished for its color alone. This shrub rose has much more to offer, though, including full, old-fashioned flowers and a relatively compact growth habit. Rounded, pink-tinged yellow buds unfurl into fully double, cupped blooms about 3½ inches across, in a soft shade of yellow that's deeper toward the center of the bloom and almost ivory at the outer petals. The sweetly fragrant flowers are held in small clusters produced in abundance in early summer, followed by moderate rebloom through the rest of the growing season. The branching canes carry medium green, semiglossy leaves. Zones 5 to 10.

HOW TO USE

'Charlotte' forms a bushy shrub that normally grows 3 to 6 feet tall and 4 to 5 feet wide. It makes a marvelous addition to a mixed border, particularly with the blue blooms of globe thistle *(Echinops ritro)* or catmints *(Nepeta* spp.) or the purple flowers of lavender or balloon flower *(Platycodon grandiflorus)*. 'Charlotte' is generally disease resistant.

❦ 'Charmian'

Syn. AUSmian
Shrub. Austin, 1983.

One of the older English roses, 'Charmian' is still appreciated for its full flowers and rich fragrance. Rounded to oval, deep pink buds open into broad-cupped to flat, fully double blooms about 3 inches across. The heady-scented, rich pink flowers appear first in late spring to early summer and continue through the summer. Arching stems bear semiglossy, medium green leaves. Zones 5 to 10.

HOW TO USE

'Charmian' is officially classified as a shrub rose, growing 4 to 8 feet tall and 4 to 6 feet wide, but its rather loose habit makes it a good candidate for use as a climber. Train it to grow against a wall or fence, or attach it to a trellis, arbor, post, or pillar, to prevent the heavy flowers from weighing down the stems. Another option is to grow 'Charmian' in groups in a mixed border or cottage garden, so the bushes can support each other. This pink rose looks superb paired with red and white flowers for a dramatic display, or with purple, blue, and yellow annuals and perennials for a cheerful combination. 'Charmian' usually has good disease resistance.

❦ 'Chevy Chase'

Hybrid multiflora. Hansen, 1939.

It blooms only once a season, but this hybrid multiflora is a real show stopper when it's in full flower! Small, rounded buds open to fully double, cupped blooms in a vibrant shade of rich crimson-red. The individual flowers are small — only about 1½ inches across — but they're held in large, tightly packed clusters. 'Chevy Chase' blooms for several weeks in late spring or early summer, making a splendid show of colorful flowers. The sturdy, prickly canes carry crinkled, medium green leaves. Zones 5 to 9.

HOW TO USE

Once classified as a rambler — a term that perfectly describes its growth habit — this vigorous rose produces long canes that can climb 12 to 15 feet in height. It makes an amazing display when trained to grow on a trellis or arbor or into a tree. 'Chevy Chase' generally has good disease resistance, though it may be susceptible to rust in some areas.

🌹 'Chicago Peace'

Syn. JOHnago
Hybrid tea. Johnston, 1962.

Take the huge, beautiful blooms of the famous hybrid tea known as 'Peace', intensify the colors a bit, and you have the lovely sport called 'Chicago Peace'. Large, pointed buds spiral open to reveal very double, high-centered flowers that are 5 to 6 inches across. The elegant blooms are generally rosy pink with yellow hearts, but they can vary widely depending on weather conditions: strong sun tends to intensify the pink, whereas cloudier conditions can produce lighter blooms in sunset shades of pink, peach, and yellow. Fragrance is slight, at best. Normally produced singly on long stems, the flowers appear in abundance in late spring or early summer, with good repeat through the rest of the season. Moderately thorny canes carry glossy, deep green foliage. Zones 5 to 9.

HOW TO USE

'Chicago Peace' grows as an upright bush that's 4½ to 6 feet tall and 3 to 4½ feet wide. It's a beauty in beds and borders, especially when planted in groups of three or more to create a drift of color. Add a few bushes to your cutting garden, as well. Overall disease resistance is moderate; black spot can be a problem, so take preventive measures in areas where this fungal disease is common.

🌹 'Child's Play'

Syn. SAVachild
Miniature. Saville, 1991.

It's probably a good thing this rose is a miniature—otherwise, its remarkable bicolored blooms could be overwhelming! The distinctive 1- to 2-inch flowers look like perfectly scaled-down hybrid tea blooms; they are high centered and semidouble to double, with white petals edged in an intense shade of deep pink. Held singly or in clusters, the stunning, sweetly scented blooms appear over a long season, from late spring or early summer well into fall. Branching stems bear dark green leaves that make a perfect backdrop for the bright blooms. Zones 4 to 10.

HOW TO USE

'Child's Play' produces a well-branched bush that generally grows 15 to 24 inches tall and 18 to 20 inches across. It's outstanding in a flower bed or border, or as an edging for a deck, patio, or walkway. Planting it in a container is also a good option, since you can admire the flowers close up. Wherever you grow it, choose its companions carefully so they don't compete with the eye-catching pink-and-white combination. White-flowered annuals, such as sweet alyssum *(Lobularia maritima)*, or those with silver foliage, such as annual dusty miller *(Senecio cineraria)*, can make pretty partners; just make sure you allow room around the rose for good air circulation. 'Child's Play' usually has excellent disease resistance.

All-America Rose Selection 1993; ARS Award of Excellence for Miniature Roses 1993

❦ 'China Doll'

Polyantha. Lammerts, 1946.

If you're looking for a low-growing, long-blooming pink rose to perk up your landscape, your search is over. This pretty polyantha offers pointed buds that open to cupped, loosely double, rosy pink blooms about 2 inches across. The flowers are only slightly fragrant, which is a bit disappointing, but this rose more than makes up for that by bearing a constant display of generously sized bloom clusters from early or midsummer through the rest of the growing season. Glossy, deep green leaves are evergreen in the South; they make this rose look handsome even when it's not in bloom. The foliage is carried on almost thornless stems. Zones 5 to 10.

HOW TO USE

'China Doll' forms a bushy, spreading mound reaching just 1 to 2 feet tall and about as wide. Its compact size makes it great choice for small gardens. It fits in just about anywhere: near the front of a bed or border, tucked into a foundation planting, or planted in groups to edge a walkway or create a landscape accent. Try it in pots to decorate a deck or patio with months of bloom. It also looks super growing as a standard (grafted atop a straight stem to create a "tree" form). Deadheading (or shearing, in the case of multiple bushes) after the first flush of bloom will help promote the best rebloom. 'China Doll' generally has excellent disease resistance.

'Climbing China Doll' (Weeks, 1977), also known as 'Weeping China Doll', is a more lax-growing form that looks charming as a ground cover, planted to cascade over a low wall, or grafted onto a 4-foot stem to create a standard.

❦ 'Chrysler Imperial'

Hybrid tea. Lammerts, 1952.

This classic hybrid tea has been around for decades, and with good reasons: namely, its dramatic color and exquisite fragrance. Elegant, tapered buds unfurl into double, high-centered blooms up to 5 inches across, in a rich, velvety, deep red. The fragrant flowers first appear in late spring to early summer and repeat through the summer, often with another good flush in fall. Semiglossy, deep green leaves held on upright, thorny canes make a perfect complement to the deep blood red blooms. Zones 6 to 9.

HOW TO USE

'Chrysler Imperial' grows anywhere from 3 to 6 feet (or even more) in height, and about 3 feet across, showing the most vigor in the warm climates it prefers. It has a fairly stiff, upright form, so it's not a rose that looks great planted by itself; for best effect, grow it in groups of three or more to get a bushier look. Its scented, long-stemmed blooms also make excellent cut flowers, so you might want to grow 'Chrysler Imperial' in a cutting garden so you can gather the blooms from there without spoiling your garden display. There is one drawback to growing this rose: its susceptibility to disease, particularly in cool climates. Give it a spot with excellent air circulation, keep the stems thinned out, and be prepared to apply protective sprays if black spot or mildew is often a problem in your area.

All-America Rose Selection 1953; James Alexander Gamble Fragrance Medal Winner 1965

❦ 'Cinderella'

Miniature. de Vink, 1953.

Think you don't have room for yet another rose? Think again: this diminutive miniature rose can fit in a smallest of spaces! Tiny, oval, pale pink buds unfurl into very double, clustered flowers less than an inch across. Newly opened blooms are pink-blushed white (the pink is especially noticeable in cool weather); they usually lose the pink tint as they age. The flowers are lightly to moderately fragrant, with a spicy scent. 'Cinderella' generally begins blooming in late spring or early summer and continues until frost (with a little help from you, in the form of regular deadheading or shearing after each flush of blooms). The thornless stems carry small, glossy, medium green leaves. Zones 5 to 9.

HOW TO USE

HOW TO USE

One of the smallest roses you can grow, 'Cinderella' creates a dense, mounded bush that's 8 to 10 inches tall and about as wide. Its compact size makes it a natural choice for container growing; try it in a pot, planter, window box, or even a hanging basket. (That's a great way to get the blooms up to eye level, so you can admire their dainty beauty and pleasing scent.) In the garden, grow 'Cinderella' in groups to dress up a flower bed, or enjoy it as an edging for a border or walkway. This rose has excellent disease resistance.

✿ 'City of York'

Syn. 'Direktör Benschop'
Large-flowered climber. Tantau, 1945.

There are few white-flowered climbing roses, and even fewer great ones, but this classic large-flowered climber is one of the best. Plump buds open into semidouble, broadly cupped blooms that are 3 to 4 inches across, with creamy white petals surrounding a cluster of sunny yellow stamens. 'City of York' is adorned with large clusters of fragrant flowers in one main flush in late spring or early summer. Scattered flowers occasionally appear later in the season as well, especially if you remove the spent flowers from the main crop of blooms. Moderately thorny canes carry the glossy, medium green leaves. Zones 5 to 9.

HOW TO USE

'City of York' produces long, vigorous canes that can grow anywhere from 8 to 20 feet in height (10 to 12 feet seems to be about average). Give it a sturdy support, such as a fence or pergola post, or a well-built trellis. It also looks marvelous trained over an arbor or on a gazebo. 'City of York' generally has good disease resistance.

✿ 'Clair Matin'

Syns. 'Grimpant Clair Matin'; MEImont
Large-flowered climber. Meilland, 1960.

In full bloom, this large-flowered climber is a truly spectacular sight. Little wonder it's one of the highest-rated climbing roses, according to the American Rose Society rankings. Pointed, reddish buds open into semi-double, cupped to flattened flowers that are 2 to 3 inches across. The blooms are pale pink at first, often taking on a salmon-pink color as they age, and they have a touch of cream on some of the wavy inner petals, which surround a cluster of showy golden stamens. The flowers are held in large clusters. Scent can vary from moderate to mild. 'Clair Matin' blooms profusely in late spring or early summer, generally followed by good rebloom through the rest of the season. Glossy, deep green leaves are carried on upright to slightly arching, branching, moderately thorny canes. Zones 5 to 10.

HOW TO USE

'Clair Matin' is usually treated as a climber, growing 8 to 12 feet tall. It makes a marvelous accent for just about any vertical structure: train it against a wall, fence, or trellis, wrap it around a pillar or pergola post, or encourage it to climb over an arbor or shed. 'Clair Matin' also adapts to life as a large shrub (about 6 feet tall and wide) if you're willing to put some work into the pruning. This rose has moderate disease resistance in most areas.

❦ 'Class Act'

Syns. 'First Class', 'White Magic'; JACare
Floribunda. Warriner, 1988.

This first-class floribunda is an elegant addition to any garden. Cream-colored buds open into semidouble, rather flattened flowers up to 4 inches across, with white petals surrounding a creamy center accented with a cluster of golden stamens. Held in small clusters, the slightly scented blooms appear first in early summer and repeat dependably through the summer. They're so prolific, in fact, that they practically cover the shiny, deep green foliage and thorny stems. Zones 5 to 9.

HOW TO USE

'Class Act' forms an upright, bushy shrub that grows 2 to 4 feet tall and about as wide. It looks great in a bed or border mixed with annuals and perennials. It combines well with a wide range of colors, but it's especially lovely in a white garden. Its compact form also makes it ideal for foundation plantings. Grow it in groups for a landscape accent or for a low, flowering hedge. 'Class Act' generally has excellent disease resistance.

All-America Rose Selection 1989

❦ 'Cocktail'

Syn. MEImick
Shrub. Meilland, 1961

The single blooms of this shrub rose aren't the biggest, but they pack a lot of punch with their stunning color combination. Pointed buds held in large clusters unfurl into simple, five-petaled, loosely cupped flowers that are 2 to 3 inches across. Newly opened blooms are scarlet red with a yellow eye surrounding golden stamens. Over time, the red deepens to crimson and the yellow eye fades to creamy white. The flowers have a light to moderate spicy scent. Blooms first appear in a large flush in late spring or early summer, followed by generous rebloom through the rest of summer and into fall. Thorny stems bear leathery, glossy, deep green leaves that may be tinged with red. Zones 5 to 9.

HOW TO USE

'Cocktail' is a vigorous rose that adapts to many different uses. As a shrub, it grows 5 to 6 feet tall and about 4 feet wide; try it as a screen or planted close together to make a tall, long-blooming hedge. 'Cocktail' also looks great trained as a short climber for a trellis or pillar, reaching about 6 to 8 feet in height. Wherever you grow it, this rose will be a knockout. 'Cocktail' offers good disease resistance.

❦ 'Compassion'

Syn. 'Belle de Londres'
Large-flowered climber. Harkness, 1972.

'Compassion' may not be the easiest rose to train, but its beautiful flowers and pleasing fragrance make it worth a little extra effort. The tapered buds of this large-flowered climber open into large, double, high-centered blooms up to 5 inches across. The sweetly scented flowers are a superb salmon pink color, usually with some peach tones toward the center. Held singly or in small clusters, the blooms begin in late spring or early summer and repeat freely through the rest of the growing season. Thorny, branching canes carry large, glossy, deep green leaves. Zones 5 to 9.

HOW TO USE

Trained as a climber, 'Compassion' generally grows 10 to 15 feet in height. Its canes are fairly stiff, so they're not well suited for wrapping around a pillar, but they look great fanned out against a wall, fence, or trellis. Hard pruning can keep 'Compassion' in a shrub form; it grows 5 to 7 feet tall and about as wide. This sturdy rose usually offers good disease resistance.

❦ 'Complicata'

Hybrid gallica. Date unknown.

Dainty the flowers may be, but there's nothing demure about the vigor of this charming hybrid gallica. Pointed pink buds open to single, broadly cupped to almost flat flowers up to 5 inches across. The bright pink, slightly folded petals are white at the base, surrounding a showy cluster of bright yellow stamens. The light to moderately fragrant flowers appear in one splendid show in late spring or early summer, followed by large, round, orange hips in fall. Large, light green leaves are held on slightly thorny stems. Zones 5 to 8.

HOW TO USE

Hybrid gallicas tend to be fairly compact bushes, but this one is distinctly more vigorous than the average, forming a relatively rampant shrub reaching 5 to 8 feet tall and about as wide. Its somewhat sprawling habit makes it a less than ideal choice for planting alone, but it looks great grown close together as an informal hedge or in a shrub border, where other plants can help support the stems. 'Complicata' also adapts well as a climber, growing to about 10 feet in height. Train it against a fence or up a pillar, or let it scramble up into a tree. This rose generally has good disease resistance.

❦ 'Comte de Chambord'

Portland. Robert & Moreau, 1860.

Rose experts debate about the proper identity of this rose: Is it best classified as a Portland or a hybrid perpetual? Or is it actually another rose altogether — a hybrid perpetual known as 'Madame Boll'? By whatever class or name you choose to give it, 'Comte de Chambord' smells as wonderful as an old rose should! Plump, pointed buds open into cupped to flat, fully double flowers that are 3 to 4 inches across. The rich pink petals are so tightly packed, they are crinkled and swirled around each other. Held singly or in clusters, the intensely fragrant flowers appear in a generous flush in late spring or early summer. More flowers appear in flushes later in the season, especially if you regularly remove the spent blooms. Moderately thorny stems carry light to medium green leaves that may show a light grayish cast. Zones 5 to 9.

HOW TO USE

'Comte de Chambord' produces a compact shrub, reaching only 3 to 5 feet in height and about the same width. It's a great choice if you love the look and scent of old roses but don't have room for the many larger-growing selections. 'Comte de Chambord' combines well with perennials and herbs in a mixed border or cottage garden. It also makes a marvelous landscape accent planted in masses or in a row for a low flowering hedge. 'Comte de Chambord' usually has good disease resistance but may develop black spot; take preventive measures if this disease is common in your area.

✿ 'Constance Spry'

Syn. AUSfirst
Shrub. Austin, 1961.

One of the first roses developed by the famous rose breeder David Austin, 'Constance Spry' shares many of the traits of his more recently released English roses, but with one exception: this beauty blooms only once a season. Rounded, reddish buds open into fully double, very cupped flowers up to 5 inches across, in a lovely shade of clear medium pink. The lavishly perfumed blooms are held in clusters and appear in one splendid show in early to midsummer. (In some areas, you may also get occasional blooms later in the season.) Thorny, arching canes carry semiglossy, deep green leaves. Zones 5 to 9.

HOW TO USE

'Constance Spry' is classified as a shrub rose, and it generally reaches 5 to 7 feet in height and width when grown unsupported. But since it is a somewhat sprawling bush, it really looks best planted in groups, so that the canes can support each other, or trained as a climber. Trained on a wall or fence, this rose can grow anywhere from 10 to 20 feet tall. 'Constance Spry' often puts on its most vigorous growth in warm climates, but it may bloom poorly there; it seems to be happiest in cooler areas. This rose is usually disease resistant.

❦ 'Cornelia'

Hybrid musk. Pemberton, 1925.

Is it pink? Is it peach? Actually, it's either or both, depending on the time of year! This lovely hybrid musk produces coral pink to coppery buds opening to small, ruffled, double blooms that eventually flatten out to about 1 inch wide. At the start of the bloom season — in late spring to early summer — the clustered flowers are mostly pale pink with a touch of yellow. The show continues through summer, usually with another generous flush of flowers in fall; the cooler weather brings out richer peachy tones in the buds and blooms. Fragrance is light to moderate. Slightly thorny canes carry dark green leaves that are often red tinged, particularly when young. Zones 6 to 9.

HOW TO USE
'Cornelia' produces long, arching canes that adapt well to training as an 8- to 12-foot climber. Wrap the stems around a pillar or pergola post, encourage them to climb over an arch or arbor, or let them spill over a wall. With a bit of pruning after the first flush of bloom, 'Cornelia' can also produce a rather airy, mounded shrub, usually reaching 4 to 6 feet in height and 5 to 7 feet in width. Enjoy it at the back of a mixed border, or use it to create an informal flowering hedge. 'Cornelia' is generally disease resistant.

❦ 'Country Dancer'

Shrub. Buck, 1973.

Dependable and practically carefree, this sturdy shrub rose is a great choice for a beginning rose gardener. It's also appreciated by experienced growers for its long bloom season and compact growth habit. Pointed, egg-shaped, reddish buds open to cupped, loosely double blooms about 3 inches across, in a pretty shade of reddish pink that ages to light pink. Held in small clusters, the moderately fragrant flowers first appear in late spring or early summer and continue well into fall. Upright canes carry glossy, deep green leaves. Zones 4 to 9.

HOW TO USE
'Country Dancer' produces a compact, bushy shrub that's usually about 3 feet tall and wide, although it can reach up to 5 feet in some areas. It is

handsome enough to stand alone as a long-blooming, easy-care land-scape accent, or as the star performer in a large planter, such as a half-barrel. It looks great in a mixed border, too, especially when paired with pink, red, and white flowers. 'Country Dancer' also makes an eye-catching low hedge. This dependable rose seldom has any disease problems.

❧ 'Cramoisi Supérieur'

Syn. 'Lady Brisbane'
Hybrid China. Coquereau, 1832.

This handsome hybrid China graces warm-climate gardens with a generous display of richly colored blooms through most of the growing season. Oval buds open into relatively small, double, cupped blossoms that are 2 to 3 inches across. The petals are blood red on top and a lighter crimson underneath; they hold their color well as they age, though occasionally you'll see a white streak on one or more. There's no consensus regarding the aroma of this rose: some say it has little or no fragrance, while other gardeners insist it has a sweet, fruity scent. Scented or not, 'Cramoisi Supérieur' is still a worthy garden rose, producing its clustered flowers abundantly from late spring or early summer to frost. Twiggy stems bear a rather sparse covering of glossy, dark green leaves. Zones 7 to 10.

HOW TO USE

'Cramoisi Supérieur' starts out in a rather unpromising manner, with somewhat angular, spreading growth, but it fills in to produce an airy, good-looking shrub. In the more northerly parts of its range, it is fairly compact, growing 3 to 4 feet tall and 2 to 3 feet wide; elsewhere, it is generally 4 to 6 feet tall and about as wide. This rose makes a handsome addition to a bed or border, planted alone or in groups of three or more. Low-growing plants with silvery or gray foliage, such as lamb's ears (*Stachys byzantina*) and *Salvia officinalis* 'Berggarten', make a beautiful backdrop for the striking flowers. This rose is generally disease resistant in most areas.

❦ 'Crested Moss'

Syns. 'Chapeau de Napoléon', 'Cristata'; *Rosa centifolia cristata, R. centifolia muscosa cristata*; Crested Provence Rose
Moss. Vibert, 1827.

You'll want to plant this rose near a path or bench so that you can get up close to admire its unusual buds. 'Crested Moss' is officially classified as a moss rose, but you'll also see it listed with centifolia roses, since it is actually a variant of *Rosa centifolia*. Regardless of what you call it, 'Crested Moss' is a very interesting rose, with mosslike growth on the edges of the sepals (the green leaflike structures that enclose the flower buds). It's a lovely contrast to the pink petals, which expand into cupped to rounded, rich pink, double flowers usually 2 to 3 inches wide. The spicy-scented blooms appear only once a season, for several weeks in late spring or early summer, but they're borne in such abundance over light green leaves that they often weigh down the arching, thorny stems. Zones 5 to 9.

HOW TO USE
'Crested Moss' produces a rather open, spreading shrub usually growing 3 to 6 feet tall and about as wide. It looks best when the canes have some kind of support. Grow it as an informal hedge so that the bushes can support each other, or enjoy it in a cottage garden setting, where it can cascade over other shrubs or stocky perennials. Another option is to train the stems against a trellis or arbor. 'Crested Moss' has moderate disease resistance; take preventive measures against black spot and mildew if these problems are common in your area.

❦ 'Crimson Bouquet'

Syn. KORbeteilich
Grandiflora. Kordes, 1999.

The rich red blooms of this award-winning grandiflora are sure to catch the eye of everyone who passes by. Large, pointed, maroon buds open to reveal double, high-centered, blood red blooms about 4 inches in diameter. The clustered flowers have little or no fragrance, but they make up for that lack by appearing abundantly over a long season, from late spring or early summer into fall. Thorny canes carry shiny, deep green leaves. Zones 5 to 9.

HOW TO USE

'Crimson Bouquet' forms a somewhat rounded, upright bush that's normally 3½ to 4½ feet tall and 3 to 4 feet across. It provides months of can't-miss color in beds and borders, and it's an amazing sight when planted in groups of three or more as a landscape accent. Don't forget to add at least one to your cutting garden for a steady supply of flowers to bring indoors. 'Crimson Bouquet' generally offers good to excellent disease resistance.

All-America Rose Selection 2000

❦ 'Crystalline'

Syns. 'Valerie Swane'; ARObipy
Hybrid tea. Christensen & Carruth, 1987.

At its best, 'Crystalline' offers the gorgeous blooms typical of hybrid teas in a crisp, snowy white that looks cool on the hottest summer day. Elegant, tapered buds unfurl into large, double flowers up to 5 inches across. They are usually held singly (although sometimes clustered) on long, straight stems, with a moderate sweet or spicy fragrance. 'Crystalline' blooms generously from late spring or early summer through the rest of the summer. If you stop deadheading in late summer, the later flowers will mature into large, rounded, orange hips. Prickly stems carry semiglossy, medium to dark green leaves. Zones 5 to 10.

HOW TO USE

'Crystalline' forms an upright bush that reaches 4 to 5 feet tall and about as wide. It is bushier than some other hybrid tea roses but still looks best planted in groups of three or more to produce a fuller look in a flower bed. Include a bush or two in your cutting garden to have a steady supply of blooms for summer arrangements. Gardeners in warm, relatively dry climates report the best results with this rose; rainy weather can lead to pink spotting on the petals. 'Crystalline' generally has moderate disease resistance; take preventive measures against black spot if this fungal disease is common in your area.

❦ 'Dainty Bess'

Hybrid tea. Archer, 1925.

There aren't too many single-flowered hybrid teas to choose from, but 'Dainty Bess' is more than a novelty; it's a truly charming garden rose. Tapered, dark pink buds open into broad, flat, single flowers usually 4 to 5 inches across, held singly or in small clusters. The slightly ruffled petals are a light rosy pink on top and slightly darker underneath, and they surround a showy cluster of golden brown to dark red stamens. Some gardeners can't detect any scent, but most agree that 'Dainty Bess' has a light to moderate, spicy fragrance. The flowers first appear in late spring or early summer and repeat through the rest of the growing season. Very thorny stems carry the semiglossy, dark green foliage. Zones 5 to 9.

HOW TO USE

'Dainty Bess' forms an upright, somewhat open bush that's usually 3 to 5 feet tall (up to 8 feet in very warm climates) and 2 to 3 feet across. It looks best planted in groups of three or more to soften the slightly stiff habit. Two often-mentioned drawbacks to 'Dainty Bess' are its tendency to drop its petals quickly in hot weather and its scanty bloom production some seasons. And while this hybrid tea generally offers good disease resistance, moderate black spot, mildew, and/or rust have been reported, so take preventive measures if any of these problems are prevalent in your area. All that being said, 'Dainty Bess' is definitely worth a try if you enjoy the simple beauty of single roses!

'Climbing Dainty Bess' (van Barneveld, 1935) is a climbing form reaching 8 to 12 feet in height.

❀ 'Dapple Dawn'

Syn. AUSapple
Shrub. Austin, 1983.

One of the few single-flowered English roses, 'Dapple Dawn' supplies an abundance of bloom through most of the growing season. Deep pink buds open into single, saucer-shaped to flattened flowers that are 4 to 5 inches across. The petals are a medium to light reddish pink, fading toward the base to produce a white eye surrounding the bright yellow stamens. The clustered flowers have only a slight scent, but they certainly aren't stingy when it comes to the bloom season, appearing in generous quantities from late spring or early summer well into fall. The abundant, dark green leaves are carried on thorny canes. Zones 5 to 9.

HOW TO USE

Technically classified as a shrub rose, 'Dapple Dawn' forms a broad-spreading, somewhat open bush growing as much as 6 feet tall and 8 feet wide in warm climates. In cool areas, 4 to 5 feet is the more common height and width. Enjoy it planted alone or in a group as a long-flowering landscape accent. It also looks super combined with other roses and shrubs in a shrub border or hedge. 'Dapple Dawn' is an outstanding addition to the back of a mixed border or cottage garden, where it blends beautifully with annuals, perennials, and herbs. This rose generally offers good disease resistance, although a bit of black spot may develop if you don't take preventive measures.

✿ 'David Thompson'

Hybrid rugosa. Svejda, 1979.

A sturdy, dependable member of the Canadian Explorer Series, this hybrid rugosa is an excellent choice for cold-climate gardeners. Pointed, egg-shaped buds unfurl into semidouble to double, shallow-cupped to flattened flowers that are 2½ inches across. The color of the flowers varies a bit but is generally deep reddish pink, sometimes showing an occasional white streak, and accented with a cluster of yellow stamens. The sweetly scented, clustered blooms appear continuously from late spring or early summer to frost. Bristly stems bear deeply veined, glossy, medium green leaves. Zones 3 to 9.

HOW TO USE

'David Thompson' forms a bushy, rounded shrub that's 3 to 5 feet tall and 3 to 6 feet wide. It makes a handsome, long-blooming hedge, and it also looks great paired with perennials in a mixed border. Silver-leaved plants, such as artemisias and lamb's ears *(Stachys byzantina),* make a striking contrast to the richly colored flowers. This easy-care rose seldom shows any disease problems.

✿ 'Delicata'

Hybrid rugosa. Cooling, 1898.

'Delicata' may not share the vigor of its hybrid rugosa relatives, but it's a pretty rose to grow if you don't have space for bigger bushes. Tapered buds open into semidouble, cupped, ruffled blooms up to 3½ inches across, in a lovely shade of light rose-pink accented with a cluster of creamy yellow stamens. Fragrance can vary from slight to strong —

apparently depending on who is doing the sniffing! Held in clusters, the flowers first appear in a generous display in late spring to early summer, then repeat well through the rest of the growing season. Fall also brings an abundant crop of large, orange hips, as well as good fall color. Thorny stems carry deeply veined, light green leaves. Zones 3 to 9.

HOW TO USE

'Delicata' creates a fairly compact bush, usually 3 to 4 feet tall and about as wide. It fits well into a bed, border, or foundation planting, providing several seasons of interest with its beautiful flowers and fruits. Be aware that gardeners report varying results with this rose: some describe it as vigorous and spreading while others say its growth is weak and straggly. If you are interested in adding 'Delicata' to your garden, try to find someone who is actually growing it in your area, or at least track down a source in your region and ask them what kind of growth you can expect. 'Delicata' generally offers good disease resistance.

✹ 'Dicky'

Syns. 'Anisley Dickson', 'Münchner Kindl'; DICkimono
Floribunda. Dickson, 1984.

Dramatic, rich color and abundant bloom make this floribunda a favorite with many gardeners. Oval pointed buds unfurl into double, high-centered, slightly fragrant flowers up to 3½ inches wide. The petals are a warm coral or salmon pink on top, with a lighter shade of the same color on the reverse side. Held in showy clusters, the blooms begin with a generous flush in late spring or early summer and repeat through the rest of the season. Slightly thorny stems carry abundant, glossy, medium to dark green leaves. Zones 5 to 10.

HOW TO USE

'Dicky' forms an upright bush growing 3 to 4 feet tall and about 3 feet wide. It makes a striking addition to a bed or border, particularly with other rich colors, such as gold- or purple-flowered perennials. 'Dicky' also makes a pretty cut flower, so consider adding it to your cutting garden. This rose is generally disease resistant.

✿'Distant Drums'

Shrub. Buck, 1985.

If you're searching for something unusual in the color department, look no further than this remarkable shrub rose. 'Distant Drums' produces pointed, purplish buds that unfurl into large, fully double, slightly cupped flowers that are 4 to 5 inches across. Newly opened blooms are a peachy brown in the center, shading to rosy purple in the outer petals; eventually, they fade to a tan center with light purple outer edges. 'Distant Drums' has a distinct fragrance that many gardeners find appealing but others consider slightly unpleasant; if possible, sniff a bloom before you buy the plant to see if you like it. Held singly or in clusters, the flowers first appear in early summer and repeat well through the rest of the season until frost. Moderately thorny canes bear dark, leathery foliage. Zones 5 to 9.

HOW TO USE

'Distant Drums' produces a mounded, bushy shrub reaching 3 to 5 feet tall with about the same spread. It makes a distinctive addition to borders, though it can be tricky to find effective companions; considering pairing it with purple foliage, such as purple-leaved heucheras and purple sage *(Salvia officinalis* 'Purpurascens'). Or give this rose a special spot of its own, where it will create an eye-catching landscape accent. Like so many of the excellent selections developed by Dr. Griffith Buck at Iowa State University, 'Distant Drums' usually has superior disease resistance.

✿'Dolly Parton'

Hybrid tea. Winchel, 1984.

This handsome hybrid tea rose is as delightful as the woman it was named for. Elegant, tapered buds spiral open to reveal double, high-centered blooms that are 5 to 6 inches across, with glowing orange-red to coral-red petals. Usually borne singly on long stems, the flowers are graced with an exceptional spicy scent. They first appear in late spring or early summer, followed by good repeat through the rest of the growing season. Sturdy, thorny canes bear semiglossy, medium to dark green leaves. Zones 5 to 9.

HOW TO USE

'Dolly Parton' forms an upright bush that's usually 3½ to 5 feet tall and 2 to 3 feet across. The vibrant color and exceptional fragrance make it a great choice for beds and borders. Like most other hybrid teas, 'Dolly Parton' looks best planted in groups of three or more to create a bushier effect. It's also a great addition to a cutting garden! Disease resistance is generally good.

❦ 'Don Juan'

Large-flowered climber. Malandrone, 1958.

The breathtaking blooms of this large-flowered climber make it a stunning sight, especially against a white or weathered gray trellis or arbor. Pointed, oval to egg-shaped, dark crimson buds open into large, fully double flowers up to 5 inches across, in a sultry shade of deep red. Held singly or in clusters, the high-centered blooms have a lovely hybrid tea shape, with the advantage of being produced closer to eye level for easier appreciation. Most gardeners consider 'Don Juan' a very fragrant rose, but there are some who can detect little or no scent. There is a profuse display of bloom at first, usually starting in spring, with moderate rebloom through the rest of the growing season. Orange hips appear in fall, adding to the show. Sturdy, thorny canes carry shiny, medium to dark green leaves. Zones 6 to 10.

HOW TO USE

'Don Juan' is a moderately vigorous climber, growing 8 to 12 feet in height in the northern parts of its range and up to 15 feet in warmer areas. It's gorgeous growing on a wall, trellis, pillar, or pergola post, and it looks super on a post-and-rail fence. Generally disease resistant, 'Don Juan' occasionally develops a bit of black spot; take preventive measures if this problem is common in your area

❦ 'Dornröschen'

Shrub. Kordes, 1960.

Southern gardeners might not be too impressed by another pink shrub rose, but rose lovers in colder climates will enjoy this hardy, long-flowering addition to their palette. 'Dornröschen' produces pointed, egg-shaped buds opening to fully double, high-centered blooms that are 3 to 4 inches across. The petals are salmon-pink on top, with a yellowish pink on the underside. Flowering starts with a generous show in late spring or early summer, with additional flushes through the rest of the growing season. The blooms are generally quite fragrant, with a spicy-sweet scent. Branching stems bear medium green, glossy leaves that have a leathery texture. Zones 4 to 9.

HOW TO USE

'Dornröschen' grows as a spreading shrub that's usually 4 to 6 feet tall and 3 to 5 feet wide; in warm climates, it may reach 6 to 8 feet or more in height and width. It is attractive enough to grow by itself as a landscape accent, but it's also splendid in a mixed border or a cottage garden. 'Dornröschen' generally has good disease resistance.

✇ 'Dortmund'

Hybrid kordesii. Kordes, 1955.

Heavy-flowering and practically problem free, this hybrid kordesii is a favorite with rose gardeners across the country. This classic climber produces long, pointed buds that open into single, slightly cupped, somewhat ruffled flowers about 3½ inches across. Each bright red bloom is accented with a white eye surrounding a cluster of showy yellow stamens. Scent is slight, at best. 'Dortmund' starts the season with a dazzling display of large, eye-catching flower clusters, usually in mid- to late spring, and repeats through the rest of the season. Blooms left on the bush mature into an attractive show of large, rounded, orange hips in late summer or fall. Very thorny stems carry small, very shiny, deep green leaves. Zones 4 to 9.

HOW TO USE

If you have the room, you could let this handsome rose grow as a shrub; it can reach 5 to 8 feet tall and about as wide. You'll most often see 'Dortmund' grown as a climber, though, since it makes such a stunning show this way. In the northern parts of its range, it generally grows 8 to 12 feet tall; in warm climates, it can shoot up to 30 feet. It's a good idea to find a garden in your area that is growing this rose so you can see what to expect in your climate. For the best display of repeat bloom, 'Dortmund' needs regular and careful deadheading during summer; this can be time-consuming, as well as challenging, owing to the thorny stems. Without deadheading, you'll get fewer later flowers, but then you'll have a great show of hips toward the end of the season. The lower parts of the stems tend to drop their leaves, so consider growing a low, leafy shrub in front of it to hide the "bare ankles." 'Dortmund' seldom has any disease problems.

❦ 'Double Delight'

Syn. ANDeli
Hybrid tea. Swim & Ellis, 1977.

Garish or gorgeous — it's your call. But if you think this hybrid tea is one of the loveliest roses you've ever seen, you have a lot of company! 'Double Delight' produces long, tapered buds that unfurl into large, high-centered, double blooms about 5 inches in diameter. As they open, the creamy white petals gradually develop a distinct cherry-red edge, creating a dramatic contrast. The amount of color that develops depends on the amount of sunlight and the age of the bloom, so each flower is slightly different. Usually held singly on long stems, the distinctive blooms are also graced with a moderate to strong scent that some describe as spicy and others refer to as fruity. Flowers first appear in late spring to early summer, usually with good repeat through the rest of the season. Moderately thorny canes bear semiglossy, deep green leaves. Zones 6 to 10.

HOW TO USE
'Double Delight' forms a somewhat spreading bush that generally reaches 3 to 5 feet in height and 2 to 4 feet in width. Its bold color combination makes it an eye-catching addition to any garden. If you enjoy bringing flowers indoors, 'Double Delight' deserves a place in your cutting garden, too; just be aware that the blooms need some sunlight to develop their showy red edging. The main drawback to growing this rose is its susceptibility to powdery mildew, particularly in cooler climates; be prepared to apply preventive sprays if this problem is common in your garden.

'Climbing Double Delight' (AROclidd; Christensen, 1982) is a once-blooming climber that makes quite a show against a wall or fence. It shares its parent's showy blooms but also its disease susceptibility.

All-America Rose Selection 1977; World Rose Hall of Fame 1985; James Alexander Gamble Fragrance Medal 1986

🌺'Dr. Huey'

Syn. 'Shafter'
Large-flowered climber. Thomas, 1914.

This large-flowered climber is a rose that many people grow but not many intentionally plant. Often used as a rootstock for grafted roses, this sturdy rose frequently lives on after the more desirable top growth dies off because of some mishap. Sometimes 'Dr. Huey' appears as a sucker even before the grafted rose dies, eventually crowding out the desired rose with its vigorous growth. Pointed, maroon buds open into semidouble, saucer-shaped, 2- to 3-inch flowers that are rich, deep red accented with yellow stamens. The slightly scented blooms usually appear just once a season, for several weeks in mid- to late spring. Long, arching canes carry semiglossy, medium to deep green leaves. Zones 4 to 9.

HOW TO USE
Given a large, sturdy support, 'Dr. Huey' can form a 12- to 18-foot climber. Try it on an arch or arbor, or against a gazebo. Left unsupported, it will form a large, rather mounded shrub that's 8 to 10 feet tall and about as wide. Its large size and short flowering season make it less interesting than many other roses for most of the year, but it certainly is a pretty sight when in full flower. Take preventive measures against black spot if this fungal disease is common in your area.

🌺'Dr. W. Van Fleet'

Large-flowered climber. Van Fleet, 1910.

It may bloom only once a season, but this large-flowered climber is still a favorite with many gardeners for its generous display of delicately colored blooms. Plump, pointed, reddish pink buds open to double, cupped, clustered flowers about 3 inches across. Newly opened blooms are an even, soft pink, with the petals fading to pink-tinted ivory as they age. The moderately fragrant flowers appear in one glorious show, generally in late spring or early summer; there is an occasional bloom here or there during the rest of the growing season, and red hips in fall. The glossy, dark green leaves are held on thorny stems. Zones 4 to 10.

HOW TO USE
'Dr. W. Van Fleet' is a vigorous rose, usually growing 15 to 20 feet in height. It's not a good selection for a small trellis—this one needs room

to ramble! It looks its best when allowed to crawl into a tree or trained to cover a pergola or shed. 'Dr. W. Van Fleet' seldom shows any disease problems.

If you like the look of 'Dr. W. Van Fleet' but would prefer a reblooming rose, consider growing its beautiful sport, 'New Dawn'.

❧ 'Dublin'

Hybrid tea. Perry, 1982.

If you're searching for outstanding fragrance combined with the classic hybrid tea form, 'Dublin' may be just the rose you're looking for! Tapered buds open to double, high-centered blooms about 4½ inches across, in a difficult-to-describe shade of medium red, with a darker tinge on the outer petals. Borne on long, straight stems, the flowers are prized for their fabulous raspberry-like fragrance. They first appear in late spring or early summer, with slow to moderate repeat through the rest of the growing season. Moderately thorny stems carry medium green leaves. Zones 6 to 10.

HOW TO USE
'Dublin' produces an upright bush, usually reaching 4 to 5 feet tall and 3 to 4 feet wide. It's a pretty addition to a flower bed or rose bed, although it's not particularly free-flowering. This hybrid tea really shines as a cut flower, so make sure you add at least one to your cutting garden. 'Dublin' has fairly good disease resistance, but take preventive measures against black spot if this problem is common in your area.

❧ 'Dublin Bay'

Syn. MACdub
Large-flowered climber. McGredy, 1975.

Considered by many to be among the best, if not *the* best, of the red-flowered climbing roses, 'Dublin Bay' deserves a special spot to show off its superb blooms. Deep red, pointed buds unfurl into double, cupped blooms that are 3 to 4 inches across, in a rich shade of blood red. Fragrance varies from light and fruity to nonexistent, depending on the growing conditions and on the person doing the sniffing. Usually held in clusters, the flowers of 'Dublin Bay' first appear in abundance in late spring to early summer, followed by a steady supply through the rest of the summer and into fall. Ample, glossy, deep green foliage is held on moderately thorny canes. Zones 4 to 10.

HOW TO USE

This large-flowered climber is often quite bushy when young, and it can form an eye-catching large shrub that's 6 to 8 feet in height, with about the same spread. It's generally encouraged to climb, however, growing 8 to 12 feet tall that way. 'Dublin Bay' looks lovely trained against a wall or fence or up a pillar or post. This selection generally offers good disease resistance.

❧ 'Duchesse de Brabant'

Syns. 'Comtesse de Labarathe', 'Comtesse Ouwaroff'
Tea. Bernède, 1857.

'Duchesse de Brabant' is one of those classics that old-rose appreciators just love. This tea rose produces red-shaded, tapered pink buds that open into large, fully double, cupped to almost rounded blooms up to 5 inches across. The color is usually a soft rose-pink, but in some conditions, the nodding blooms are closer to salmon pink. Held in clusters, the heavily perfumed blooms generally begin in mid- to late spring; after that, they appear continuously through the rest of the growing season. Twiggy, moderately thorny stems bear wavy, semiglossy, light green leaves. Zones 7 to 10.

HOW TO USE

'Duchesse de Brabant' generally produces a vigorous, bushy to somewhat spreading shrub. In the northern parts of its range, a height and spread of 3 to 5 feet is common; in warmer climates, 6 to 8 feet is more likely. 'Duchesse de Brabant' is pretty enough to grow by itself as a long-blooming landscape accent, but it also looks magnificent blended with perennials and other plants in a mixed border or cottage garden. This rose is prone to mildew in cooler areas but generally has good resistance to black spot.

❧ 'Duet'

Hybrid tea. Swim, 1960.

'Duet' has been around a while, but it has held its own against many newer hybrid teas, thanks to its beautiful blooms and excellent disease resistance. Tapered, deep pink buds open to double, high-centered flowers to 4 inches in diameter. The petals are light coral pink on top and a darker shade on the underside, giving the blooms a two-toned appearance. The flowers have little or no fragrance, but they're produced generously over a long season, starting in late spring to early summer. Thorny stems carry glossy, medium to dark green leaves that have a leathery texture. Zones 5 to 10.

HOW TO USE

'Duet' grows as an upright to somewhat spreading bush that's 3 to 6 feet tall and 2 to 5 feet wide. Its long season of bloom makes it a welcome addition to a flower bed. The long-stemmed flowers are also excellent for arrangements, so 'Duet' deserves a place in the cutting garden, too. Best of all, this hybrid tea generally has excellent disease resistance.

All-America Rose Selection 1961

✿ 'Earthquake'

Syn. MORquake
Miniature. Moore, 1983.

Here's an eye-catching little rose that will definitely shake up a staid garden planting! This distinctive miniature produces pointed buds that open into double, high-centered blooms that are about 1½ inches across. There's no fragrance, but you'll hardly miss it: instead, you'll be admiring the striking red-and-yellow-striped flowers. The stripes vary widely in size and somewhat in color as well — the red parts tend to be more pink in cooler weather, and hot sun can cause fading) — so every bloom is unique. Held singly or in clusters, the blooms appear from late spring or early summer through the rest of the growing season. Moderately thorny stems bear small, bright green, glossy leaves. Zones 6 to 10.

HOW TO USE

'Earthquake' forms a small, upright bush that's usually 15 to 18 inches tall and about 12 to 15 inches wide. Plant it in groups as a vibrant edging along a walkway or around a deck or patio, or enjoy it in a pot or planter. It's tricky to find companions that won't clash with the vivid blooms, so you might want to grow this one by itself — it certainly can hold its own in the flower-power department! 'Earthquake' is most vigorous in warm climates, but its blooms are brightest when shaded from direct sun, so try to give it a spot with a bit of shade during the hottest part of the day. This miniature rose generally has good disease resistance.

'Climbing Earthquake' (MORshook; Moore, 1990) produces arching canes that are 2 to 3 feet long. Train them as a low climber against a wall or fence, or let the bush grow by itself to form a low, spreading shrub.

❦ 'Earth Song'

Grandiflora. Buck, 1975.

Considered by many to be one of Dr. Griffith Buck's best roses, 'Earth Song' is a favorite with many gardeners in both warm and cool climates. This glorious grandiflora produces elegant, tapered, reddish buds that open to high-centered, double flowers up to 4½ inches across, held singly or in small clusters. As the blooms age, their deep rosy pink petals age to a lighter pink, and they develop a cupped form that's accented with a cluster of yellow stamens. The flowers have a light to moderate, sweet scent. Bloom starts in late spring or early summer and continues freely until heavy frost. Thorny stems carry dark green, glossy leaves that have a leathery texture. Zones 4 to 9.

HOW TO USE
'Earth Song' forms an upright, bushy shrub reaching 3 to 5 feet tall and about as wide. Plant it by itself as a landscape accent, or enjoy it in groupings as a mass planting or hedge. This remarkable rose makes a valuable addition to a mixed border, adding months of color to complement perennials, grasses, and other plants. Its rich rose-pink flowers look especially good with purple and blue blooms, such as those of sages (*Salvia* spp.) and bellflowers (*Campanula* spp.). 'Earth Song' shares the excellent disease resistance that Buck roses are known for.

❦ 'Eden Climber' See 'Pierre de Ronsard'

❦ 'Elegant Beauty'

Syns. 'Delicia', 'Kordes' Rose Delicia'; KORgatum
Hybrid tea. Kordes, 1982.

A lovely name for a lovely rose! This handsome hybrid tea produces long, tapered, rich yellow buds that unfurl into double, high-centered flowers about 4 inches in diameter. The broad petals are a soft shade of light yellow, sometimes with a light pink blush. The lightly fragrant flowers first appear in late spring to early summer, and they repeat well through the rest of the growing season, often with a particularly good display in fall. The large, deep green leaves are carried on thorny stems. Zones 5 to 9.

HOW TO USE
'Elegant Beauty' has the rather stiff, upright habit shared by most hybrid tea roses, generally growing 3 to 5 feet tall and 2 to 3 feet wide. Planted in groups, it could be a pretty addition to a flower bed, but it's best known for its use as a cut flower; make sure you include at least one in your cutting garden for a supply of wonderful long-stemmed blooms. 'Elegant Beauty' usually has moderate disease resistance.

❦ 'Elina'

Syns. 'Peaudouce'; DICjana
Hybrid tea. Dickson, 1984.

'Elina' offers the best of both worlds: the elegant blooms of a hybrid tea on a handsome, bushy plant. Pointed, creamy yellow buds unfurl into huge, high-centered, double blooms up to 6 inches across. Opened blooms are pale yellow with a slightly deeper yellow center, aging to ivory, and they appear from late spring or early summer well into fall. Moderately thorny stems carry abundant, deep green, glossy leaves that make a beautiful background for the delicately colored blooms. Zones 5 to 10.

HOW TO USE
'Elina' produces a vigorous bush growing 3 to 5 feet tall and 2½ to 4 feet across. Held singly on sturdy stems, the lightly fragrant, long-lasting blooms make lovely cut flowers, so this rose is a super selection for a cutting garden. Its bushy habit also makes it a good choice for adding height and months of beautiful blooms to a flower bed. 'Elina' generally has good disease resistance, but it may develop some mildew toward the end of the growing season in some areas.

❦ 'Elizabeth Taylor'

Hybrid tea. Weddle, 1985.

This marvelous hybrid tea is a winner with gardeners who enjoy its rich color and elegant form. 'Elizabeth Taylor' produces long, tapered buds that open to large, double, high-centered blooms that are 4 to 5 inches in diameter, with a light to moderate, somewhat spicy fragrance. The petals are a rich deep pink with darker edges as they open; occasionally they are marked with a white or light pink stripe. Usually held singly on long stems, the flowers begin in late spring or early summer, with good repeat through the rest of the growing season. Moderately thorny stems bear semiglossy, deep green leaves. Zones 5 to 9.

HOW TO USE

'Elizabeth Taylor' has the typical hybrid tea habit, producing an upright and somewhat spreading bush usually 4 to 5 feet tall and about 3 feet wide. Planted in groups, it can make a tall accent for a flower bed. It really shines as a cut flower, though, so it's a wonderful choice for a cutting garden. You'll delight in the steady supply of long-stemmed, perfectly formed flowers. 'Elizabeth Taylor' generally has good disease resistance, but without preventive sprays, it may develop a bit of mildew in some areas.

❦ 'Elmshorn'

Shrub. Kordes, 1951.

It's hard to beat 'Elmshorn' for pure flower power: this first-class shrub rose is practically smothered with blooms for months. Oblong buds open into double, cupped rosettes 1 to 2 inches across, in a vibrant shade of deep reddish pink aging to lighter rose-pink. The individual flowers may be small, but they're held in large clusters, making a splendid show from late spring or early summer through the rest of the growing season. Some gardeners can detect a light to moderate applelike scent; others describe 'Elmshorn' as lacking fragrance. Moderately thorny, upright to arching canes carry a generous covering of glossy, light green, slightly wrinkled leaves. Zones 5 to 9.

HOW TO USE

'Elmshorn' forms a vigorous, bushy shrub that usually reaches 4 to 6 feet tall and is about as wide. It's handsome enough to stand alone as a landscape accent, but it also looks great in groups as a mass planting or hedge. Its free-flowering habit also makes it an excellent choice for planting in a mixed border. Use it to add zip to a planting of pastel yellow-flowered and blue-flowered perennials, or let it hold its own against brighter golds and purples. This versatile rose also adapts to training as a climber, reaching to 10 feet or more. 'Elmshorn' generally has excellent disease resistance.

❦ 'Empress Josephine'

Syns. 'Francofurtana', 'Impératrice Josephine', 'Souvenir de l'Impératrice Josephine'; *Rosa francofurtana*
Miscellaneous old garden rose. Introduced before 1815.

Rose experts may not be able to agree on a single name or classification for this rose, but many gardeners agree that it's a real charmer! The American Rose Society officially classifies 'Empress Josephine' as a miscellaneous old garden rose, but you'll usually find it listed with the gallica roses in catalogs. Rounded, reddish buds open to double, 3- to 4-inch-wide blooms with loosely arranged, crinkled and slightly wavy petals. The lightly fragrant flowers are reddish pink in the center and lighter pink on the outer edges. They appear just once a season, usually for a few weeks in early summer, but they're followed by an abundant crop of large hips in late summer to fall. The nearly thornless stems carry an ample covering of dark green leaves that have a grayish cast. Zones 3 to 9.

HOW TO USE
'Empress Josephine' forms a branching, bushy shrub that's usually 4 to 5 feet tall and about as wide. Enjoy it as a hedge, or let its flowers and fruits add seasonal interest to a mixed border or shrub border. 'Empress Josephine' generally has good disease resistance.

❦ 'Enfant de France'

Hybrid perpetual. Lartay, 1860.

If you're fond of poking through a variety of reference books in your quest to learn about interesting roses, you'll eventually notice that there are actually several different selections with this name. As you may guess, this has caused a bit of confusion! The rose we're talking about here is a hybrid perpetual that was introduced in the mid-1800s, and this is the one you're most likely to get when you buy 'Enfant de France' today. Its plump, reddish pink buds open into very double, somewhat flattened, 5-inch flowers filled with swirls of petals in a lovely shade of light, clear pink. This rose is prized for its strong old-rose scent, as well as its long bloom season: it starts in late spring to early summer and repeats moderately through the rest of the growing season. Matte green leaves provide good covering for the stout, thorny canes. Zones 5 to 9.

'Enfant de France' has an upright but relatively compact habit, generally growing 4 to 5 feet tall and 3 to 4 feet wide. It's a beautiful addition to a mixed border or cottage garden, especially if you enjoy the fragrance and flower form of old-fashioned roses but want more than a single flush of summer bloom. This adaptable selection can even grow well in a large container. 'Enfant de France' usually has good disease resistance, but it may develop a bit of powdery mildew in some areas.

ᚦ 'English Garden'

Syn. AUSbuff
Shrub. Austin, 1990.

Do you love the full look of old-fashioned roses but want one in the yellow-apricot range? That's a tough bill to fill with a true antique, but the modern English rose called 'English Garden' may be just the thing for you! Plump, pointed, red-blushed yellow buds unfurl into fully double, clustered flowers that are 3 to 4 inches across. Tightly packed with folded petals, the blooms start out broadly cupped and open to a nearly flat form, with a soft yellow to peachy yellow center and a creamy white perimeter. Reports on its fragrance vary widely: some claim the scent is very light, while others describe it as strong. Thorny stems carry an ample covering of light green leaves. Zones 5 to 9.

HOW TO USE
'English Garden' tends to have a fairly upright, bushy habit, generally growing 3 to 4 feet in height and width. It looks best when planted in groups of three or more, grown in a mass for a landscape accent, set out in a row for a charming low hedge, or sited in the middle of a mixed border. The delicately shaded blooms blend beautifully with soft pink-, blue-, and white-flowered perennials. 'English Garden' can also grow well in a large container, such as a half-barrel planter. Its disease resistance is usually good, but take preventive measures against black spot and rust if either of these problems is common in your area.

ᚦ 'English Miss'

Floribunda. Cants of Colchester, 1977.

Here's a real charmer: a cute little floribunda that just blooms its heart out! 'English Miss' produces rounded to oval, reddish pink buds that open to beautifully formed, fully double flowers that are 2 to 3 inches across. The clustered blooms are a light rose-pink when new, aging to creamy pink. Most who have grown this rose agree that it has a noticeable fragrance, but they don't always concur on the *type* of scent; some describe it as sweet while others insist it is spicy. 'English Miss' blooms freely for months, usually starting in late spring or early summer and producing several more flushes of flowers through the rest of the growing season. Branching stems bear leathery, glossy, deep green leaves. Zones 5 to 9.

HOW TO USE

'English Miss' forms a compact bush, usually reaching just 2 to 3 feet in height and width; this makes it a delightful addition to beds and borders, especially in gardens where space is at a premium. 'English Miss' looks particularly good planted in groups for more impact, but it's pretty enough to stand alone. Its small stature also makes it a natural choice for growing in a large container. If you enjoy making small arrangements, this floribunda deserves a place in your cutting garden as well. 'English Miss' generally has excellent disease resistance.

❦ 'Erfurt'

Hybrid Musk. Kordes, 1939.

The charming ruffled flowers and excellent fragrance of this dependable hybrid musk earn it a place in any garden. 'Erfurt' offers long, pointed, reddish buds that unfurl into large, semidouble, saucer-shaped blooms that are 4 to 5 inches across. The clustered flowers are reddish pink when new; as they open, they age to a lighter rosy pink fading to white at the base of the petals. The center of each flower is accented with a cluster of golden yellow stamens. 'Erfurt' is generally known for its strong fragrance, but there are a few gardeners who can't detect much scent. Expect a prolific first flush of bloom in late spring to early summer, followed by moderate summer repeat and often another showy flush in fall. Rounded, orange-red hips also appear in late summer to fall. Arching, thorny canes carry an ample covering of leathery, dark green, semiglossy leaves that sometimes hold a reddish tint. Zones 6 to 9.

HOW TO USE

'Erfurt' forms a vigorous, spreading shrub that's usually 4 to 5 feet tall and wide, though it may reach 6 feet or more over time. It makes a pretty background for a mixed border, and its flowers and fruit add months of interest to a shrub border. Left unattended, 'Erfurt' can look a bit untidy, but pruning can help shape it into a denser shrub. The arching stems also adapt to training on a pillar. This rose seldom shows any disease problems.

❦ 'Escapade'

Syn. HARpade
Floribunda. Harkness, 1967.

The delicately shaded blooms of this delightful selection have the dainty charm of a wild rose, but they're borne in profusion on a compact floribunda that can fit into just about any part of your landscape. Tapered, rosy pink buds open into slightly cupped to flat, semidouble flowers that are about 3 inches across, in a soft shade of purplish pink. The center of each bloom is accented with a white eye surrounding a cluster of golden yellow stamens. Held in large clusters, the lightly fragrant flowers appear first in late spring to early summer and repeat almost continually through the rest of the growing season. (Hot sun tends to fade the flowers quickly, so expect the early- and late-season blooms to have the best color.) Moderately thorny canes bear shiny, light green leaves. Zones 5 to 9.

HOW TO USE

'Escapade' has a shrubby, upright habit, generally growing 2½ to 4 feet tall and about 3 feet across. Plant it alone or in masses for a long-blooming landscape accent; tuck it into beds, borders, and foundation plantings; or grow it in a row to create a charming low hedge. It looks great in a planter, too! Along with all of its other great features, 'Escapade' also offers excellent disease resistance.

❦ 'Étoile de Hollande'

Hybrid tea. Verschuren, 1919.

'Étoile de Hollande' may not be the easiest rose to grow well, but its richly colored blooms and strong fragrance have kept it in circulation for over 80 years. This hybrid tea produces tapering buds that unfurl into double, bright to deep red blooms that are around 3 inches across. The cupped blooms are somewhat looser than the typical hybrid tea form, and they're held singly or in small clusters on short, thin stems that tend to bend with the weight of the fully opened flowers. The heavily scented blooms usually put on their best display from late spring or early summer through mid- to late summer; some gardeners report good rebloom while others say the late season show is sparse. The deep green leaves are carried on thorny stems. Zones 5 to 9.

HOW TO USE

'Étoile de Hollande' forms a somewhat open, upright bush, usually reaching 2 to 3 feet tall and wide. It's an interesting addition to a collection of classic roses, and it could be suitable for use in a flower bed. While often touted as disease resistant, 'Étoile de Hollande' frequently develops mildew if you don't take preventive measures in areas where this fungal disease is a common problem.

Nowadays, you're more likely to find 'Climbing Étoile de Hollande' (Leenders, 1931) listed in catalogs. Unfortunately, this selection shares the mildew susceptibility of the bush form, but some gardeners are willing to overlook that flaw: if you really want a red climber with hybrid tea–form blooms that have good fragrance, there aren't many other choices. When the canes are trained on a pillar, trellis, fence, arch, or arbor, the nodding flowers are displayed to advantage. 'Climbing Étoile de Hollande' can grow anywhere from 8 to 18 feet tall. Zones 6 to 9.

❧ 'Europeana'

Floribunda. deRuiter, 1963.

If your color preferences fall in the pastel range, 'Europeana' is probably not to your taste, but it's just the ticket if you're searching for an eye-catching accent plant. This free-flowering floribunda offers plump, pointed, maroon buds that open into semidouble to double, cupped rosettes about 3 inches across, in a spectacular shade of clear red. The fully opened blooms are highlighted with a showy clump of bright yellow stamens in the center. You'll be dazzled by the sizable clusters of stunning blooms that are produced freely from late spring until heavy frost. Scent is usually slight, at best. While many roses produce reddish new growth, the leaves of 'Europeana' seem to hold their reddish tint longer, turning deep green just before the flowers bloom atop the branching, thorny stems. Zones 5 to 9.

HOW TO USE

'Europeana' forms a dense, rounded shrub that's 2 to 3 feet in height and spread. This compact form makes it a super choice for adding drama to a bed, border, or foundation planting. This adaptable rose makes a splendid low hedge, and it also grows well in a container. It's great as a cut flower, too. What more could you ask for? Perhaps better disease resistance: take preventive measures against powdery mildew and black spot if either of these problems is common in your area.

All-America Rose Selection 1968

❦ 'Evelyn'

Syn. AUSsaucer
Shrub. Austin, 1992.

Ask ten people who've grown this inarguably beautiful English rose what they think of it, and you're liable to get a dizzying array of opinions on its exact color, fragrance, habit, and general garden worthiness. 'Evelyn' produces rounded, peachy yellow buds that open to reveal very double, 3- to 5-inch flowers that start out as shallow cups and open to a rosette form. The color is basically a blend of peach and yellow, although various weather conditions can bring out more pink in the petals. Some say the scent is only mild, although most rave about the good to intense, rosy-fruity fragrance. 'Evelyn' flowers freely in late spring or early summer; rebloom can range from sparse to generous. Moderately thorny, upright to arching canes carry semiglossy, medium green leaves. Zones 5 to 9.

HOW TO USE

In the coolest parts of its range, 'Evelyn' forms a rather upright shrub that's 3 to 4 feet tall and about as wide. In warmer areas, expect a larger, somewhat sprawling shrub that's 5 to 6 feet tall and wide, or even a 6- to 9-foot climber. It's definitely wise to find someone in your area who is already growing this rose so that you can learn what to expect in your conditions. Disease resistance is usually only moderate; take preventive measures against black spot and powdery mildew if these problems are common in your area.

❦ 'Eyepaint'

Syns. 'Eye Paint', 'Tapis Persan'; MACeye
Floribunda. McGredy, 1975.

This vivid floribunda is not for the faint of heart. 'Eyepaint' offers egg-shaped buds that open to single, flattened flowers that are 2 to 3 inches across, in a spectacular shade of scarlet-red accented with a white eye and showy golden stamens. The clustered, slightly fragrant flowers appear freely from late spring or early summer through the rest of the growing season. Somewhat arching, thorny stems carry an ample covering of glossy, medium green leaves. Zones 5 to 9.

HOW TO USE

'Eyepaint' produces a vigorous, rather rounded shrub that's usually 3 to 4 feet tall and about as wide. Its strong, striking color makes it challenging to combine with other colors, so it's easiest to give this one a spot by itself. A grouping of 'Eyepaint' makes a can't-miss landscape accent or low hedge. Or try planting it atop a low wall or raised bed so that its arching canes can cascade over the side. This rose is often billed as being disease-free, but don't count on that; be prepared to take preventive measures if black spot is a serious problem in your area.

'Fair Bianca'

Syn. AUSca
Shrub. Austin, 1983.

Do you adore the full, fragrant flowers of antique roses but wish they'd bloom for more than a few weeks? If so, 'Fair Bianca' may be just the rose for you. This lovely English rose offers maroon-blushed, rounded buds opening to fully double, cupped rosettes that are 3 to 3½ inches across. The flowers are generally a clear to creamy white, though sometimes they show a hint of pink in the center or on the outermost petals. When the clustered blooms are fully open, a small green center is visible. The flowers are strongly scented; most gardeners find the fragrance delightful, but a few think it's somewhat too strong, so you might want to sniff a bloom before you decide to buy. 'Fair Bianca' blooms in quick flushes, usually starting in late spring or early summer and continuing through the rest of the growing season. Prickly canes carry light to medium green, semiglossy leaves. Zones 5 to 9.

HOW TO USE

'Fair Bianca' is much more restrained than many of the English roses, forming an upright, bushy shrub that's usually 3 to 5 feet tall and 3 to 4 feet wide. It's a marvelous addition to a mixed border, blending beautifully with annuals, perennials, bulbs, herbs, and other roses. For best effect, plant 'Fair Bianca' in groups of three or more to create a drift of delicate color. If you enjoy their fragrance, the blooms also make excellent long-lasting cut flowers. 'Fair Bianca' has moderate disease resistance; it may develop some mildew, black spot, or rust if you don't take preventive measures in areas where these diseases are common problems.

❦ 'Fairy' See 'The Fairy'

❦ 'Fame!'

Syn. JACzor
Grandiflora. Zary, 1998.

This glorious grandiflora hasn't been around for long, but it's certainly attracted its share of attention, and little wonder: It's impossible to miss those vibrant blooms. 'Fame!' produces large, pointed, coral pink buds that unfurl into large, double, perfectly formed flowers up to 5 inches across, in a vivid shade of deep pink. The single or clustered blooms are generally only lightly scented, though the fragrance seems to get a bit stronger as the flowers age. Bloom begins in late spring to early summer and repeats through summer into fall. Upright stems bear glossy, deep green leaves. Zones 5 to 9.

HOW TO USE
'Fame!' creates a tall, bushy plant, usually reaching 4 to 6 feet tall and 3 to 4 feet across. A drift of three or more bushes makes an outstanding display, either as a mass planting in a landscape or as a color accent in a bed or border. The long-stemmed blooms are also excellent as cut flowers. 'Fame!' seems to have good disease resistance.

All-America Rose Selection 1998

❦ 'Fantin-Latour'

Centifolia. Date unknown.

This exquisite old rose blooms only once a season, but it's certainly worth waiting for! 'Fantin-Latour' is officially classified as a centifolia, but experts agree that it's more likely a hybrid. Regardless of its questionable parentage, it's a glorious garden rose. Plump, red-blushed pink buds unfurl into 3- to 4-inch flowers full of swirled, soft pink petals. The flowers are cupped when new; as they open, the outer petals fold back and the inner petals become broadly cupped, revealing a button of tightly packed, small petals in the center. Fans of 'Fantin-Latour' generally agree that the flowers have an intense, sweet scent, although a few can detect only a light fragrance. This rose produces one prolific show for several weeks each year, starting in mid- to late spring in mild climates and early to midsummer in cooler areas. Large, dark green leaves are borne on long, arching, slightly thorny canes. Zones 5 to 8.

HOW TO USE

'Fantin-Latour' normally forms a bushy, mounded shrub. In warm climates, growth is fairly restrained: 3 to 5 feet in height and width. In the cool climates it favors, 'Fantin-Latour' can grow much larger: 5 to 6 feet tall and wide is common, though it may get up to 8 feet tall and wide where it is very happy. Pruning after flowering can help keep the size under control, but this rose really looks best where it has the room to spread out its graceful, arching canes. Site it at the back of a mixed border or cottage garden; it looks especially lovely combined with old-fashioned perennials such as lady's mantle *(Alchemilla mollis)* and red valerian *(Centranthus ruber)*. 'Fantin-Latour' can also make a charming 8- to 10-foot climber; train it to a fence or pillar to help the canes support the weight of the heavy flowers. Disease resistance is moderate; take preventive measures against mildew or black spot if these problems are common in your area.

'Felicia'

Hybrid musk. Pemberton, 1928.

Fragrant and free flowering, 'Felicia' is a marvelous addition to just about any warmer-climate garden where pastel colors are prominent. This hybrid musk produces pointed, coral-pink buds that open into double, 3-inch, clustered blooms with a moderate to strong scent. The newer flowers have a clear light pink to peachy pink color and something of a hybrid tea shape; they open to a looser ruffled form and fade to cream as they age. 'Felicia' blooms abundantly in late spring to early summer, with moderate rebloom in summer and often another big flush in fall. The cool weather of fall also brings out richer colors in the flowers, and they last longer then too. Large, rounded, red hips also appear in fall. Medium to dark green, leathery leaves are carried on long, arching canes. Zones 6 to 10.

HOW TO USE

'Felicia' forms a broad, branching shrub that can grow anywhere from 3 to 8 feet tall and 4 to 9 feet wide, depending on your climate and how much pruning you're willing to do. Before you plant it, it's a good idea to find a specimen or two growing in conditions similar to yours; that way, you'll have a better idea of how much room to allow and how much maintenance to expect. Give it a spot by itself to enjoy it as a landscape accent, or try it in a row to create a charming informal hedge. 'Felicia' also looks great trained on a fence or pillar as an 8- to 10-foot climber. This lovely rose usually offers excellent disease resistance.

☙ 'Félicité Parmentier'

Alba. Parmentier, 1834.

'Félicité Parmentier' is a perfect choice for gardeners who love the delicate colors and scent of alba roses but who don't have room for a full-sized selection. Plump, creamy white buds tinged with yellow or light green open into rather flattened to nearly rounded, very double, 2-inch flowers packed with many folded petals. Clear, light pink when newly opened, the flowers fade to blush white around the edges; in hot weather, the entire bloom may quickly bleach to almost white. Fragrance lovers generally consider 'Félicité Parmentier' to be among the best of the old garden roses for scent. The flowers appear in one main flush, normally starting in late spring or early summer and lasting four to six weeks. Sturdy, thorny canes carry an abundant covering of handsome, dark green leaves that have a bluish tint. Zones 4 to 8.

HOW TO USE

'Félicité Parmentier' is a vigorous but relatively compact rose, usually reaching just 4 to 5 feet in height and 3 to 4 feet in spread. Its more restrained size and upright habit make it an excellent alba for a smaller garden. Enjoy it as a low hedge, or add it to mixed borders or cottage gardens. It looks just splendid combined with early-summer perennials, such as foxgloves (*Digitalis* spp.) and catmints (*Nepeta* spp.). It even grows well in a large container. 'Félicité Parmentier' appreciates a bit of afternoon shade in warm climates. Like other albas, this one can tolerate some shade in other areas as well, but it's more prone to mildew there than its relatives. It may also develop a bit of rust in areas where this fungal disease is common.

❦ 'Fimbriata'

Syns. 'Diantheflora', 'Dianthiflora', 'Phoebe's Frilled Pink'
Hybrid rugosa. Morlet, 1891.

Here's a rose that hardly looks like a rose at all! This hybrid rugosa produces tapered, light pink buds that open into semidouble, loosely cupped blooms that are about 3 inches across. The clustered flowers are usually white but are often blushed with pale pink, and they're generally quite delightfully fragrant. What really makes the flowers of 'Fimbriata' distinctive, though, is the fringed edge on each of the petals; they look very much like florists' carnations *(Dianthus caryophyllus)*. This rose produces its best show in late spring or early summer, with moderate rebloom through the rest of the season. A few orange-red hips may also appear in fall, but don't depend on an abundant display. Upright to somewhat arching, bristly canes carry large, light green, deeply veined leaves. Zones 4 to 8.

HOW TO USE

'Fimbriata' forms a bushy, upright plant that grows 4 to 5 feet in height and width. This is not a rose to grow if you're looking for a spectacular garden show; rather, it's a charming, subtle accent for a shrub or mixed border. Make sure you site it where you can get close enough to admire the unusual blooms. Like many of its rugosa relatives, 'Fimbriata' seldom develops serious disease problems.

❦ 'First Edition'

Syns. 'Arnaud Delbard'; DELtep
Floribunda. Delbard, 1976.

The richly hued blooms of this lovely floribunda make an outstanding color accent in almost any garden. 'First Edition' produces egg-shaped, pointed, deep coral pink buds that unfurl into double, coral-shaded orange flowers that are 2 to 3 inches across. The blooms are high centered at first; as they open, they reveal a cluster of yellow stamens surrounded by a ring of short inner petals and a cup of large outer petals. The slightly fragrant flowers are held singly or in clusters, starting in late spring to early summer and repeating through the rest of the growing season. Moderately thorny, branching canes carry glossy, olive green leaves. Zones 5 to 9.

HOW TO USE

'First Edition' forms an upright, somewhat rounded bush that's about 3½ to 5 feet tall and 3 to 4 feet wide. A group of three or more plants makes a dramatic drift of color in a bed or border. For even more impact, try 'First Edition' as a spectacular flowering hedge. Gardeners in cooler areas report the best success with this rose; very hot summers seem to cut down on flower production and lead to some fading on the blooms that do form, although the show is still fairly good. This low-maintenance rose generally offers excellent disease resistance.

All-America Rose Selection 1977

❧ 'First Kiss'

Syn. JACling
Floribunda. Warriner, 1991.

It may take a bit of searching to find this floribunda, but you'll know it's worth the hunt when you see it in full bloom! 'First Kiss' produces pointed buds that open into slightly fragrant, double flowers up to 4 inches across, with medium to light pink petals that are touched with peach toward the middle of the bloom. The flowers are high centered when new, then open to a more informal, cupped shape. Blooming begins in late spring or early summer and continues freely for the rest of the season. Upright, branching stems bear abundant, medium green leaves. Zones 5 to 9.

HOW TO USE

'First Kiss' forms a compact bush that's usually 2 to 4 feet in height and spread. Enjoy it in groups of three or more as an outstanding color accent in a flower bed or mixed border. Silver-leaved companions, such as dusty miller *(Senecio cineraria)* or lamb's ears *(Stachys byzantina),* are particularly effective partners for the brightly colored blooms. This easy-care rose offers good disease resistance.

❧ 'First Prize'

Hybrid tea. Boerner, 1970.

This hybrid tea may not be a good choice if you're looking for a good garden display, but if you want nearly perfect blooms for cutting, 'First Prize' is a winner. Long, tapered, reddish pink buds unfurl into double, high-centered flowers that are usually 4 to 6 inches across, in various shades of rosy pink with a lighter pink to cream center to each petal. The color is richest in cool weather; intense sun can cause the pink to fade quickly. Slightly scented flowers appear in abundance — often in impressive sprays — in late spring or early summer, with moderate repeat bloom through the rest of the season. Thick, very thorny stems carry medium to dark green, semiglossy leaves that have a leathery texture. Zones 6 to 9.

HOW TO USE
'First Prize' forms a vigorous, upright to slightly spreading bush that usually reaches 3 to 5 feet in height and spread. This rose generally isn't a great performer in the landscape, but it's wonderful for a cutting garden; the long-stemmed, long-lasting flowers are excellent for arrangements. Be prepared to watch for disease problems, though; 'First Prize' is moderately susceptible to black spot and may also develop some powdery mildew if you don't take preventive measures.

All-America Rose Selection 1970

❦ 'Fisherman's Friend'

Syn. AUSchild
Shrub. Austin, 1987.

In a group of roses famous for their fragrance, this dramatic English rose is among the most powerfully perfumed. 'Fisherman's Friend' produces pointed, maroon buds that open into very double blooms full of folded petals. The rich, deep color is somewhere between maroon and deep reddish pink, with a lighter shade of the same color on the backs of the petals. Usually 4 to 5 inches in diameter but up to 6 or 7 inches across in cool weather, the single or clustered flowers are cupped at first, opening to a somewhat flattened, rosette form. Bloom usually starts with a good show in early summer, followed by good repeat bloom through the rest of the summer into fall. Stout, thorny canes carry semiglossy, dark green leaves. Zones 5 to 9.

HOW TO USE
'Fisherman's Friend' forms an upright, bushy shrub that generally reaches 3 to 4 feet tall and 2½ to 4 feet wide. It's a handsome addition to a mixed border, particularly when paired with white flowers or silvery fo-

liage to show off the large, deep red blooms. 'Fisherman's Friend' also adapts to training against a fence or other support. This beautiful rose seems to do best in warm, dry areas; take preventive measures against black spot, mildew, and rust in areas where these problems are prevalent.

❧ 'Flower Carpet'

Syns. 'Heidetraum', 'Pink Flower Carpet'; NOAtraum
Shrub. Noack, 1989.

This free-flowering, easy-care shrub rose is an excellent choice for a beginning rose gardener, but it's pretty enough to earn the appreciation of experienced rose growers as well. Small, rounded buds open into semi-double, 1½-inch, cupped to flattened flowers in a vibrant shade of deep pink. When fully opened, the petals reveal a small white eye and a cluster of yellow stamens. The flowers are only slightly fragrant, but they're held in large clusters, and they appear in flushes over a very long season: from late spring or early summer until frost. Small, rounded, red hips also adorn the plants in fall. Glossy, deep green leaves are held on sprawling stems. Zones 5 to 10.

HOW TO USE

'Flower Carpet' produces a vigorous, low, spreading shrub that's usually 2 to 3 feet tall and 3 to 4 feet across. It looks great planted in groups of three or more to create a drift of color: enjoy it as a landscape accent, a groundcover for a gentle slope, or an eye-catching low hedge or foundation planting. The trailing canes also show off well when allowed to spill over a low wall or out of a container planting. 'Flower Carpet' is generally touted as disease resistant or even disease-free, but gardeners do report some mildew or black spot on unprotected bushes, mainly in warm, moist climates.

Since the release of 'Flower Carpet', several other colors have been introduced, including 'Flower Carpet Appleblossom' (deep pink buds and light pink flowers) and 'Flower Carpet White' (with white buds and flowers).

❦ 'Folklore'

Syn. KORlore
Hybrid tea. Kordes, 1977.

This handsome hybrid tea takes up its share of space, but if you have the room, you'll glory in its striking, sunset-shaded blooms. Long, pointed, bright orange buds unfurl into very double, high-centered flowers that are 4½ to 5 inches across, in an exquisite shade of salmon pink with peachy yellow on the backs of the petals. The delightfully fragrant flowers generally first appear in early summer, with moderate bloom in summer and good repeat in fall. Strong, very thorny stems carry glossy, medium to deep green leaves. Zones 5 to 9.

HOW TO USE

'Folklore' is a vigorous rose with a vase-shaped to spreading habit; it can reach anywhere from 6 to 10 feet in height and about 4 to 6 feet in spread. Before you choose a planting spot, try to find a bush already growing in conditions similar to yours to see what to expect from this rose in your area. You'll probably end up placing it at the back of a border, or even training it as a climber. It is also effective as a tall hedge. Held on long stems, the flowers are excellent for cutting. 'Folklore' is seldom bothered by diseases.

❦ 'Foxi Pavement' See 'Buffalo Gal'

❦ 'Fourth of July'

Syns. 'Crazy for You'; WEKroalt
Large-flowered climber. Carruth, 1999.

Keep the excitement of Independence Day going all summer long with this amazing large-flowered climbing rose. Pointed, reddish buds open into semidouble blooms that are 2 to 4 inches across, with golden stamens surrounded by ruffled white petals that are streaked and speckled with bright red. The clustered flowers generally have a somewhat sweet scent. They appear in a spectacular flush in early summer, followed by good repeat bloom into fall. Moderately thorny canes carry glossy, deep green leaves. Zones 5 to 10.

HOW TO USE

'Fourth of July' is a moderately vigorous climber, reaching 10 to 15 feet tall in most areas. It's handsome enough to grow by itself on an arbor, a large fence, or a sturdy trellis, but it also looks great paired with white- or red-flowered climbing roses. The dramatic flowers of 'Fourth of July' show off beautifully against both dark and light backgrounds (except perhaps orange-hued brick). This climber normally has good disease resistance, but some gardeners report that black spot can be a problem if you don't use preventive sprays.

All-America Rose Selection 1999

🌹 'Fragrant Cloud'

Syns. 'Duftwolke', 'Nuage Parfumé'; TANellis
Hybrid tea. Tantau, 1967.

Who says old garden roses are the only ones with good fragrance? This award-winning hybrid tea ranks right up there in the American Rose Society's top-ten list of fragrant roses. Pointed, oval, bright red buds unfurl into double, high-centered blooms up to 5 inches across. The clustered flowers are a hard-to-describe color: somewhere between soft brick red and purplish red, depending on the age of the bloom. Every photograph you see of this rose looks different, so if color is critical, find a bush growing in your area and take a look for yourself before you buy. For most gardeners, though, color is a secondary consideration to this rose's outstanding scent. 'Fragrant Cloud' blooms freely from late spring or early summer to fall. Thorny stems bear glossy, deep green leaves. Zones 5 to 9.

HOW TO USE

This powerfully perfumed selection has a fairly stiff, upright habit, growing 3 to 5 feet tall and 2 to 3 feet wide. Grow it in a group of three or more for a fragrant accent in a flower bed or border. This rose really shines as a cut flower, so make sure you try at least one in your cutting garden. 'Fragrant Cloud' has moderate disease resistance: take preventive measures against black spot and powdery mildew if these problems are common in your area.

James Alexander Gamble Rose Fragrance Medal 1969; World Rose Hall of Fame 1981

✼ 'Fragrant Delight'

Syn. 'Wisbech Rose Fragrant Delight'
Floribunda. Wisbech Plant Co., 1978.

Here's another must-have if fragrance is high on your wish list when choosing roses. This delicately colored floribunda produces bright rose-pink buds that open into double, 3-inch blooms with a loose, cupped form. The clustered flowers are a soft peachy pink when new (especially during cool weather), aging to more of a clear pink and opening to reveal a yellow heart accented with golden stamens. The highly perfumed blooms appear abundantly in late spring or early summer and continue into fall. Moderately thorny canes bear an ample covering of shiny, medium green leaves. Zones 5 to 9.

HOW TO USE

'Fragrant Delight' has an upright, somewhat narrow habit, usually growing 3 to 4 feet tall and 2½ to 3½ feet wide. Enjoy its exquisite scent and lovely color in a flower bed or border (it looks best in groups of three or more). It blends beautifully with many other colors but looks especially pretty with blues and purples. 'Fragrant Delight' is generally disease resistant but may develop some mildew in fall.

✼ 'Frau Dagmar Hartopp'

Syns. 'Frau Dagmar Hastrup', 'Fru Dagmar Hastrup'
Hybrid rugosa. Hastrup, 1914.

Months of blooms, showy fruits, splendid fall color, compact growth, and excellent disease resistance — this hybrid rugosa has it all! 'Frau Dagmar Hartopp' produces long, tapered, reddish pink buds that unfurl into single, cupped to saucer-shaped blooms that are 3 to 4 inches across, accented with a cluster of yellow stamens in the center. New flowers are bright rosy pink, softening to lighter pink as they open. The moderately fragrant blooms appear abundantly in late spring to early summer and continue until heavy frost. Round, red hips also ripen among the blooms in late summer and fall. The show isn't over yet — there's still an excellent display of fall color to enjoy. The semiglossy, rich green leaves held on bristly stems usually turn yellow or bronze, but they may also show shades of red, orange, or purple. Zones 3 to 8.

HOW TO USE

'Frau Dagmar Hartopp' forms a dense, spreading shrub that grows 3 to 5 feet tall and 4 to 6 feet across. Established plants tend to produce suckers, creating a bushy clump that's an effective low hedge, a marvelous mass planting for a landscape accent, or a good tall groundcover for a gentle slope. The heat and salt tolerance make 'Frau Dagmar Hartopp' a great choice for planting in tough sites, such as along driveways or streets. This lovely rose also looks splendid planted in a mixed border or shrub border. Best of all, it's rarely bothered by diseases.

❦ 'Frau Karl Druschki'

Syns. 'F. K. Druschkii', 'Reine des Neiges', 'Snow Queen', 'White American Beauty'
Hybrid perpetual. Lambert, 1901.

This hybrid perpetual produces an outstanding show of pristine blooms that add a touch of class to any planting. Plump, pointed buds tinged with reddish pink unfurl into fully double, 3- to 5-inch blooms that are high centered when new and cupped when fully open. The flowers are snowy white, sometimes with a blush of palest pink or yellow in the center, and accented with a cluster of golden stamens. They normally have little or no scent. Blooms appear in abundance in late spring and often again in fall, with moderate rebloom during the summer. Round, red hips also appear in fall. Thorny stems carry leathery, medium green leaves. Zones 5 to 9.

HOW TO USE

'Frau Karl Druschki' produces a vigorous, slightly arching shrub, generally reaching 4 to 6 feet tall and 3 to 4 feet wide, though it can get much larger where it's happy. It's a good idea to find someone in your area who is growing this rose and ask about their experience with its size before you select a planting site. It looks best planted in groups of three or more for a bushier effect; try it at the back of a mixed border for its elegant, multiseason interest. It also adapts to training as a climber, reaching 8 to 10 feet in height. 'Frau Karl Druschki' has moderate disease resistance; take preventive measures against black spot, powdery mildew, and rust if these problems are common in your area.

❦ 'Fred Loads'

Shrub. Holmes, 1968.

Subtle it isn't; stunning it is! This eye-catching shrub rose produces pointed buds that open to single, cupped to saucer-shaped blooms that are 3 to 3½ inches across. Beginning in a brilliant shade of orange-red, the flowers age through clear orange to a soft salmon color, accented with a small white eye and yellow stamens. Held in large, heavy clusters, the blooms appear almost continuously from late spring or early summer through the rest of the growing season. They have little or no scent, but that's not much of an issue in the garden, since they're produced at the tops of tall, moderately thorny canes that are often over head-height anyway. The abundant, glossy, light green leaves make a perfect backdrop for the bright blooms. Zones 5 to 10.

HOW TO USE

'Fred Loads' forms a vigorous, upright bush that can grow anywhere from 4 to 8 feet tall and 3 to 6 feet across. (Hard pruning during the dormant season can help control the height.) It makes an amazing color accent for the back of a mixed border paired with other tall, bright companions: good candidates include goldenrods *(Solidago* spp.), bronze fennel *(Foeniculum vulgare* 'Purpureum'), and dark-leaved cannas, such as 'Red King Humbert' *(Canna × generalis* 'Red King Humbert'). 'Fred Loads' also adapts well to training as a climber or pillar. This dramatic rose is seldom bothered by diseases.

❦ 'French Lace'

Syn. JAClace
Floribunda. Warriner, 1980.

This lovely floribunda can be a little hard to please, but many gardeners feel that's a small price to pay for the exquisite flowers. Elegant, tapered cream-colored buds are blushed with pink or peach; they open to double, high-centered, 3- to 4-inch blooms that are ivory with a hint of peach in the center. Held in clusters or singly on long stems, the slightly scented flowers are produced freely from late spring or early summer to fall. Moderately thorny stems carry semiglossy, deep green leaves. Zones 7 to 10.

HOW TO USE

'French Lace' produces an upright bush that grows 2½ to 4 feet tall and 3 to 4 feet across. It will grow in Zone 6 with good winter protection, but this tender rose really performs best in warmer climates. It looks good enough to plant alone as a landscape accent or low hedge, but it also blends beautifully into beds and borders. Include one in your cutting garden, too: The long-lasting blooms are excellent for arrangements. Apart from its dislike of cold winters, 'French Lace' is generally trouble-free.

All-America Rose Selection 1982

⚜'Frühlingsgold'

Syn. 'Spring Gold'
Hybrid spinosissima. Kordes, 1937.

The bloom season of this hybrid spinosissima may be brief, but it's nothing short of spectacular! Pointed yellow buds blushed with red open into saucer-shaped, single, 3- to 4-inch flowers. The blooms are a clear buttery yellow when new, quickly aging to creamy white in warm conditions, and they are accented with a cluster of golden yellow to golden brown stamens. 'Frühlingsgold' produces one outstanding show of delightfully fragrant flowers, generally for two to three weeks starting in mid- to late spring. A few additional blooms may appear here and there later in the season, along with some dark, rounded hips. Arching, thorny canes carry large, light green leaves. Zones 4 to 9.

HOW TO USE

This vigorous rose has a bushy, upright to arching habit, reaching anywhere from 6 to 8 feet tall and 5 to 9 feet wide. It looks best when allowed to grow with minimal pruning, so make sure you give it plenty of room; try to find an established bush in your area to see what size to expect in your climate. Give 'Frühlingsgold' a spot in a shrub border as a seasonal accent, or use it as an informal hedge. This big and beautiful rose seldom develops serious disease problems.

❦ 'Frühlingsmorgen'
Syn. 'Spring Morning'

Hybrid spinosissima. Kordes, 1942.

If you have the room for it, 'Frühlingsmorgen' is an attractive garden addition for its glorious easy-season show. This hybrid spinosissima produces long, pink buds that unfurl into single, saucer-shaped to flattened flowers that are 3 to 4 inches across and accented with a cluster of reddish orange stamens. Color varies from bright to soft rosy pink with a soft yellow to cream center, depending on the weather. The moderately fragrant flowers appear mainly in one splendid show, usually in late spring; you may also see occasional flowers through the rest of the growing season or even another smaller flush of bloom in late summer. Some large, oblong hips may also appear in late summer and fall. Dark grayish green leaves are carried on moderately thorny, arching canes. Zones 5 to 9.

HOW TO USE

'Frühlingsmorgen' has a rather open, branching habit. In most areas, it reaches 5 to 7 feet in height and spread, but it can get even larger in ideal conditions. Try to find an existing bush growing in conditions similar to yours so that you can see what to expect and plan accordingly. If you have the space, enjoy 'Frühlingsmorgen' as a seasonal accent at the back of a mixed border, include it in a shrub border, or try it as a mass planting. It also makes an effective hedge or screen. 'Frühlingsmorgen' generally has good disease resistance, although it may get mild to moderate black spot if you don't take preventive measures in areas where this disease is a common problem.

❦ 'Galway Bay'
Syn. MACba
Large-flowered climber. McGredy, 1966.

The pretty pink flowers of this large-flowered climber are a perfect choice for dressing up a vertical surface. Pointed, deep pink buds unfurl into double, open-cupped, 3½-inch blooms in a rich shade of deep to medium pink. The slightly scented, clustered flowers appear in abundance almost continually from late spring or early summer to fall. Rather stiff, branching stems carry a generous covering of medium to dark green, glossy leaves. Zones 5 to 9.

HOW TO USE

'Galway Bay' is a vigorous climber, generally growing 8 to 12 feet tall. It's a glorious sight adorning an arbor, dressing up a fence, or perking up a pillar. This selection is not seriously troubled by diseases; a bit of black spot may develop but it is seldom severe.

✿ 'Gartendirektor Otto Linne'

Shrub. Lambert, 1934.

There's nothing stingy about the bloom display on this superb shrub rose! 'Gartendirektor Otto Linne' produces pointed, pink buds that open to small, double rosettes that are 2 inches across. Held in huge clusters on long, strong stems, the flowers are a warm shade of rosy pink with a touch of yellow or white at the base of the petals. This splendid show of color first appears in late spring to early summer, and it repeats in flushes through the rest of the summer and into fall. Slightly thorny, arching stems carry light green, semiglossy leaves that have a leathery texture. Zones 5 to 9.

HOW TO USE

'Gartendirektor Otto Linne' has a vigorous, upright habit. Grown as a shrub, it usually reaches 4 to 6 feet tall and wide; try it as a hedge, or enjoy it as a long-blooming color accent at the back of a mixed border. This rose also adapts to training as a climber in mild climates, where it can reach up to 10 feet in height. 'Gartendirektor Otto Linne' generally has excellent disease resistance.

✿ 'Gemini'

Syn. JACnepal
Hybrid tea. Zary, 1999.

Lovers of bicolored blooms will jump at the chance to grow this distinctive hybrid tea. 'Gemini' bears large, cream-colored buds that are tinged with reddish pink, unfurling into exquisite, double, high-centered blooms that are up to 4½ inches across. New blooms are creamy white with a narrow edging of coral-pink to orange-pink on each petal; as the flowers age, the edging darkens and expands to cover more of the petal. The blooms have a light, sweet to fruity fragrance, and they're normally produced singly on long stems, though sometimes two or three flowers will appear together. The show starts in late spring to early summer, with good repeat through the rest of the season. Look for the biggest blooms and best color contrast in cool weather. Thorny stems bear semiglossy, deep green leaves. Zones 5 to 9.

HOW TO USE

‘Gemini’ forms an upright bush, growing anywhere from 3 to 6 feet tall and 2 to 3 feet wide. It makes a dramatic display in a flower bed or border, especially when planted in groups of three or more to create a broader, more shrublike clump. Try it as a cut flower, too. ‘Gemini’ seems to have good disease resistance in most areas.

All-America Rose Selection 2000

✿‘Gene Boerner’

Floribunda. Boerner, 1968.

‘Gene Boerner’ is classified as a floribunda, but you might not guess that by looking at its elegant, hybrid tea–like flowers. Egg-shaped, deep pink buds unfurl into high-centered, double blooms that are 3 to 3½ inches across, held singly or in clusters. The beautiful blooms generally have little scent, but they’re produced prolifically in late spring or early summer, with excellent repeat through the rest of the summer and into fall. Thorny stems carry light to medium green, glossy leaves. Zones 5 to 9.

HOW TO USE

‘Gene Boerner’ has a slender, upright habit, usually growing 4 to 5 feet tall and 2 to 3 feet wide. It’s a great choice for tucking into a narrow spot, such as a foundation planting or a container. Try it in groups of three of more to create a drift of color near the back of a mixed border. The long-lasting blooms also make marvelous cut flowers, so consider adding a bush to your cutting garden for an ample supply of arranging material. ‘Gene Boerner’ generally has good disease resistance, though it may develop a touch of black spot or mildew if you don’t take preventive measures.

All-America Rose Selection 1969

❦ 'Geranium'

Hybrid moyesii. Royal Horticultural Society, 1938.

If you have the space, this hybrid moyesii is an outstanding garden addition, for its fruits as much as its flowers. 'Geranium' produces pointed buds that open into single, saucer-shaped blooms that are 2 inches across. Some plants distributed under this name have pink or orange-pink flowers, but the true 'Geranium' bears brilliant red to scarlet blooms, accented with orange-yellow stamens and held in small clusters. They have little or no scent and only appear once a season, in late spring or early summer, but the best is yet to come: they produce a dazzling display of elongated, orange-red fruits in late summer to fall. Arching stems carry light green leaves that make a beautiful contrast to the bright flowers and fruits. Zones 5 to 8.

HOW TO USE

'Geranium' has an upright, somewhat vase-shaped habit. It usually grows 6 to 8 feet tall and 5 to 8 feet across, but it can reach up to 10 feet tall where it's really happy. It's a smart idea to find someone in your area who is growing this rose so that you can find out what size to expect before you choose a planting site. You might also want to find out the source of the bush and buy from the same source so that you can be sure you'll get the true geranium red 'Geranium'. This rose makes a magnificent multiseason show at the back of a mixed border. If you don't have the room to let the stems arch naturally, try training them up a pillar or against a fence. 'Geranium' generally doesn't have serious disease problems, although it may develop a bit of mildew in some areas.

❦ 'Gertrude Jekyll'

Syn. AUSboard
Shrub. Austin, 1986.

One of the most well known of the English roses, this shrub rose is lovely but needs care to look its best. Plump, deep reddish pink buds open into fully double, slightly cupped to flattened rosettes that are 4 to 5 inches across and full of folded petals. The clustered blooms are usually deep pink in the center, softening to medium or light pink on the outer edges; the color is richest during cool weather. Gardeners agree that this rose is powerfully perfumed, though their judgments vary as to the type of fragrance: some say it is sweet and others describe it as a classic old-rose scent. The best show of blooms appears in late spring or early summer to midsummer; later bloom tends to be much less abundant. Stiff, thorny canes carry medium green, semiglossy leaves. Zones 5 to 9.

HOW TO USE

'Gertrude Jekyll' (pronounced JEE-kul) forms a somewhat open shrub that's usually 4 to 5 feet tall and 3 to 4 feet wide in cool climates; in warmer areas, it often works better trained as an 8- to 10-foot climber. Either way, it's certainly a splendid sight in the early-summer garden, livening up a mixed border or adorning a wall or fence. If you're using this rose as a shrub, cutting it back by half after its first flush of flowers can help control size and increase later blooming. 'Gertrude Jekyll' has moderate disease resistance; take preventive measures against black spot and mildew in areas where these diseases are common.

꤈'Giggles'

Syn. KINgig
Miniature. King, 1987.

You'll often hear or see 'Giggles' referred to by its code name, KINgig, to distinguish it from another miniature rose also called 'Giggles'. This popular little selection produces tiny deep pink buds that open into small, double blooms resembling tiny hybrid tea flowers to just 1½ inches across. Usually held singly but sometimes in clusters, the slightly scented blooms appear in light to medium rose-pink (or sometimes peachy pink) with a darker shade of the same color on the underside of the petals; as they age, they fade to a light, creamy pink. Flowering generally starts in late spring and continues freely through the rest of the growing season. Light to medium green leaves are carried on thorny stems. Zones 5 to 9.

HOW TO USE

'Giggles' has a vigorous, upright habit, generally growing 18 to 24 inches tall and 16 to 18 inches across. It's a lovely addition to a flower bed, particularly near a deck or patio or a bench where you can sit and admire the elegant blooms. You could also try growing it in a container to raise it up closer to eye level. This little charmer makes a great cut flower, too. 'Giggles' generally has good disease resistance.

❦ 'Glowing Amber'

Syn. MANglow
Miniature. Mander, 1996.

It may be classified as a miniature, but there's nothing small about the appeal of this splendid little rose! 'Glowing Amber' produces pointed buds that open into double, high-centered blooms, each about 2 inches across. The flowers are a magnificent rich red with a yellow center and a golden yellow flush on the outside of each petal, creating an amazing two-color effect. As the flowers open, the petal edges roll back along the sides to create a pointed tip, giving the blooms a starlike outline. The long-stemmed, lightly fragrant flowers generally begin in late spring, with good repeat though the rest of the growing season. Moderately thorny stems carry dark green, glossy leaves, which make a beautiful backdrop for the bright flowers. Zones 5 to 10.

HOW TO USE
'Glowing Amber' has a bushy, upright habit, growing anywhere from 15 to 30 inches in height and about 12 to 18 inches in width. Enjoy it as an accent in a bed or border, as an edging for a deck, patio, or walkway, or in a container. Try combining it with yellow flowers — such as 'Lemon Gem' marigold (*Tagetes tenuifolia* 'Lemon Gem') — to echo the yellow tones in the blooms. (Just make sure you leave room around the rose for good air circulation.) 'Glowing Amber' generally has good disease resistance.

❦ 'Golden Celebration'

Syn. AUSgold
Shrub. Austin, 1993.

The splendid flowers of this superb English rose offer an old-fashioned form in a relatively modern color. Plump, yellow buds blushed with red open to reveal very double, 3- to 6-inch blooms with cupped inner petals and reflexed outer ones. The color is commonly a deep egg-yolk yellow, but it may also be blushed with peach or pink to create a rich coppery yellow. Held in small, often nodding clusters, the flowers offer a moderate to strong perfume that hovers somewhere between spicy and fruity. 'Golden Celebration' flowers generously in late spring to early summer with frequent repeat flushes through the rest of the growing season. The lightly to moderately thorny, arching canes bear glossy, medium green leaves. Zones 5 to 9.

HOW TO USE

'Golden Celebration' forms a rounded to somewhat spreading shrub, generally reaching 4 to 5 feet tall and wide in the cooler parts of its range and 6 to 7 feet tall and wide in warmer areas. It's a beautiful addition to a mixed border — try it combined with lavender or with violet sage *(Salvia × superba)* — and it also makes a good cut flower. Disease resistance is generally good, but consider taking preventive measures if black spot is a problem in your area.

❦'Golden Showers'

Large-flowered climber. Lammerts, 1956.

This large-flowered climber is a great choice for adding sunny color to just about any warmer-climate garden. Long, pointed, bright yellow buds open to double, 3½- to 4½-inch blooms accented with a cluster of golden stamens. The flowers start out bright yellow with high centers, quickly opening to a loosely ruffled form and fading to light cream. Flowers at all different stages appear on the bush at the same time, giving an interesting bicolored effect. Some gardeners detect a moderate to strong sweet or licorice scent; others don't notice any fragrance. Held singly or in clusters, the flowers first appear in a generous flush in late spring to early summer, usually followed by moderate rebloom through summer and often another flush in fall, continuing until frost. Deep green, glossy leaves are carried on somewhat thorny canes. Zones 6 to 9.

HOW TO USE

'Golden Showers' is a fairly vigorous climber, generally growing 6 to 10 feet tall but occasionally reaching up to 14 feet. Use it to adorn an arch or arbor, dress up a wall or fence, or wrap around a pillar. Young bushes tend to have a rather bushy habit, and you can encourage them to keep that shrubby form with regular pruning, if desired. Disease resistance is moderate; take preventive measures against black spot and mildew where these fungal diseases are common.

All-America Rose Selection 1957

❦ 'Golden Wings'

Shrub. Shepherd, 1956.

The soft-colored, simple flowers may look delicate, but this sturdy shrub rose generally has a trouble-free constitution. 'Golden Wings' produces long, pointed buds that open to single, saucer-shaped blooms 3 to 5 inches across, in a lovely shade of light butter yellow accented with orange to red stamens. The lightly to moderately fragrant flowers are held in small clusters. Bloom usually begins in mid- to late spring and continues moderately but steadily to heavy frost; it's a rare day that there isn't at least one bloom! Thorny stems carry light green leaves. Zones 4 to 8.

HOW TO USE

'Golden Wings' forms a bushy, somewhat rounded shrub that generally grows 4 to 6 feet tall and 3 to 5 feet across. This adaptable rose looks super in many parts of the garden: plant it alone as a landscape accent, or enjoy it in a cottage garden or mixed border, where it looks especially lovely with spring bulbs and with blue-flowered companions, such as bellflowers (*Campanula* spp.). 'Golden Wings' also looks great in groups as a mass planting or hedge. You can even train it to grow on a wall or fence. This rose usually resists diseases but may develop a bit of black spot in humid climates if you don't take preventive measures.

❦ 'Gold Medal'

Syn. AROyqueli
Grandiflora. Christensen, 1982.

If you love the golden glow of yellow roses, give 'Gold Medal' a try: this glorious grandiflora is one of the best around! Long, pointed, golden buds tinged with red unfurl into double, 4- to 5-inch blooms that have the classic, high-centered form of a hybrid tea. New flowers are a rich golden yellow, often with delicate reddish or orange edging to the outer petals; they eventually fade to light yellow or near white. The slightly scented, long-stemmed blooms are sometimes held singly but more often in small clusters. Flowering starts in late spring or early summer, with good repeat through the rest of the growing season. Nearly thornless stems carry deep green, semiglossy foliage. Zones 5 to 9.

HOW TO USE

'Gold Medal' has a fairly stiff, upright habit, usually growing 4 to 6 feet tall and 3 to 5 feet across. It looks best planted in groups of three or more to create a bushier mass, making a dramatic drift of color in a bed or border. The long-lasting flowers are also excellent for arrangements, so consider adding a bush or two to your cutting garden for a steady supply of golden blooms through the summer. 'Gold Medal' can grow in Zone 5 (and even some areas of Zones 4), but winter protection is critical in these cold climates. It has above-average disease resistance for a yellow rose, but it still may develop a touch of black spot or mildew if you don't take preventive measures.

❦ 'Gourmet Popcorn'

Syns. 'Summer Snow'; WEOpop
Miniature. Desamero, 1986.

This cute little miniature may be small in stature, but it's certainly not lacking in the charm department! Hundreds of tiny, rounded, ivory buds that are sometimes touched with pink open to small, semidouble, 1-inch rosettes. The flowers are bright white accented with a cluster of golden yellow stamens, and they're held in large, puffy clusters that look rather like masses of popped popcorn (if you use a bit of imagination). Reports on the fragrance vary, so you might want to find a bush in bloom and take a test sniff before you buy if scent is important to you. But really, when you consider the abundance of bloom this rose produces from late spring or early summer well into fall, minimal scent is mostly a minor issue. Glossy, dark green leaves are held on somewhat slender stems that arch under the weight of the bloom clusters. Zones 4 to 9.

HOW TO USE

'Gourmet Popcorn' has a compact, bushy, mounded habit, generally reaching 18 to 30 inches in height and 15 to 24 inches in spread. Enjoy it anywhere you could use a splendid show of white blooms all season long: this mini looks super cascading out of a container planting or over a low wall. Tuck it into beds and borders, or plant it in a drift of three or more for a low landscape accent. 'Gourmet Popcorn' is an easy-care rose that seldom has any disease problems.

❦'Graham Thomas'

Syns. 'English Yellow', 'Graham Stuart Thomas'; AUSmas
Shrub. Austin, 1983.

This gorgeous shrub is one of the most popular of the English roses, and
it's also one of the most variable. Its plump buds range in color from
peach to red, opening into cupped, double, 3- to 4-inch blooms packed
with petals. The flowers are usually a deep golden yellow when new —
they may have a touch of peach in some conditions — aging to lighter
yellow; at any one time, you'll see blooms of different ages in many
shades of yellow on the same bush. The clustered flowers have a moderate
to strong fragrance that some people like and others don't. Flowers appear in abundance in late spring to early summer, usually with moderate
rebloom through the rest of the growing season. Long, arching stems
carry glossy, medium to dark green leaves. Zones 5 to 9.

HOW TO USE

'Graham Thomas' has a vigorous, upright habit. In the coolest parts of its
hardiness range, it generally grows as a shrub that's about 5 to 6 feet tall
and 4 to 5 feet wide, making a handsome addition to a mixed border. In
warm climates, it tends to send up very long canes, reaching 8 to 12 feet in
height — ideal for a wall, fence, or pillar. Grown in moderate climates,
this rose may show both characteristics: let the canes stretch and train
them onto a support, or try cutting them back by half after the first flush
of flowers to encourage bushy growth. Some gardeners claim that using
own-root rather than grafted plants can also help keep the shrubby habit.
'Graham Thomas' generally has good disease resistance, but it may develop a bit of black spot or mildew if you don't take preventive measures.

❦'Great Maiden's Blush'

Syns. 'Cuisse de Nymphe', 'Incarnata', 'La Virginale', 'Maiden's Blush'
Alba. Introduced before 1600.

If you love the full-flowered look of antique roses, this elegant alba belongs in your garden! It produces creamy pink, rounded to egg-shaped
buds that open into very double, 3-inch blooms filled with cupped or
gently folded petals. New blooms are light to medium pink, with an almost rounded form; fully opened blooms are flattened and softened to
blush pink around the outer edge. The clustered, sweetly scented flowers

appear in one splendid show, usually in late spring. Arching, prickly stems bear matte, bluish green leaves. Zones 3 to 8.

HOW TO USE

'Great Maiden's Blush' starts out upright, then develops a somewhat fountain-like habit as the heavy blooms weigh down the ends of the canes. It generally grows 6 to 8 feet tall and 5 to 6 feet across. The old-fashioned flowers blend beautifully into a cottage garden setting; they also add a soft touch of seasonal color to mixed borders. 'Great Maiden's Blush' is pretty enough to stand alone as a landscape accent, but it also looks super planted in masses or used as a hedge or screen. It makes a great cut flower, too! Take preventive measures against black spot in humid conditions; otherwise, this rose is generally quite disease resistant.

'Maiden's Blush' (also known as 'Small Maiden's Blush'; Kew Gardens, 1797) is virtually identical, except that its flowers are slightly smaller and it is more compact, generally growing 4 to 6 feet tall and 3 to 5 feet wide.

❦ 'Green Ice'

Miniature. Moore, 1971.

Here's a crisp green-and-white combination that looks cool even on the hottest summer day. This miniature produces pointed, white buds often blushed with red, opening into 1-inch, double, ruffled rosettes that start out white (sometimes with a light pink blush) and age to light green. The flowers are held in large clusters, so you'll have white and green blooms right next to each other in the same bunch. They don't have much scent, if any, but they're produced prolifically in late spring to early summer with good repeat though the rest of the summer and into fall. Long, sprawling canes carry a dense covering of glossy, dark green leaves. Zones 5 to 10.

HOW TO USE

'Green Ice' has a bushy, spreading habit, generally growing 1 to 2 feet tall and spreading 18 to 24 inches. This compact, easy-care rose fits in just about anywhere: near the front of a bed or border; as an edging for a path or walkway; atop a low wall; or cascading out of a container. You can even train it as a low climber against a fence or trellis. Deadheading will help encourage generous rebloom. 'Green Ice' is rarely bothered by diseases.

🐛 'Grüss an Aachen'

Floribunda. Geduldig, 1909.

'Grüss an Aachen' may look like an antique rose, but it's actually relatively modern. This floribunda produces pointed, light orange or pink buds that unfurl into fully double, 3-inch, cupped flowers that open nearly flat to an almost rounded form. The new blooms are usually soft pink to pale peach, perhaps even with a touch of yellow, and they turn cream as they age. In strong sun, they may become almost white. Reports of their scent range from light to potent. Flowers first appear in late spring to early summer, with good repeat through the rest of the growing season. Mostly smooth canes carry glossy, deep green leaves. Zones 4 to 9.

HOW TO USE

'Grüss an Aachen' has an upright, bushy habit, forming a low shrub that ranges in size from 1½ to 3 feet tall and about as wide. Its old-fashioned, soft-colored flowers look lovely in a mixed border or cottage garden, planted singly or in groups of three or more to create a drift of color. Try it in a row as a low hedge, or enjoy it as a container plant or a deck or patio. 'Grüss an Aachen' appreciates a bit of shade during the hottest part of the day in warm climates. It may develop a touch of powdery mildew, black spot, or rust, but it is seldom seriously bothered by any of these problems.

🐛 'Grüss an Teplitz'

Syn. 'Virginia R. Coxe'
Bourbon. Geschwind, 1897.

'Grüss an Teplitz' is officially classified as a Bourbon rose, although it's actually a hybrid that shows characteristics common to some other rose classes. It produces small, egg-shaped buds opening to loosely double, cupped blooms that are 3 to 3½ inches across. The flowers are a bright red that ages to deep red — this darkening is a trait common to the China roses in this rose's background — and are borne on short, slender stems that tend to nod under the weight of the flower. Produced singly or in small to medium-size clusters, they generally have a noticeable, spicy scent. 'Grüss an Teplitz' flowers over a long season, starting in late spring to early summer and continuing until heavy frost; the fall show is often especially good. Long canes carry semiglossy, medium green leaves. Zones 5 to 10.

HOW TO USE

'Grüss an Teplitz' has a vigorous, upright habit that adapts to life either as a shrub or as a climber. Left to its own devices, it forms a somewhat open shrub that usually reaches 5 to 6 feet in height and 4 to 5 feet in width. Try it in a mixed border or cottage garden — silver foliage and white flowers make particularly pretty companions — or use it as an informal hedge. Trained as a climber on an arbor or pillar, this rose can grow 10 to 12 feet tall. 'Grüss an Teplitz' generally has good disease resistance, but mildew and/or black spot may develop in cool or humid areas if you don't take preventive measures.

❦ 'Guy de Maupassant'

Syns. 'Romantic Fragrance'; MEIsocrat
Floribunda. Meilland, 1996.

Classified as a floribunda by the American Rose Society, 'Guy de Maupassant' is marketed as a Romantica rose, one of a group of roses developed fairly recently in France. It's a very pretty selection, with plump, pink buds that produce old-fashioned flowers packed with over 100 petals. The 2½- to 3-inch, clustered flowers start out strongly cupped, opening to a flattened form with a circular outline. The fragrance is generally moderate to strong, and it's often likened to that of apples. Flowering begins with a generous display in late spring to early summer, with reasonable to good repeat bloom through the rest of the season. Moderately thorny canes carry glossy, deep green leaves. Zones 5 to 9.

HOW TO USE

'Guy de Maupassant' has a bushy, upright habit. Gardeners in different areas report differences in this rose's vigor: 4 to 6 feet in height and spread seems to be common, though it may be as compact as 3 feet or as much as 8 feet in height and spread. It's a relatively new introduction, so it may take some experimenting to find out how this rose will grow in your area; keep that in mind when you choose a planting site. It would make a charming addition to a flower bed or mixed border. 'Guy de Maupassant' seems to have good disease resistance.

❦ 'Handel'

Syns. 'Haendel', MACha
Large-flowered climber. McGredy, 1965.

If you're looking for a distinctive climber to accent a special site, 'Handel' may be just the rose for you. The pointed, reddish buds of this large-flowered climber unfurl into loosely double, 3½-inch blooms that start with high centers and widen to an open-cupped form. New flowers are creamy white with yellow centers and a delicate reddish pink rim brushed onto the edge of each petal; as they age, the pink often spreads to cover much of the petals, especially in warm weather. Blooms of all different ages are visible at one time, creating an eye-catching display from late spring or early summer to fall. The blossoms have little or no scent. Slightly thorny stems bear medium to deep green, glossy leaves. Zones 5 to 9.

HOW TO USE

'Handel' is a rather stiff, branching climber, generally growing 10 to 15 feet in height. It looks especially lovely trained on a light-colored support, such as a white pillar or post or a weathered gray arbor. Choose a planting site where you can get up fairly close to admire the unique blooms. 'Handel' has moderate disease resistance; it may develop black spot and powdery mildew if you don't take preventive measures.

❦ 'Hansa'

Hybrid rugosa. Schaum & Van Tol, 1905.

Tough and trouble-free, 'Hansa' is about as close to a no-maintenance rose as you can get! This hardy hybrid rugosa produces slender, pointed, deep reddish pink buds that unfurl into 3- to 4-inch, loosely double, informal rosettes on short, slender stems that tend to nod under the weight of the bloom. The flowers are a hard-to-describe color that's somewhere between purplish magenta and bright purplish red. The powerfully perfumed blooms appear in abundance in late spring to early summer, with moderate to good rebloom in summer and often another flush in fall. Large, plump, reddish hips ripen among the blooms towards the end of the growing season. Very thorny, arching canes carry deeply veined, semiglossy, bright green leaves that turn yellow, orange, or deep purpled-red in fall. Zones 3 to 8.

HOW TO USE

'Hansa' has an upright, vase-shaped habit, eventually forming a mounded outline. It tends to be relatively compact in cool climates, usually reaching 4 to 5 feet tall and 3 to 4 feet wide; in warmer areas, it may stretch to 10 feet or more. Try to find an established bush growing in your area so that you know what size to expect before you select a planting site. 'Hansa' is a handsome addition to a mixed border, and its informal blooms look right at home in a cottage garden setting. This rose tends to spread by suckers, making a dense hedge or screen that offers multiseason interest. 'Hansa' offers excellent disease resistance in most areas.

❦ 'Happy Child'

Syn. AUScomp
Shrub. Austin, 1994.

A lovely color, superb foliage, pleasing fragrance, and a compact growth habit: What more could you ask for? This English rose is a real charmer, with rather rounded buds that open into fully double, 3- to 4-inch, wide-cupped flowers composed of swirls of folded petals. The clustered blooms of 'Happy Child' are bright yellow, with lighter yellow around the outer edge, and their fragrance is generally described as delightful. Flowering starts in late spring to early summer, with moderate to good repeat bloom through the rest of the season. Moderately thorny, slightly arching canes carry glossy, medium green leaves. Zones 5 to 9.

HOW TO USE

'Happy Child' produces a bushy, upright shrub that usually reaches 3 to 4 feet in height and spread. It's a wonderful addition to a mixed border, particularly when paired with blue- or purple-flowered perennials, such as catmints (*Nepeta* spp.) or sages (*Salvia* spp.). Planting in groups of three or more helps create a denser drift of color. Its compact growth habit also makes it a good candidate for foundation planting. 'Happy Child' generally offers good disease resistance.

☙'Harison's Yellow'

Syns. 'Harisonii', 'Pioneer Rose'; *Rosa foetida harisonii, R. x harisonii,
R. lutea hoggii;* Yellow Rose of Texas
Hybrid foetida. Introduced around 1830.

Developed in New York, this adaptable hybrid foetida was carried west-ward by pioneers and planted around their homesteads, where it thrived with virtually no care. Despite its tough-as-nails constitution, this is actually a very delicate-looking rose, at least when in bloom. Oval, bright yellow buds that are sometimes blushed with pink open into semidouble, cupped flowers that are 2 to 2½ inches in diameter. They have a moderate to strong scent that some find appealing and others find appalling, so you might want to think twice about planting it near a path or window! 'Harison's Yellow' produces a glorious display of flowers that lasts several weeks, starting in early spring to early summer, depending on where you live. Bristly, black hips ripen in late summer to fall among the small, light to medium green leaves that are borne on long, slender, thorny canes. Zones 3 to 9.

HOW TO USE

'Harison's Yellow' has an upright to arching habit, varying in size from 4 to 6 feet tall and 3 to 5 feet wide in cooler areas to as much as 8 to 10 feet tall and 6 to 8 feet wide in warm climates. It's smart to find an established bush growing in conditions similar to yours to see what you can expect before you decide on a planting site. Use it as an early-season accent in a border or cottage garden, or enjoy it as an informal hedge. 'Harison's Yellow' may develop some black spot, but the problem is seldom serious.

☙'Heidelberg'

Syns. 'Grüss an Heidelberg'; KORbe
Hybrid kordesii. Kordes, 1959.

This trouble-free hybrid kordesii makes a bright and beautiful accent for just about any sunny site. Deep red, pointed buds open into double, 4-inch, glowing pinkish red blooms that start out with high centers and gradually develop a flattened form. The lightly fragrant flowers are produced in clusters on strong stems over a long season: the generous late spring or early summer show is followed by sporadic to good repeat into fall. Sturdy canes carry glossy, dark green leaves. Zones 5 to 9.

HOW TO USE

'Heidelberg' has a bushy, upright habit. It's most often trained as a 6- to 8-foot-tall climber on a wall or pillar, but with a little pruning, it can also form a shrub that's about 6 feet tall and 5 feet across. Combine it with other roses and shrubs to create a handsome screen planting. 'Heidelberg' is seldom bothered by diseases.

❦ 'Helmut Schmidt'

Syns. 'Goldsmith', 'Simba'; KORbelma
Hybrid tea. Kordes, 1979.

If yellow roses are your weakness, you'll definitely want to consider growing this beautiful hybrid tea in your garden. Large, long, pointed buds unfurl to display double, high-centered blooms that are 4 to 5 inches across, with clear, bright to buttery yellow petals. Usually produced singly on strong stems, the flowers have a mild to moderate fragrance. They first appear in late spring or early summer, with additional flushes of bloom through the rest of the growing season. Lightly thorny canes carry medium green foliage. Zones 5 to 9.

HOW TO USE

'Helmut Schmidt' has a bushy, upright habit. In most areas, it grows 3 to 4 feet tall and about as wide, but it can be as short as 2 feet or stretch up to 5 feet. The long-lasting blooms make it a good choice for the cutting garden, and it's a beauty in beds and borders as well. 'Helmut Schmidt' generally offers good disease resistance.

❦ 'Henri Martin'

Syn. 'Red Moss'
Moss. Laffay, 1862.

The short, slender, bristlelike growths on the stems and buds of 'Henri Martin' show why it is classified as a moss rose. Plump, deep red buds open into double, nearly flat, 3-inch flowers in glowing, deep pinkish red accented with a cluster of golden stamens. The richly fragrant blooms are loosely arranged in large clusters that appear in one glorious show lasting several weeks, starting in spring or early summer. Red hips ripen in late summer or fall among the abundant, deep green leaves that cover the thorny, arching canes. Zones 4 to 9.

HOW TO USE

'Henri Martin' produces a vigorous, spreading shrub that generally grows 5 to 6 feet tall and 4 to 5 feet wide. It looks best with some kind of support, so consider giving it a trellis to grow on or planting it in clumps of three or more so that the bushes can hold each other up and create a drift of early-season color. Enjoy the grouping as a landscape accent or as an informal hedge. 'Henri Martin' generally has good disease resistance.

☙ 'Henry Hudson'

Hybrid rugosa. Svejda, 1976.

It's hard to believe that such a charming rose could be so easy to grow! This hybrid rugosa is part of the Canadian Explorer Series — a group of roses selected for their hardiness and disease resistance — and it's truly a first-class garden rose. Egg-shaped, rosy pink buds unfurl into double, cupped to nearly flat flowers that are 2½ to 3 inches across, with a cluster of yellow stamens in the center. The wonderfully fragrant blooms are soft pink when new, usually aging to white (they may keep a pink tinge in cool weather). Bushes burst into bloom in late spring or early summer, with moderate to good rebloom through the rest of the growing season. Low-growing canes are practically obscured by a generous covering of glossy, rich green leaves. Zones 2 to 8.

HOW TO USE

'Henry Hudson' has a compact, bushy habit, forming a spreading shrub that's 2 to 3 feet tall and 3 to 4 feet across. This sturdy little selection looks magnificent in a bed or border, in a mass as a landscape accent, or as a low hedge. Enjoy it as an edging along a path or walkway or around a deck or patio. It's perfectly in scale for foundation plantings, too. Perhaps its only drawback is its tendency to hold on to its old petals; removing these petals will help keep the bush looking its best. 'Henry Hudson' has outstanding disease resistance.

☙ 'Heritage'

Syn. AUSblush
Shrub. Austin, 1985.

One of the most beloved of the English roses, this lovely shrub is prized for its splendid, old-fashioned blooms and its delightful fragrance.

Plump, light pink or peach buds that are sometimes tinged with red open into double, 3- to 5-inch-wide blooms that are mostly cupped, but with a ring or two of reflexed outer petals. The clustered flowers bloom in shades of light pink, usually with rose-pink in the center and softening to pale pink on the outermost petals. They are quite fragrant, often with a bit of lemon in the scent. 'Heritage' starts the season with a prolific flush of flowers in late spring to early summer, followed by moderate to good rebloom through the rest of the growing season. Arching, slightly thorny canes carry glossy, deep green leaves. Zones 5 to 9.

HOW TO USE
'Heritage' produces a bushy, upright shrub that's usually 4 to 5 feet tall and 3 to 4 feet wide in cool climates and 5 to 7 feet tall and 4 to 5 feet wide in warmer areas. It's a splendid addition to the back of a mixed border, and it looks right at home in a cottage garden setting. In warm climates, the bushes tend to send up long canes in mid- to late summer; if this is common in your area, consider training 'Heritage' on a post or pillar to show it off to advantage. The only drawback to this delightful rose is its only moderate disease resistance: black spot, mildew, and rust have all been reported, so take preventive measures if any of these problems are common in your area.

❦'Hermosa'

Syns. 'Armosa', 'Melanie Lemaire', 'Mme. Neumann'
Hybrid China. Marcheseau, before 1837.

'Hermosa' is officially classified as a hybrid China, but it also shares a number of traits with Bourbon roses. This lovely little rose doesn't care how you group it, as long as you appreciate its beautiful blooms and long-flowering habit. Pointed, egg-shaped, deep pink or reddish pink buds expand into light purplish pink, double blooms that are 2 to 3 inches across. They are deeply cupped to almost rounded when newly open; as they age, some of the outer petals roll back, and the cup widens a bit. Some gardeners can't detect any fragrance, while others rave about the moderate to strong, sweet scent. Flowering generally begins in late spring to early summer (closer to early spring in the Deep South) and continues through the rest of the growing season. The show is often best early and late in the season, but it's a rare day that doesn't bring at least one bloom. Upright, slightly thorny canes bear semiglossy, medium green to grayish green leaves. Zones 6 to 10.

HOW TO USE

'Hermosa' has a shrubby, compact habit, growing 2 to 4 feet tall and wide. It looks good enough to stand alone as a landscape accent but really shines when planted in multiples of three of more as a mass or hedge. Try a grouping in a mixed border to add months of delicate color, or enjoy it as a container plant. 'Hermosa' generally has good disease resistance, but it may develop some black spot if you don't take preventive measures.

❦ 'Hippolyte'

Hybrid gallica. Introduced before 1842.

This hybrid gallica blooms only once a season, but what a show! Rounded, pink buds open into double, ball-shaped, 3-inch blooms that become broadly cupped to nearly flat with a tight "button" at the center. At first the loosely held petals are a deep reddish purple with white bases; they age to a medium purplish pink. The clustered flowers usually have a moderate to strong fragrance, and they appear over a period of a few weeks in late spring or early summer. Dark green leaves are carried on long, slender, almost thornless canes. Zones 4 to 9.

HOW TO USE

'Hippolyte' forms a somewhat open, outward-arching shrub that's about 4 to 6 feet tall and wide. It generally looks best with some kind of support, so consider training it around a pillar or post or planting it against a fence. Or set it at close spacings to form an informal hedge that offers a stunning early-season show. 'Hippolyte' normally doesn't develop major disease problems, but you'll occasionally see some mildew.

❦ 'Honorine de Brabant'

Bourbon. Date unknown.

The exquisitely striped and spotted blooms of this Bourbon rose demand close inspection to reveal their true beauty. Plump buds open into double, 2- to 3-inch-wide blooms held in small clusters. The flowers are loosely filled with folded, pale pink petals that are streaked and flecked with a deep reddish pink that ages to lilac-purple. A cluster of yellow stamens is visible in the center of fully open blooms. Graced with a moderate to powerful perfume, the distinctive flowers appear in abundance in late spring to early summer, usually followed by sporadic summer bloom and often another flush in fall. Rounded, orange-red hips also appear in late summer to fall. Slender, slightly thorny canes carry light to medium green leaves. Zones 6 to 9.

HOW TO USE
'Honorine de Brabant' forms a loose, somewhat sprawling shrub that usually reaches 6 to 8 feet in height and 5 to 7 feet in width. Its intriguing blooms make a striking accent at the back of a mixed border. This rose also makes a handsome short climber: try it on a pillar or trained against a fence. However you use it, make sure you can get up close to admire the individual flowers: each one is different. Mildew can be a slight problem in some areas; otherwise, 'Honorine de Brabant' generally has good disease resistance.

❦ 'Hoot Owl'

Syn. MORhoot
Miniature. Moore, 1990.

There's nothing small about the garden effect of this dazzling miniature rose! 'Hoot Owl' produces pointed buds that unfurl into single, flattened, 1½-inch flowers that are bright red, accented with a white eye and a cluster of golden stamens. They have little or no fragrance. Held singly or in small clusters, the long-lasting blooms practically smother the semiglossy, deep green leaves from mid- or late spring to frost. Zones 6 to 10.

HOW TO USE
'Hoot Owl' forms a bushy, rather rounded plant that's 1 to 2 feet tall and about as wide. It's a little tricky to blend the bright blooms with other colors, so consider using this miniature alone in groups of three or more to create an eye-catching accent planting around a deck or patio or along a path. If you do want to use it in a bed or border, possible partners might include white-flowered companions, such as sweet alyssum (*Lobularia maritima*), or perhaps silver or gray foliage, such as that of dusty miller (*Senecio cineraria*) — just make sure you don't let the companions crowd the rose. 'Hoot Owl' also looks super in containers. It generally has excellent disease resistance.

❦ 'Hot Tamale'

Syns. 'Sunbird'; JACpoy
Miniature. Zary, 1993.

Is it yellow, or orange, or pink? Actually, it's all three! This spectacular miniature rose goes through some amazing changes as it matures. Small, pointed buds open into high-centered, 1- to 2-inch, double flowers that start out mostly yellow, then develop shadings of orange, rose-red, and pink as they mature. Held singly or in clusters, the vibrant blooms have little or no scent, but they're produced generously from late spring or early summer through the rest of the growing season. Slightly thorny stems carry semiglossy, deep green leaves. Zones 6 to 10.

HOW TO USE

'Hot Tamale' has a bushy, compact habit, generally growing 18 to 30 inches tall and about as wide. It's an eye-catching addition to a bed or border, where its ever-changing blooms blend readily with a variety of other bright colors. Tuck one into your cutting garden too; the blooms are great for small arrangements. 'Hot Tamale' is seldom bothered by diseases.

ARS Award of Excellence for Miniature Roses 1994

❦ 'Iceberg'

Syns. 'Fée des Neiges', 'Schneewittchen'; KORbin
Floribunda. Kordes, 1958.

'Iceberg' has been around for over 40 years, and it's still one of the most popular floribundas ever introduced. The long, pointed, white buds unfurl into double, 3-inch-wide blooms that are high centered when new and loosely cupped when mature. The clustered flowers are clear white in most conditions, though both they and the buds may be tinged with pink in cool weather, and they are accented with yellow stamens. Fragrance ranges from light to moderate. This free-blooming floribunda starts flowering early (midspring to early summer) and continues freely until heavy frost. Slightly thorny stems bear shiny, light to medium green leaves. Zones 4 to 9.

HOW TO USE

'Iceberg' forms a bushy, upright, rather rounded shrub. In most areas, expect 3 to 5 feet in height and width; where it's really happy, though, it can reach as much as 6 to 8 feet tall and wide. 'Iceberg' is pretty enough to stand alone as a landscape accent or hedge, but it also blends beautifully into mixed borders. It's practically a must-have for an all-white garden! The long-lasting flowers are also good for cutting. 'Iceberg' is generally disease resistant, but it may develop a touch of black spot or mildew in some conditions.

'Climbing Iceberg' (Cant, 1968) is similar but grows 10 to 15 feet tall. It looks splendid trained up a pillar or post or against a fence or shed.

World Rose Hall of Fame 1983

❦ 'Ingrid Bergman'

Syn. POUlman
Hybrid tea. Poulsen, 1984.

Considered by some to be one of the finest red hybrid tea roses available, 'Ingrid Bergman' has just about everything you could ask for, except perhaps excellent fragrance. Long, tapered buds spiral open to reveal double, high-centered, deep red blooms that are 4 to 6 inches in diameter, held singly on long stems. The fragrance is usually mild, although some gardeners claim they detect a moderate or even strong scent. All agree that bloom production is plentiful, with good repeat bloom from late spring or early summer through the rest of the growing season. Well-branched, moderately thorny canes carry semiglossy to glossy, deep green leaves. Zones 5 to 9.

HOW TO USE

'Ingrid Bergman' forms an upright bush that's usually 2 to 4 feet tall and about as wide. Tuck it into beds, borders, and foundation plantings—anywhere you'd enjoy the rich red color. It looks especially lovely with silvery foliage or white flowers. The long-lasting blooms are also delightful for cutting. 'Ingrid Bergman' generally offers exceptional disease resistance.

World Rose Hall of Fame 2000

❦ 'Intrigue'

Syn. JACum
Floribunda. Warriner, 1982.

'Intrigue' may not be the easiest rose to grow well, but many gardeners are willing to overlook this floribunda's weaknesses for its appealing color and fabulous fragrance. Deep reddish purple, tapered buds unfurl into double blooms up to 3½ inches across, with a somewhat loose but high-centered form. At its best, 'Intrigue' is a velvety, rich reddish purple; in some conditions, it has more of a magenta hue. The purple seems to be most noticeable in cool conditions. The delightfully fragrant flowers are produced singly or in clusters starting in late spring or early summer, with sporadic to good repeat through summer and into fall. Moderately thorny canes carry semiglossy, medium to deep green leaves. Zones 5 to 9.

HOW TO USE

'Intrigue' has a bushy, rather rounded habit, usually reaching 3 to 4 feet in height and about 3 feet wide. Where it grows well, 'Intrigue' offers captivating color and superb scent to beds and borders. Even where it is less vigorous, it can still be a good choice for the cutting garden. Some gardeners find 'Intrigue' to be very susceptible to black spot, although others report good overall disease resistance.

All-America Rose Selection 1984

❦ 'Irresistible'

Syn. TINresist
Miniature. Bennett, 1989.

This magnificent little miniature rose is certainly well named: its beautiful blooms really are irresistible! Small, egg-shaped buds open into double, high-centered flowers that look just like hybrid tea blooms, but they're perfectly scaled down to just 1½ inches across when fully open. The blooms are white with a pale pink blush in the center; a faint green or pink tinge may also appear on the outer petals. Borne singly or in clusters, the moderately fragrant flowers appear freely from late spring to early summer, with good repeat through the rest of the growing season. Thorny stems carry semiglossy, medium green leaves. Zones 5 to 10.

HOW TO USE

'Irresistible' forms an upright, fairly large bush (for a miniature), generally reaching 2 to 3 feet in height and 20 to 24 inches in width. The long-lasting, long-stemmed blooms are ideal for arrangements, so it's a super choice for cutting, but don't stop there: 'Irresistible' also looks lovely in the garden. Try planting a group of three or more in a flower bed or border as a long-blooming accent, perhaps underplanted with pink and white sweet alyssum *(Lobularia maritima)* to echo its delicate colors. (Just leave plenty of room around the rose for good air circulation.) It also makes a pretty addition to a foundation planting where a full-size hybrid tea might be too large. 'Irresistible' appears to have excellent disease resistance as well.

❦ 'Ispahan'

Syns. 'Isfahan', 'Pompon des Princes'
Damask. Introduced before 1832.

If you're interested in growing antique roses, this damask is a great place to start. Plump, reddish pink buds open into double, 2- to 3-inch flowers that are bright pink and high centered when new, aging to lighter pink with a slightly cupped to nearly flat form filled with swirled petals. Held in clusters, the richly perfumed blooms appear over a period of six to eight weeks, starting in late spring or early summer. ('Ispahan' is considered a once-blooming rose, but its flowering period is still quite generous!) Slender, arching, thorny stems carry semiglossy, medium green leaves. Zones 5 to 9.

HOW TO USE

'Ispahan' forms a fairly dense, bushy shrub, generally reaching 4 to 6 feet tall and 3 to 5 feet wide. Plant a group of three or more to add summer color and fragrance to the back of a mixed border. The chartreuse blooms and gray-green leaves of lady's mantle *(Alchemilla mollis)* make an especially pretty partner to the pink flowers, both in the garden and in arrangements. 'Ispahan' also adapts to training on a pillar, where it can reach 6 to 8 feet in height. It may develop a touch of mildew in some areas but overall is seldom bothered by diseases.

'Ivory Fashion'

Floribunda. Boerner, 1958.

'Ivory Fashion' has remained in fashion for a good many years, thanks to its elegant, delicately shaded flowers. This floribunda produces clusters of ivory white to light yellow, egg-shaped buds that unfurl into semidouble to double flowers that are 3½ to 4½ inches across. The newly opened flowers are creamy white with high centers that are shaded with light yellow; older blooms are nearly flat, revealing a cluster of showy orange-red stamens. Opinions on its fragrance vary widely: some say there's no scent, whereas others describe it as moderate to strong and either spicy or sweet. Flowering starts with a generous show in late spring to early summer, followed by good repeat through the rest of the growing season. Medium to deep green, semiglossy leaves are carried on slightly thorny stems. Zones 5 to 9.

HOW TO USE

'Ivory Fashion' has a bushy, upright habit, usually reaching 2 to 4 feet in height and width. Plant a group of three or more to create a drift of color in a bed or border, or enjoy this rose as a low hedge. It also grows well in a container, and it makes a wonderful cut flower, too. 'Ivory Fashion' generally has good disease resistance.

All-America Rose Selection 1959

'Jean Kenneally'

Syn. TINeally
Miniature. Bennett, 1984.

The exquisitely formed flowers of this outstanding miniature rose are prized by exhibitors and gardeners alike. Pointed buds open into double, high-centered, 1½-inch blooms in varying shades of pale to medium peach, often with a slight tinge of pink in cool weather. The lightly to moderately fragrant, long-lasting flowers are sometimes held singly but are most often produced in clusters, from late spring or early summer through the rest of the growing season. Well-branched canes carry semiglossy, medium green leaves. Zones 5 to 10.

HOW TO USE

'Jean Kenneally' is a very upright, bushy mini, generally growing 2 to 3 feet in height and 12 to 18 inches across. Its delicately colored blooms blend beautifully with soft yellow-, blue-, and purple-flowered companions, as well as silvery foliage. A group of three or more bushes will create a handsome effect tucked into a bed, border, or foundation planting, or used as an edging for a deck, patio, or walkway. This rose is also a must-have for a cutting garden. 'Jean Kenneally' has good disease resistance.

ARS Award of Excellence for Miniature Roses 1986

✿'Jeanne Lajoie'

Climbing miniature. Sima, 1975.

The flowers may be small, but there's nothing else diminutive about this vigorous, free-blooming climbing miniature rose! Long, pointed, deep pink buds open into double, high-centered, slightly scented blooms that are a pretty medium pink on top, with a slightly darker pink on the undersides of the petals. Held singly or in clusters, the individual flowers are just 1 to 2 inches across, but they're produced in abundance in late spring or early summer, with moderate to good repeat bloom through the rest of the summer and into fall. Vigorous, branching stems carry deep green, glossy leaves. Zones 5 to 10.

HOW TO USE

'Jeanne Lajoie' makes an unusually charming climber, reaching 6 to 8 feet in most areas. It looks particularly good with its canes trained horizontally along a fence, wall, or trellis, since that encourages even more flowers. Left unsupported, this rose can also make an attractive, arching shrub that's 4 to 6 feet tall and about as wide. 'Jeanne Lajoie' is seldom bothered by diseases.

ARS Award of Excellence for Miniature Roses 1977

✿'Jens Munk'

Hybrid rugosa. Svejda, 1974.

Northern gardeners, here's a great rose for you: it's amazingly hardy and adaptable, and it's quite beautiful as well — just what you'd expect from a hybrid rugosa rose that's part of the Canadian Explorer Series. Tapered, bright pink buds unfurl into semidouble, saucer-shaped blooms that are 3 inches across. The flowers are bright pink, aging to medium pink, with occasional white streaks in the petals and a cluster of showy yellow stamens in the center. Some gardeners rave about the spicy-sweet fragrance, though others say they don't detect any scent. Flowers first appear in late spring to early summer, with good repeat through the rest of the growing season. A few red hips may appear in fall. Arching stems carry glossy, bright green leaves that have attractive fall color. Zones 2 to 8.

HOW TO USE

'Jens Munk' forms a bushy shrub with a rather rounded outline, usually reaching 4 to 6 feet in height and spread. It tends to be a bit sprawling when young, but it develops into a fairly dense bush that looks lovely at the back or a mixed border or used as an informal, long-flowering hedge. 'Jens Munk' offers excellent disease resistance.

❦ 'John Cabot'

Hybrid kordesii. Svejda, 1978.

Cool-climate gardeners don't have many colorful, hardy climbers to choose from, so this sturdy, adaptable hybrid kordesii from the Canadian Explorer Series is definitely worth a look. Clustered, egg-shaped buds open into broadly cupped, double blooms that are 2 to 3 inches across, in a deep shade of reddish pink or purplish pink highlighted with showy yellow stamens. Reports on the scent range from mild to strong. 'John Cabot' blooms abundantly from late spring or early summer into midsummer, with some rebloom later in the season. Thorny, arching canes carry a generous covering of light to medium green leaves. Zones 3 to 9.

HOW TO USE

'John Cabot' is a vigorous, versatile rose. As a shrub, it generally reaches 4 to 6 feet in height and spread (closer to 8 feet in warm climates). Try it as an informal hedge, or enjoy it in a casual cottage-garden setting. It also adapts well to use as a climber, reaching 6 to 10 feet when supported by a pillar, post, trellis, arbor, or fence. This sturdy, easy-care rose offers excellent disease resistance.

❧ 'John Davis'

Hybrid kordesii. Svejda, 1986.

Another amazingly hardy member of the Canadian Explorer Series, this handsome hybrid kordesii adapts to life as either a shrub or a climber. Deep reddish pink, pointed buds open into double, 3- to 4-inch blooms that have high centers and reflexed outer petals. The clustered flowers are medium pink, shading to light yellow or cream at the base. Some gardeners say they can't detect any scent; others describe it as moderate to strong and spicy or spicy-sweet. Expect a splendid show of bloom for several weeks starting in late spring to early summer, followed by moderate to good rebloom through the rest of the season. Long, arching, thorny canes carry medium to deep green, glossy leaves. Zones 3 to 9.

HOW TO USE
'John Davis' grows as either a large spreading shrub (about 4 to 7 feet tall and 6 to 8 feet across) or an 8- to 10-foot climber. Enjoy it unsupported as a landscape accent or an informal hedge, or train it on a pillar, trellis, fence, or arbor. 'John Davis' generally has good disease resistance, but you may want to take preventive measures against black spot and powdery mildew in areas where these diseases are common problems.

❧ 'Joseph's Coat'

Large-flowered climber. Armstrong & Swim, 1969.

There's certainly nothing subtle about the ever-changing blooms of this eye-catching climber. Pointed, reddish buds open into double, loosely ruffled, 3- to 4-inch flowers that open nearly flat, with yellow to orange petals that are quickly blushed with cherry red where touched by the sun. Held in clusters that often nod, the slightly scented blooms appear in a spectacular first flush in late spring, generally followed by sporadic repeat through the rest of the growing season. Very thorny canes bear glossy, medium to deep green leaves. Zones 5 to 9.

HOW TO USE
'Joseph's Coat' has a vigorous, upright growth habit. It's often used as an 8- to 10-foot climber to adorn a fence or trellis, but it also works well trained to a pillar or post or left unsupported to form a large, arching shrub about 7 feet tall and wide. Be aware that 'Joseph's Coat' can be quite

susceptible to both black spot and mildew. Some gardeners report that unsprayed plants may recover on their own from these problems, but in the meantime, you may be left with an expanse of leafless canes.

☙ 'Just Joey'

Hybrid tea. Cants of Colchester, 1972.

Take one look at the superbly shaded blooms of this hybrid tea and you'll see right away why it's one of the world's favorite roses! 'Just Joey' produces elegant, pointed, orange buds that unfurl into large, double, high-centered but loose blooms that are 4 to 6 inches across. The wavy-edged petals are a rich peachy orange or cantaloupe color when new, softening to light peach or peachy pink at the outer edges as the blooms mature. Sometimes held singly but more often in clusters, the flowers have a delightful fruity fragrance. Bloom season starts in late spring to early summer, with quick repeat flushes through the rest of the summer and into fall. Thorny, branching stems bear glossy, dark green leaves. Zones 5 to 9.

HOW TO USE

'Just Joey' has a bushy, somewhat spreading to rounded habit. It generally grows 3 to 4 feet tall and about 3 feet wide, though it may stay as small as 2 feet tall and wide or stretch to 5 feet where it's really happy. 'Just Joey' is just glorious in flower beds and borders, and its long-stemmed flowers make it a great candidate for cutting. 'Just Joey' generally has good disease resistance.

World Rose Hall of Fame 1994

☙ 'Kaleidoscope'

Syn. JACbow
Shrub. Walden, 1998.

You might not think that orange, pink, and purple sounds like an attractive color combination, but once you've seen this unique shrub rose in person, you're liable to find it quite appealing. Pointed, orange-pink buds open into very double, high-centered to ruffled flowers that are 2 to 3 inches across. The coppery yellow petals quickly develop a purplish pink edge that gradually extends over the entire petal. The clustered flowers have little fragrance, but they're produced in abundance over a long season, from late spring or early summer into fall. Thorny canes carry glossy, deep green leaves. Zones 5 to 10.

HOW TO USE

'Kaleidoscope' produces a rounded to spreading bush that's generally 2 to 4 feet tall and about as wide. It's a pretty addition to beds and borders, although it can be challenging to find good companions for its multicolored flowers. Consider pairing it with yellow miniature roses, such as soft yellow 'Yantai' or bright yellow 'Cal Poly', or perhaps with the green blooms of *Nicotiana* 'Lime Green'. 'Kaleidoscope' makes a marvelous hedge planting, where its intriguing flowers can be admired in mass. Disease resistance is generally good, although some black spot has been reported in some areas.

All-America Rose Selection 1999

❦ 'Kardinal'

Syns. 'Kardinal 85', 'Kordes' Rose Kardinal'; KORlingo
Hybrid tea. Kordes, 1986.

'Kardinal' started out as a favorite with cut-flower growers, but it's also a gem in the garden. Tapered, deep red buds unfurl into double, bright red blooms with the classic, high-centered hybrid tea form. Reaching 3 to 4½ inches in diameter, the lightly fragrant flowers are usually produced singly on long stems. They start in late spring to early summer, with regular flushes of repeat bloom through the rest of the growing season. Sturdy, thorny stems carry deep green, semiglossy leaves. Zones 5 to 8.

HOW TO USE

'Kardinal' forms an upright bush, usually reaching 4 to 5 feet tall and 2½ to 3 feet wide. It looks best planted in groups of three or more for a denser effect, creating a splendid red accent in beds and borders. Pair it with other hybrid teas in sunny yellows and bright oranges for a sizzling summer display, or create a more elegant look with partners in white and shades of pink. The long-lasting blooms are perfect for cutting, too. 'Kardinal' generally has good disease resistance, but you might want to take preventive measures against black spot and powdery mildew.

❦ 'Kathleen'

Hybrid musk. Pemberton, 1922.

This beautiful hybrid musk produces delicate-looking blooms, but there's nothing dainty about its size: it gets to be a large shrub or even a climber. Egg-shaped, reddish pink buds open into single, flattened flowers that are just 1 to 1½ inches across. They are light pink when new, aging to near white with just a hint of pink on the backs of the petals, and each flower is crowned with a cluster of golden stamens in the center. Some gardeners can't detect any scent, whereas others rave about the rich perfume. The individual blooms are small, but they're produced in large clusters over a long season. The show is usually best in late spring or early summer and again in fall, with scattered bloom in between. A generous crop of small, orange hips appears along with the flowers in fall. Gently arching canes carry dark green leaves. Zones 6 to 9.

HOW TO USE

'Kathleen' has a vigorous, somewhat sprawling habit. Left unpruned, it can form a large shrub anywhere from 4 to 8 feet tall and about 6 to 8 feet across. It also adapts well to training as a climber on an arbor or shed, reaching 8 to 15 feet in height. 'Kathleen' seldom has any disease problems, and it tolerates some shade.

❦ 'Keepsake'

Syns. 'Esmeralda', 'Kordes' Rose Esmeralda'; KORmalda
Hybrid tea. Kordes, 1981.

Light pink, medium pink, and deep pink: this pretty hybrid tea has them all! Tapered buds unfurl into double, high-centered blooms that are 3 to 4 inches across. The newly opened flowers are deep pink, gradually softening to light pink; the color change begins in the petal centers and spreads outward to the petal tips, creating a somewhat bicolored effect. Blooms at all color stages can be on the bush simultaneously, creating an intriguing display. Reports on the scent of 'Keepsake' range from light to strong, with most gardeners agreeing it has a moderate, sweet fragrance. Held singly or in small clusters on long stems, the blooms first appear in late spring to early summer, with good repeat bloom through the rest of the growing season. Thorny canes carry medium to dark green, glossy leaves. Zones 5 to 10.

HOW TO USE

'Keepsake' has an upright to somewhat spreading, bushy habit. It can vary quite a bit in size, growing just 2½ to 3 feet high and 2 feet wide in some areas, while stretching to 4 to 6 feet tall and about 3 to 4 feet wide in other areas. Try it in groups of three or more to create a pretty-in-pink drift of color in a bed or border. The flowers are also excellent for cutting. 'Keepsake' generally has good disease resistance, though it may develop a touch of black spot if you don't take preventive measures.

❦ 'Knock Out'

Syn. RADrazz
Shrub. Radler, 1999.

If you're searching for a trouble-free rose with knock-your-socks-off color, 'Knock Out' may be just the thing for you! This super shrub rose offers generous clusters of pointed buds that open into semidouble, broadly cupped to nearly flat flowers, each 2½ to 3½ inches across. The brilliant blooms are an electric shade of cherry red, accented with a tiny touch of white at the base of the petals and centered with a cluster of showy gold stamens. The fragrance is on the mild side, but you can hardly complain about that when you consider the abundance of flowers produced freely from mid- or late spring up to frost. Rarely a day goes by without at least one bloom! Branching, thorny canes carry dark green leaves that turn reddish purple in fall. Later in the season, you'll enjoy the show of orange-red hips that last well into winter, adding yet another season of interest. Zones 4 to 9.

HOW TO USE

'Knock Out' has a compact, bushy, mounded habit, generally reaching 3 feet tall and about as wide. Enjoy it alone or in masses as a multiseason landscape accent; tuck it into foundation plantings; or try it as a long-flowering low hedge. It's also stunning in a beds and borders, particularly when paired with white flowers or silvery or gray foliage. 'Knock Out' looks great in containers, too. Best of all, this rose offers outstanding disease resistance.

All-America Rose Selection 2000

'Königin von Dänemark'

Syns. 'Belle Courtisane', 'Queen of Denmark', 'Reine du Dänemark'
Alba. Booth, 1826.

This lovely old alba is prized for its beautiful blooms and exquisite fragrance. 'Königin von Dänemark' produces red-tinged, light pink buds that open into fully double, 2½- to 3½-inch flowers filled with folded, clear pink petals that age to pale pink or nearly white. Fully opened flowers have a rather flattened form, with outer petals that fold back and center petals that curl in tightly to form a "button" eye. The sweetly scented blooms appear in one glorious show in late spring or early summer, followed by large red hips in late summer to fall. Blue-green leaves are carried on thorny, arching stems. Zones 4 to 8.

HOW TO USE

'Königin von Dänemark' has an upright, slender habit that can become somewhat open when the heavy blooms weigh down the stems. It generally grows 4 to 6 feet tall and 4 to 5 feet wide. This rose is pretty enough to stand alone as a landscape accent, but it's also lovely in multiples for a mass planting or hedge. It's also pretty at the back of a mixed border or even trained against a wall or fence. The flowers add color and fragrance to arrangements as well. 'Königin von Dänemark' has excellent disease resistance.

'Kristin'

Syn. BENmagic
Miniature. Benardella, 1992.

When you see the eye-catching blooms of this charming miniature, you'll know why it's won its share of prizes at rose shows, as well as an Award of Excellence from the American Rose Society. Elegant, pointed buds unfurl into high-centered, double flowers that are 1 to 2 inches across, with white petals that are deeply edged with bright cherry red. In cooler areas, the flowers open just halfway, then hold that classic form for several days. Held singly or in small clusters, the blooms have little or no scent, but they're produced freely from late spring or early summer through the rest of the growing season. Upright stems bear glossy, deep green foliage. Zones 5 to 10.

HOW TO USE

'Kristin' has a bushy habit, growing 18 to 30 inches tall and 15 to 24 inches wide. It makes a handsome small shrub for just about any part of a landscape, from a bed or border to a foundation planting, a low edging, a mass planting, or a container. Add a bush to your cutting garden, too: the long-lasting blooms are ideal for arrangements. 'Kristin' seems happiest in warm, dry areas; elsewhere, the color contrast may be less intense, and mildew may be a problem if you don't take preventive measures.

ARS Award of Excellence for Miniature Roses 1993

'La Belle Sultane'

Syns. 'Gallica Maheca', 'Violacea'
Hybrid gallica. Introduced around 1795.

'La Belle Sultane' may not be a long-blooming rose, but this gorgeous hybrid gallica is popular with many old-rose appreciators for its dramatic color. Oval to egg-shaped buds open into semidouble, rather flat flowers that are 3½ to 5 inches across. New blooms are a rich, deep maroon or reddish violet, accented with a small white eye and a cluster of showy yellow stamens; as they age, they fade to pale purple or violet. Fragrance ranges from light to strong. This pretty rose produces one abundant show of blooms starting in late spring or early summer and usually lasting 6 to 8 weeks. Some red hips may appear in late summer. Flexible, arching stems carry grayish green leaves that turn reddish or orange in fall. Zones 4 to 8.

HOW TO USE

'La Belle Sultane' generally grows 4 to 6 feet tall and 4 to 5 feet wide, with an upright, somewhat open habit. It's especially handsome used as a hedge or screen, if you have the space. It is also pretty at the back of a mixed border, but it does tend to spread by suckers, so it can develop quite a thicket over time. 'La Belle Sultane' tends to drop its leaves during hot spells in summer but will recover quickly when cooler temperatures return. Diseases are seldom a problem.

❧ 'Lace Cascade'

Syn. JACarch
Large-flowered climber. Warriner, 1992.

There aren't many white-flowered climbing roses to choose from, so this large-flowered climber is a valuable addition to the list. Egg-shaped, cream-colored buds open into double, 3- to 4-inch blooms with crisp white petals that open wide to display a crown of golden stamens. The clustered flowers have little scent. They're produced in profusion from late spring or early summer through the rest of the growing season. Long, arching, thorny canes carry medium to dark green, semiglossy leaves. Zones 5 to 9.

HOW TO USE

'Lace Cascade' is a vigorous rose, growing as either a large spreading shrub (about 5 to 7 feet tall and wide) or a 10- to 12-foot climber. It looks particularly lovely trained against a support, such as a wall, fence, arch, or pillar. 'Lace Cascade' is generally disease resistant.

❧ 'La Marne'

Polyantha. Barbier, 1915.

Looking for a free-flowering, easy-care rose that is ideal for a warm-climate garden? 'La Marne' may be just the rose for you! This dependable polyantha produces plump, reddish buds that open into single or semi-double, cupped blooms that are 2 inches across. The petals are rose- or salmon-pink at the edges, paling to near white at the center, and they age to pale pink or almost white. The colors tend to be most intense in cool weather and faded in hot weather. The flowers usually don't have much fragrance, but they're held in large, showy clusters starting in late spring to early summer and continuing freely until hard frost in fall. Nearly thornless, upright stems carry shiny, dark green leaves. Zones 6 to 9.

HOW TO USE

'La Marne' forms an upright, bushy shrub that ranges widely in size, growing 3 to 4 feet tall and 2 to 3 feet wide in the cooler parts of its range and 4 to 6 feet tall and 3 to 5 feet wide in warmer areas. This adaptable rose looks great alone or in masses as a landscape accent, or used as a hedge. It also adds months of color to a mixed border. 'La Marne' may develop a bit of mildew, but it's normally not seriously affected by disease.

❦ 'Lamarque'

Noisette. Maréchal, 1830.

Warm-climate gardeners take note: Here's a winner for you! This excellent Noisette produces an abundance of long, tapered, white buds that unfurl into double, loosely ruffled flowers that are 3 to 4 inches across. New blooms are white with a lemon yellow center; after a day or two, the center fades to cream or white to match the rest of the flower. Reports on the type and amount of fragrance vary, but most gardeners detect at least a moderate scent. This remarkable rose has an amazingly long bloom season, with a splendid show in spring and fall and moderate rebloom in the heat of summer. It may even flower well into winter, until nipped by heavy frost. Long, slightly thorny canes carry light to medium green leaves. Zones 7 to 10.

HOW TO USE

'Lamarque' is a vigorous, fast-growing climber, reaching anywhere from 10 to 30 feet in height. It's smart to find someone else in your area who is growing this rose to learn what size to expect before choosing a planting site. The plant may take a year or two to settle in, but after that, it will quickly cover a large arch or arbor. The young canes are fairly flexible and easy to train; older stems get quite stiff. 'Lamarque' generally has good disease resistance, although you may want to take preventive measures against black spot.

❦ 'La Reine Victoria'

Syn. 'Reine Victoria'
Bourbon. Schwartz, 1872.

If fragrance is high on your wish list when choosing roses, 'La Reine Victoria' is definitely one to consider. This regal Bourbon beauty produces rounded, reddish pink buds that open into globe-shaped to deeply cupped, double, rose-pink blooms that are 3 to 3½ inches across. The richly fragrant flowers appear abundantly in late spring or early summer, with light to moderate rebloom during the heat of summer and usually another good show in fall. Long, arching canes bear matte, light to medium green leaves. Zones 5 to 9.

HOW TO USE

'La Reine Victoria' forms an upright shrub with a vase-shaped habit, generally growing 4 to 6 feet tall and 3 to 4 feet wide. It looks best planted with some kind of support, since the heavy blooms can weigh down the stems; try it on a wall, fence, or trellis. Removing the spent flowers will help keep the bush neat and encourage rebloom. 'La Reine Victoria' is susceptible to black spot and may also get mildew, but it doesn't seem to be seriously weakened by either problem; still, it's wise to consider taking preventive measures.

❦ 'La Sévillana'

Syn. MEIgekanu
Floribunda. Meilland, 1978.

There's no missing this bright-blooming floribunda when it's in its full glory! Pointed buds unfurl into semidouble, cupped blooms that are 2 to 3 inches across, in a brilliant shade of clear red. The clustered flowers have little or no scent, but they're produced freely in late spring to early summer with excellent repeat through the rest of the growing season. An abundant crop of scarlet hips appears in fall and hangs on into winter, extending the season of interest. Bushy, upright stems carry glossy, dark green leaves that are often tinged with red. Zones 6 to 9.

HOW TO USE

'La Sévillana' has a dense, somewhat spreading habit, growing 3 to 4 feet tall and 3 to 5 feet wide. It's excellent for adding multiseason interest to a landscape as a compact hedge or in a mass or foundation planting. Or use it to jazz up a mixed border paired with other hot-colored partners, such as orange cosmos (*Cosmos sulphureus*), 'Lemon Gem' marigolds (*Tagetes* 'Lemon Gem'), and crocosmias (*Crocosmia* spp.). 'La Sévillana' generally has good disease resistance.

❦ 'Lavaglut'

Syns. 'Intrigue', 'Lavaglow'; KORlech
Floribunda. Kordes, 1978.

The name may not be particularly appealing, but this floribunda is definitely a beauty in the garden. Deep red buds open into broadly cupped, double blooms that are 2½ inches across, in a rich shade of dark red accented with golden stamens that are visible when the flowers are fully open. The clustered blooms don't have much scent, if any, but they're produced generously from late spring or early summer well into fall. Upright, thorny stems carry glossy, deep green leaves that make a gorgeous backdrop for the glowing red blooms. Zones 4 to 9.

HOW TO USE

'Lavaglut' forms a bushy shrub that's usually 3 to 4 feet tall and 2 to 3 feet across. Enjoy it as a dramatic, long-blooming accent in a bed or border. It pairs perfectly with pink or white flowers and makes a dramatic combination with silvery foliage, such as that of artemisias or lamb's ears *(Stachys byzantina)*. It also makes a handsome hedge. 'Lavaglut' can develop black spot if you don't take preventive measures, but overall it has good disease resistance.

'Lavender Dream'

Syn. INTerlav
Shrub. Interplant, 1984.

"Lavender" may be a bit of an overstatement, but this long-blooming shrub rose is a lovely addition to any garden. Deep reddish pink, egg-shaped buds open into semidouble, nearly flat flowers that are 2 to 3 inches across. Bright medium pink petals touched with the slightest hint of blue surround a showy cluster of golden yellow stamens. The flowers have little or no fragrance, but they're held in large clusters that appear abundantly in late spring or early summer, with excellent repeat bloom through the rest of the growing season. Arching canes with few thorns carry matte, light green leaves. Zones 4 to 9.

HOW TO USE

'Lavender Dream' has a bushy, mounded habit, generally growing 3 to 5 feet tall and about as wide. Enjoy its long flowering season in a bed or border, or use it alone or in masses as a multiseason landscape accent or hedge. 'Lavender Dream' generally has excellent disease resistance, but it may develop a touch of mildew in some seasons.

'Lavender Lassie'

Hybrid musk. Kordes, 1960.

This free-flowering hybrid musk makes a marvelous climber or a handsome large shrub. Red-blushed, pink buds open into double, 3-inch blooms filled with loose swirls of lilac-pink to rosy pink petals. The open-cupped to flattened flowers are held in large clusters, and they generally have a moderate to strong fragrance. 'Lavender Lassie' produces a splendid show in late spring or early summer and again in fall, with good rebloom in between. Medium green, semiglossy leaves are held on long, slightly thorny stems that arch under the weight of the blooms. Zones 6 to 9.

HOW TO USE

'Lavender Lassie' grows as a 10- to 15-foot climber or a somewhat open, spreading shrub that's 5 to 8 feet tall and about as wide. Train its long canes to an arbor, arch, fence, wall, or pillar, or use as a large shrub in a screen planting or hedge. This rose can tolerate a bit of shade, so it's a good choice for a site that is bright but doesn't have full sun all day. 'Lavender Lassie' generally has good disease resistance.

'La Ville de Bruxelles'

Syn. 'Ville de Bruxelles'
Damask. Vibert, 1849.

'La Ville de Bruxelles' blooms only once a season, but it's worth waiting for the richly fragrant, petal-packed flowers. This lovely damask produces rounded, reddish pink buds that open to medium to deep pink, 3- to 5-inch blooms full of swirled petals. The petals at the outer rim of the bloom fold back, while those in the very center curl in tightly to form a "button" eye. There is just one bloom season — in late spring or early summer in most areas — but the flowers create a lovely display in their nodding clusters, and they have a strong, sweet scent. Light to medium green, semiglossy leaves are borne on moderately thorny canes that arch under the weight of the flowers. Zones 5 to 9.

HOW TO USE

'La Ville de Bruxelles' has a somewhat open, spreading habit, generally reaching 3 to 5 feet in height and width. It tends to be a bit sprawling if left unsupported, so consider planting it in groups of three or more so that the bushes can support each other. Enjoy it in a collection of other antique roses, or as a single-season accent in a mixed border. Disease resistance is moderate to good; mildew can be a problem in some areas.

🌵 'L. D. Braithwaite'

Syns. 'Braithwaite', 'Leonard Dudley Braithwaite'; AUScrim
Shrub. Austin, 1993.

Richly hued blooms set this shrub apart from many of the softer-colored English roses. Rounded, deep red buds open to reveal fully double, 3- to 4-inch flowers that are broadly cupped and filled with loose swirls of dark red petals. In cool conditions, the red color lasts for several days; in hot weather, it quickly changes to a deep purplish red or purplish deep pink. Opinions on the fragrance vary from light to strong. The scent may be stronger in older flowers. Held singly or in clusters, the flowers aren't particularly abundant, but they do last fairly long; they first appear in late spring or early summer with rebloom through the rest of the summer into fall. Moderately thorny, upright stems carry medium to dark green leaves. Zones 5 to 9.

HOW TO USE

'L. D. Braithwaite' forms a bushy to somewhat spreading shrub that generally grows 3 to 5 feet tall and 4 to 6 feet wide in cooler areas and 5 to 6 feet tall and 6 to 8 feet wide in warmer zones. It looks super at the back of a mixed border, especially when planted in groups of three or more to create a drift of luxuriant color. Disease resistance is generally good, but take preventive measures against powdery mildew and black spot where these fungal diseases are common problems.

🌵 'Leander'

Syn. AUSlea
Shrub. Austin, 1983.

'Leander' offers a splendid show of fragrant, old-fashioned flowers that add an elegant touch to the summer garden. This English rose produces plump, warm pink buds that open into very double, 3-inch, broad-cupped to nearly flat flowers filled with folded, wavy petals. Color ranges from deep peachy pink to creamy pink. The clustered flowers have a moderate, fruity fragrance and appear most abundantly in late spring or early summer, with moderate rebloom through the rest of the summer. Thorny stems bear medium to dark green, glossy leaves. Zones 5 to 9.

HOW TO USE

In the cooler parts of its range, 'Leander' forms a somewhat open, spreading shrub that's usually 5 to 7 feet tall and about 6 feet wide. Its soft color blends beautifully with yellow, blue, purple, and pink flowers in a bed or border. In warm areas, the canes can get quite long, creating a 12- to 14-foot climber that looks lovely on a wall, fence, or pillar. Disease resistance is generally good, but you may want to take preventive measures against black spot.

❦ 'Léda'

Syn. 'Painted Damask'
Damask. Introduced before 1827.

If you love the informal look of antique roses but have limited space, consider adding this compact damask to your collection. Reddish, rather rounded buds open into double, ruffled-looking, 3-inch blooms that are nearly ball shaped when fully open, with a cluster of tightly incurved petals forming a "button" eye in the center. The tips of the white petals are irregularly touched with red, creating a dramatic contrast. The delightfully perfumed blooms appear in one dramatic show in late spring or early summer; occasional blooms may appear in late summer or fall as well. Dark gray-green leaves are carried on thorny stems. Zones 4 to 9.

HOW TO USE

'Léda' is a small, slightly sprawling shrub that generally stays 3 to 4 feet tall and wide. Enjoy it as a single-season accent in a bed, border, or cottage garden, or try it as a low climber trained against a trellis. It looks great in a container, too. This rose normally has good disease resistance; in some areas, a bit of powdery mildew may appear but usually isn't serious.

❦'Lilian Austin'

Syn. AUSmound
Shrub. Austin, 1981.

With its generous show of sunset-shaded blooms, this English rose
blends beautifully with a wide range of companions. Oval, deep pink
buds unfurl into semidouble to double, 4- to 5-inch-wide rosettes with
loose swirls of wavy petals. The flowers are an eye-catching coral pink to
salmon pink lightly shaded with gold or peach. Yellow stamens are visible
when the flowers are fully open. Held singly or in small clusters, the
lightly scented blooms appear in abundance in late spring or early summer, with good repeat in summer and fall. Arching, thorny canes carry
glossy, deep green leaves. Zones 5 to 9.

HOW TO USE
'Lilian Austin' has a fairly compact, mounded habit, usually growing just
3 to 4 feet tall and 4 to 5 feet wide. It's a splendid sight planted alone or in
masses as a landscape accent, and it makes a handsome, long-blooming
hedge too. It's an outstanding choice for a mixed border or foundation
planting as well. In warmer areas, the long canes even adapt to training
on a fence or trellis. Black spot can be a problem if you don't take preventive
measures; otherwise, 'Lilian Austin' generally has good disease resistance.

❦'Linda Campbell'

Syns. 'Tall Poppy'; MORten
Hybrid rugosa. Moore, 1990.

In a group of roses commonly known for their purplish, pink, or white
flowers, 'Linda Campbell' stands out with its glowing red blooms. This
hybrid rugosa produces pointed red buds that unfurl into double, 3-inch,
cupped flowers. The blooms are clear red with a slightly lighter red on the
backs of the petals and a crown of showy yellow stamens in the center.
Fragrance is minimal, but the flowers appear in generous clusters to create a dazzling display from late spring or early summer into fall. Arching,
slightly thorny stems bear semiglossy, dark green leaves. Zones 4 to 9.

HOW TO USE
'Linda Campbell' forms a bushy, upright to spreading shrub or moderate
climber. Shrub size varies from 3 to 5 feet tall and 4 to 6 feet wide in cooler

areas to 6 feet tall and 8 feet wide in warm climates. Enjoy it alone as a landscape accent, in a row as a hedge, or combined with other roses and shrubs as a screen planting. When trained on a trellis, arch, or arbor, it can grow 8 to 10 feet tall. Without preventive measures, this heat-loving rose may develop some mildew or black spot where these problems are common; otherwise, disease resistance is generally good.

❦ 'Little Artist'

Syns. 'Top Gear'; MACmanly, MACmanley
Miniature. McGredy, 1982.

Each beautifully shaded bloom of this magnificent miniature is a masterpiece in itself! Small, red buds open to display semidouble, broadly cupped to flat flowers that are just 1 inch across, accented with showy yellow stamens in the center. The petals are basically white with a red-brushed edge on the upper half; as they age, the red area increases. Each flower is marked slightly differently, creating what is often called a "hand-painted" effect. The blooms have little or no scent, but they're produced in large clusters that appear freely from late spring or early summer through the rest of the growing season. Semiglossy, medium to dark green leaves are carried on upright stems. Zones 5 to 10.

HOW TO USE
'Little Artist' forms a spreading mound that's usually 12 to 18 inches tall and about as wide. It looks magnificent in a mass planting or used as an edging for a pathway, deck, or patio. Try it in a container, too, so that it's easy to get up close to admire the unique blooms. 'Little Artist' is seldom bothered by diseases.

❦ 'Little Darling'

Floribunda. Duehrsen, 1956.

'Little Darling' is a perfect name for this lovely, delicately colored floribunda. Oval to egg-shaped, reddish pink buds unfurl into high-centered, double, 3-inch blooms that are rosy pink shaded with peach and yellow near the middle. The moderately fragrant, clustered blooms appear in a generous show in late spring or early summer, followed by good repeat bloom through the rest of the summer and into fall. Shiny, deep green leaves are held on flexible stems that may arch under the weight of the bloom clusters. Zones 5 to 10.

HOW TO USE

'Little Darling' may look dainty in bloom, but it's a vigorous rose with a shrubby, somewhat spreading habit. Height is generally 4 to 6 feet, with a similar spread. It blends beautifully with a wide variety of companions in a mixed border or flower bed. Soft blues and purples such as lavenders (*Lavandula* spp.) and catmints (*Nepeta* spp.) are particularly pretty growing around the base of this rose. 'Little Darling' also makes a handsome flowering hedge, and it's great for cutting as well. Disease resistance is generally quite good.

☙'Little White Pet' See 'White Pet'

☙'Livin' Easy'

Syns. 'Fellowship', HARwelcome
Floribunda. Harkness, 1992.

Eye-catching, season-long color on a great-looking, easy-care bush: What more could you ask for? This choice floribunda offers elegant, tapered, orange buds that unfurl to display double, cupped, 3-inch blooms with wavy petals surrounding a crown of showy golden stamens. Newly opened, moderately fragrant blooms are an amazing, glowing orange; they lighten to rich peach as they age. The show starts in late spring or early summer and continues in regular waves through the rest of the growing season. Thorny stems carry glossy, medium green leaves. Zones 5 to 9.

HOW TO USE

'Livin' Easy' has an upright, rather spreading habit, generally growing 3 to 5 feet tall and 3 to 6 feet wide. Grown alone or in masses, it creates a can't-miss landscape accent. In a bed or border, try it combined with bright yellows and purples for a vibrant show that lasts for months. 'Livin' Easy' looks super as a hedge, and it's good for cutting, too. This rose is seldom bothered by diseases.

All-America Rose Selection 1996

❦ 'Louise Odier'

Syn. 'Mme. de Stella'
Bourbon. Margottin, 1851.

This beautiful Bourbon rose combines the full, fragrant flowers of an antique rose with a flowering season that rivals those of many of the best modern roses. Rounded, deep pink buds open to double, rich rose-pink blooms that are 2½ to 3½ inches across. New blooms are cupped, then open to a rather flat and circular form that shows off the swirls of petals within. The clustered, slightly nodding flowers are graced with a delightful fragrance. An abundant show in late spring or early summer is followed by moderate to good repeat through the rest of the summer and into fall. Orange-red hips add extra interest near the end of the season. Light to medium green leaves are borne on slightly thorny, arching canes. Zones 5 to 10.

HOW TO USE

'Louise Odier' has a tall, fountainlike to somewhat sprawling habit. Height and spread range from 4 to 8 feet tall and 3 to 6 feet wide. Before you choose a planting site, try to find an established bush growing in conditions similar to yours so that you know what size to expect in your area. This rose looks beautiful at the back of a mixed border or as an informal hedge. The slender stems also adapt to training as a climber on a trellis, arch, or pillar. Disease is seldom a problem, except for a bit of black spot in some conditions.

❦ 'Louis Philippe'

China. Guérin, 1834.

This handsome China rose is an excellent choice for warm-climate gardens. Round, red buds open into globe-shaped to cupped, double, 3-inch blooms that are deep red with a lighter red center. Reports of its fragrance range from light to strong. Flowering starts in mid- to late spring and continues freely until heavy frost. Slender, thorny canes carry small, glossy, medium green leaves. Zones 7 to 10.

HOW TO USE

'Louis Philippe' forms a bushy shrub that's usually 2 to 3 feet tall and wide in the cooler parts of its range and 3 to 5 feet tall and wide in warmer areas. Tuck it into a foundation planting, or use it to add months of color to a flower bed or mixed border. 'Louis Philippe' generally has good disease resistance.

✿ 'Loving Touch'
Miniature. Jolly, 1983.

'Loving Touch' offers elegantly shaped flowers in various shades of apricot on a compact bush that can find a place in any garden. This award-winning miniature rose produces tapered, orange buds that unfurl into double, high-centered 1½-inch blooms. Held singly or in small clusters, the slightly scented flowers are almost orange in cool conditions and more of a creamy peach color in hot weather. They're produced freely over a long period, usually starting in late spring or early summer and continuing through the rest of the growing season. Branching stems bear semiglossy, medium green leaves. Zones 5 to 10.

HOW TO USE
'Loving Touch' forms a compact, bushy shrub with a height and spread that ranges between 12 and 30 inches. It's a magnificent addition to beds and borders, providing months of pretty, pastel blooms that blend beautifully with both bright and soft yellows, blues, pinks, and purples. It also forms a charming edging for a path or patio. 'Loving Touch' generally has excellent disease resistance.

ARS Award of Excellence for Miniature Roses 1985

✿ 'Magic Carrousel'
Syns. MORrousel, MOORcar
Miniature. Moore, 1972.

It's been around for decades, but 'Magic Carrousel' retains the charm that has made it one of the most popular miniature roses produced to date. Small, pointed, creamy yellow buds tipped with red unfurl into semi-double to double, cupped rosettes that open to flat, 2- to 2½-inch flowers with golden stamens in the center. The creamy white or pale yellow petals are distinctly marked with a red or dark pink edge. The color contrast tends to be most intense in cool weather. The clustered flowers have little or no scent, but they're produced generously in late spring or early summer, with good repeat through the rest of the growing season. Branching, thorny canes carry glossy, medium to dark green leaves. Zones 5 to 10.

HOW TO USE

'Magic Carrousel' has an upright, bushy habit. Left alone, it can grow 24 to 30 inches tall and 18 to 24 inches wide; with regular pinching, it will stay much more compact (12 to 18 inches tall and about 9 to 12 inches wide). This distinctive miniature makes an eye-catching addition to many parts of the garden: in beds and borders, as a low hedge, around a deck or patio, or in a planter. It's also excellent as a cut flower. 'Magic Carrousel' has moderate disease resistance; black spot may be a problem if you don't take preventive measures.

ARS Award of Excellence for Miniature Roses 1975; Miniature Rose Hall of Fame 1999

'Maiden's Blush' See 'Great Maiden's Blush'

'Marchesa Boccella'

Syns. 'Marquise Boccella', 'Marquise Boçella'
Hybrid perpetual. Desprez, 1842.

Here's a rose with a bit of an identity problem: some experts classify it as a hybrid perpetual whereas others list it with the Portland roses. There is also some confusion between this rose and a Portland known as 'Jacques Cartier'. 'Marchesa Boccella' is a lovely old rose with plump, deep pink buds that open into fully double, 3- to 4-inch, light pink flowers packed with petals. New blooms have a flattened rosette form; as they age, the outer petals fold back, giving the blooms a rather rounded appearance. The flowers are held on a very short peduncle (the stem under the bloom), so they look as though they are sitting right on the uppermost leaves — an attractive and identifying feature of this rose. The wonderfully perfumed blooms are held in clusters over a long season, from late spring or early summer with moderate to good repeat well into fall. Light green leaves are held on stout, thorny, upright canes. Zones 5 to 9.

HOW TO USE

'Marchesa Boccella' forms a compact, somewhat vase-shaped shrub. In most areas, it generally grows 3 to 4 feet tall and about 3 feet wide; in very warm areas, expect 5 to 6 feet in height and 3 to 4 feet in spread. Use it to add months of soft color and great fragrance to a bed or border, or enjoy it as an informal hedge. Diseases usually aren't a problem, although a bit of black spot may develop if you don't take preventive measures.

❦ 'Margaret Merril'

Syn. HARkuly
Floribunda. Harkness, 1977.

This first-class floribunda is a favorite in many gardens across the country. 'Margaret Merril' produces elegant, pointed, yellow buds that are blushed with pink, unfurling into double, 4-inch-wide blooms that are white with a faint pink tint in the center. New blooms have a high-centered form, becoming cupped and then flat as they age. Most gardeners agree that this rose is delightfully fragrant, but there are a few who can detect only a slight scent. Held singly or in clusters, the flowers first appear in late spring or early summer, with excellent repeat bloom through the rest of the season. Moderately thorny canes carry dark green, semiglossy foliage. Zones 5 to 9.

HOW TO USE

'Margaret Merril' has an upright, bushy habit. Its height can be rather variable, depending on your climate; expect 3 to 5 feet in height and 2 to 4 feet in width in most areas. It's handsome enough to stand alone as a landscape accent, but it also looks marvelous planted in masses, used as a flowering hedge, or tucked into beds and borders. Add one to your cutting garden for a steady supply of beautiful blooms to enjoy indoors. Black spot can be a problem if you don't take preventive measures; otherwise, disease resistance is generally quite good.

❦ 'Marie Louise'

Damask. Introduced before 1813.

'Marie Louise' may be petite in stature, but there's nothing demure about this damask's beautiful blooms! Plump, pink buds open into very double, rose-pink flowers that are 4 to 5 inches across and so heavy that they tend to nod. New flowers have a flattened form, with swirled petals and a tight "button" eye; the outer petals gradually fold back, giving the blooms a ball-shaped effect. There's only one flowering season, usually in mid- to late spring, but the richly perfumed, clustered blooms are worth waiting for. Light green leaves are carried on moderately thorny, slender canes that arch under the generous display of blooms. Zones 4 to 9.

HOW TO USE

'Marie Louise' forms a rather loose shrub that looks best with some kind of support. Height and spread can range from 3 to 6 feet. Try it in a cottage garden or at the back of a mixed border (give it a tripod of stakes for support), or set bushes about 3 feet apart as a hedge so that they can lean on each other. It also looks pretty spilling over a low retaining wall. 'Marie Louise' generally doesn't have much problem with diseases, except for a bit of mildew in some climates.

✿ 'Marie Pavié'

Polyantha. Allégatière, 1888.

'Marie Pavié' has pretty much everything you could ask for in a rose: a long flowering season, good fragrance, good disease resistance, and almost no thorns. This choice polyantha produces pointed, pink buds that open into semidouble or double, shallowly cupped, 2-inch blooms. The clustered, fragrant flowers are light pink when new, aging to cream or white with golden stamens. The show starts in late spring, with excellent repeat into fall. Nearly thornless stems bear deep green leaves that make a handsome backdrop for the delicately colored blooms. Zones 5 to 9.

HOW TO USE

'Marie Pavié' makes a compact, bushy shrub that's 2 to 4 feet tall and 2 to 3 feet across. Its delightful fragrance and nearly smooth stems make it an excellent rose for planting along paths, around a patio or garden bench, or in a container on a deck. It also looks great in a bed, border, or foundation planting, or when used as a low hedge. You may notice a bit of black spot in some areas, but this easy-care rose is seldom seriously troubled by disease problems.

❦ 'Marijke Koopman'

Hybrid tea. Fryer, 1979.

This handsome hybrid tea may be a puzzle to pronounce (it's something like mah-RYE-kuh, by the way), but it's a hit in the garden. Long, pointed, deep pink buds unfurl to reveal loosely double, high-centered blooms that are 4 to 5 inches across, in a clear shade of medium to deep pink. Reports of its scent range from slight to intense. Held singly or in small clusters, the blooms first appear in late spring or early summer and repeat almost continuously through the rest of the growing season. Glossy, dark green leaves are held on thorny canes. Zones 5 to 9.

HOW TO USE
'Marijke Koopman' has a somewhat stiff, upright habit, generally growing 4 to 6 feet tall and 2 to 3 feet wide. It looks best planted in groups of three or more to create a bushier effect in a bed or mixed border. It combines beautifully with the pinks and pink blends found in many other hybrid tea roses. It's a marvelous addition to a cutting garden, too: the long-lasting, long-stemmed blooms are great in arrangements. Disease resistance is usually good.

❦ 'Mary Rose'

Syn. AUSmary
Shrub. Austin, 1983.

One of the earliest English roses, 'Mary Rose' remains quite popular for its pretty blooms. This charming shrub produces plump, deep pink buds that open into very double, 3- to 5-inch, rose-pink flowers with a loosely swirled center surrounded by cupped outer petals. Some gardeners rave about the wonderful fragrance, whereas others say the scent is mild to moderate. In some places it produces its best show in late spring or early summer and again in fall; in others, it repeats well through the whole growing season. Branching, thorny stems bear matte, medium green leaves. Zones 5 to 9.

HOW TO USE
'Mary Rose' forms a bushy, rounded shrub that's 4 to 6 feet tall and about as wide. Its old-fashioned flowers blend beautifully into a cottage garden setting, and a group of three or more makes a charming sight in a mixed

border. Good candidates for companions include pinks (such as *Dianthus* 'Bath's Pink'), catmints (*Nepeta* spp.), and lady's mantle (*Alchemilla mollis*), to name just a few. Disease resistance is moderate in most areas; take preventive measures against black spot and powdery mildew where these fungal diseases are common problems.

❧ 'Max Graf'

Hybrid rugosa. Bowditch, 1919.

Though best known for its use in the breeding of many modern hardy, disease-resistant roses, this hybrid rugosa is still worth growing in its own right. Pointed, bright pink buds open into single, cupped to flat flowers that are 2 to 3 inches across, with bright pink petals that pale to near white at the base, around a crown of creamy yellow stamens. The clustered blooms have a moderate spicy-fruity fragrance. 'Max Graf' generally only blooms once a season, for about 6 weeks starting in early summer. Trailing, thorny canes are abundantly clad in glossy, medium green, deeply veined leaves. Zones 3 to 8.

HOW TO USE

'Max Graf' forms a very low, broad, spreading bush that's 1 to 2 feet tall and 8 to 10 feet across. The stems tend to root where they touch the ground, eventually forming a dense carpet that makes a great groundcover. Use it to fill space in a low-maintenance area or to cover a gentle slope. This vigorous, adaptable rose can tolerate light shade, and it's rarely bothered by diseases.

❧ 'Mermaid'

Hybrid bracteata. Paul, 1918.

This hybrid bracteata can take a few years to get established, but once it gets going, stand back! 'Mermaid' is a vigorous grower with sharply pointed, cream-colored buds (sometimes blushed with pink) that open into single, saucer-shaped to flat flowers up to 6 inches across. Held singly or in clusters, the moderately to strongly scented flowers are light yellow to ivory with a deeper yellow eye and impressive yellow-orange to golden brown stamens. Bloom generally begins with a splendid show in late spring, with additional flushes of flowers through the rest of the growing season; in warm climates, flowering may continue well into winter. Glossy, deep green, nearly evergreen leaves are held on stout canes well armed with large, hooked thorns. Zones 7 to 10.

HOW TO USE

'Mermaid' is generally grown as a climber, reaching from 6 to 10 feet tall in the northern parts of its range and 20 to 30 feet tall in warmer areas. This is not a rose to plant on a small trellis or archway; it will easily overwhelm a small space, and its thorns can be a menace in a high-traffic area. Instead, use it where you need a thorny barrier, or let it beautify an unsightly outbuilding or boring, large wall. 'Mermaid' can survive the winter in Zone 6 and even colder areas with protection, but then you'll have to deal with pruning out dead (but still thorny) top growth, and that's not a pleasant job. It's best to plant this rose where pruning needs are minimal! 'Mermaid' is seldom bothered by diseases.

🌿 'Midas Touch'

Syn. JACtou
Hybrid tea. Christensen, 1992.

Lovers of yellow roses can hardly find enough good things to say about this superb hybrid tea. Long, pointed buds unfurl to reveal elegant, double, high-centered flowers that are about 4 inches across, with golden yellow petals. The blooms usually have a moderate fragrance that some describe as musky and others as fruity, and they're normally produced singly on long, sturdy stems. Flowering begins in late spring or early summer, with fairly quick repeat flushes of bloom through the rest of the growing season. Moderately thorny canes carry semiglossy, medium to deep green leaves. Zones 5 to 10.

HOW TO USE

'Midas Touch' has a bushy, upright habit. It generally grows 4 to 5 feet tall and 3 to 4 feet wide, but it can be as compact as 3 feet or as tall as 6 feet or more. Its brilliant yellow blooms are a delight for cutting, and they add can't-miss color to beds and borders. Pair them with vibrant red, orange, and violet for a sizzling hot-color combination, or soften them with silvery blues and purples, such as English lavender (*Lavandula angustifolia*) and catmints (*Nepeta* spp.). One downside to this rose is that the flowers tend to open too quickly in warm temperatures. You may notice a bit of mildew in some areas, but in most conditions, 'Midas Touch' offers excellent disease resistance.

All-America Rose Selection 1994

❦ 'Millie Walters'

Syn. MORmilli
Miniature. Moore, 1983.

'Millie Walters' stands out among miniatures with its intriguing, brick-colored blooms. Pointed, coral red buds unfurl into very double, 1½-inch flowers with a classic hybrid tea form in a muted shade of orange-red or orange-pink. Fragrance is minimal, but the bush makes up for that by blooming generously in late spring or early summer with good repeat into fall. Matte, medium green leaves amply cover the slender, thorny canes. Zones 5 to 10.

HOW TO USE

'Millie Walters' has a bushy, somewhat sprawling habit, growing just 1 to 2 feet tall and about as wide. It makes a striking color accent near the front of a bed or border, and it looks super cascading out of a container or spilling over a low wall. Try it with rich purple or blue flowers, such as veronicas or annual lobelia *(Lobelia erinus),* for a dramatic combination, or pair it with silvery foliage, such as lamb's ears *(Stachys byzantina)* or dusty miller *(Senecio cineraria).* Mildew may be a problem in cool climates; elsewhere, disease resistance is generally good.

❦ 'Minnie Pearl'

Syn. SAVahowdy
Miniature. Saville, 1982.

This perky, pint-sized miniature is a real charmer, both in the garden and in arrangements. 'Minnie Pearl' offers long, tapered, light pink buds that are tipped with rose-red, opening into double, high-centered blooms that are just 1½ inches across. The flowers are generally creamy pink, shading to yellow near the center and brushed with reddish pink on the edges of the outer petals. Held singly or in clusters, the slightly scented, long-lasting blooms appear in abundance in late spring or early summer, followed by good repeat through summer and into fall. Slender, thorny stems carry semiglossy, medium green leaves. Zones 5 to 9.

HOW TO USE

'Minnie Pearl' forms an upright bush that's usually 1 to 2 feet tall and about as wide. Enjoy its delicate color in beds and borders, or use it to outline a pathway or patio edge. Planting it in a container brings the charming blooms closer to eye level for easy appreciation. The strong, straight stems make the flowers excellent for cutting, too! 'Minnie Pearl' looks best with some protection from strong sun in hot climates; otherwise, it fades quickly. Take preventive measures against powdery mildew if this problem is common in your area; otherwise, expect good disease resistance.

✿'Mirandy'

Hybrid tea. Lammerts, 1945.

This older hybrid tea isn't as free flowering as many of its modern classmates, but many gardeners still consider it worth growing for its exceptional fragrance. Dark red, pointed buds unfurl into double, high-centered, deep wine red blooms that are 5 to 6 inches across, with an intense old-rose perfume. Flowering usually begins in late spring or early summer, with a few additional flushes of bloom through the rest of the growing season. Well-branched, moderately thorny canes bear semiglossy, deep green leaves. Zones 5 to 9.

HOW TO USE

'Mirandy' produces an upright bush that's usually 4 to 5 feet tall and about 4 feet across. It's a favorite for the cutting garden, even though the flower stems are sometimes bent and strong sun may cause the outer petals to turn black; the good blooms are so gorgeous and fragrant that they make up for the drawbacks. Where it grows well, 'Mirandy' can also be pretty in beds and borders. Black spot, mildew, and rust have all been reported on unprotected plants, although gardeners in some areas report excellent disease resistance. If you enjoy growing fragrant roses, it's worth giving this one a try to see how it does for you!

All-America Rose Selection 1945

❧ 'Miss Flippins'

Syn. TUCkflip
Miniature. Tucker, 1997.

The rich red flowers are fairly small, but this outstanding exhibition miniature actually forms a fairly sizable bush. 'Miss Flippins' produces long, pointed buds that unfurl into double, high-centered blooms that are about 1½ inches across, with cardinal red petals that are deep reddish pink underneath. They have little or no fragrance, but they're produced abundantly in late spring or early summer, with good repeat into fall. Moderately thorny stems carry glossy, deep green leaves. Zones 5 to 10.

HOW TO USE

'Miss Flippins' has a dense, bushy habit; expect a height and spread of 2 to 3 feet. It fits easily into a foundation planting or a flower bed or border. Try it with purple-leaved heucheras (such as *Heuchera* 'Plum Pudding') and bright orange zinnias *(Zinnia angustifolia)* to create a stunning summer combination. Or pair it with pink and white flowers — perhaps sweet alyssum *(Lobularia maritima)* and *Dianthus* 'Bath's Pink' — for an elegant color grouping. 'Miss Flippins' usually has good disease resistance, although mildew may be a problem in some areas.

❧ 'Mister Lincoln'

Hybrid tea. Swim & Weeks, 1964.

Introduced well over thirty years ago, 'Mister Lincoln' is still beloved by gardeners for its color and fragrance. Elegant, maroon buds unfurl to reveal double, velvety maroon red to cherry red flowers that are 4 to 6 inches across. Held singly on long stems, the powerfully perfumed blooms start out with high centers, opening to a cupped form accented with yellow stamens. Flowering starts in late spring or early summer, with good repeat through summer and into fall. Tall, thorny stems bear matte, dark green foliage. Zones 5 to 9.

HOW TO USE

'Mister Lincoln' produces gorgeous flowers, but the bush itself isn't particularly pretty. It has a fairly stiff, upright habit, generally growing 4 to 6 feet tall and 2 to 3 feet wide. In the garden, it looks best planted in groups of three or more to create a bushier effect at the back of a border. Make sure you grow at least one in your cutting garden, too, so that you can enjoy the superbly scented blooms indoors. Disease resistance is usually just moderate — consider taking preventive measures against powdery mildew, black spot and rust. Many gardeners are willing to take this extra effort in exchange for the exquisite blooms!

All-America Rose Selection 1965

✵ 'Mme. Alfred Carrière'

Noisette. Schwartz, 1879.

One of the hardiest of the Noisette roses, 'Mme. Alfred Carrière' is prized for its long bloom season and wonderful fragrance. Plump, pink-tinged buds open into double, broadly cupped to flat flowers that are about 4 inches across. The loose, somewhat ruffled-looking blooms are usually creamy white touched with pink (the pink is most noticeable in cool conditions), and with a bit of yellow near the center. Very fragrant flowers first appear in mid- or late spring, with moderate to good repeat bloom continuing well into winter in warm areas. Light green, semiglossy leaves are held on long, slender, slightly to moderately thorny canes. Zones 6 to 10.

HOW TO USE

'Mme. Alfred Carrière' may take a few years to get established, but after that it grows vigorously, forming either a 10- to 20-foot climber or a large shrub ranging from 6 to 10 feet in height and spread. (Since its size can vary so widely, it's smart to find a bush already growing in your area so that you can see what to expect in your conditions.) Train it against a wall or fence or on a pillar or pergola post. Older canes tend to be somewhat stiff, so it's best to train them while they are young and still flexible. This rose tolerates some shade, so it's a great choice for a spot that gets lots of bright light but not much direct sun. Both mildew and black spot can occur on unprotected plants, but they seldom seriously weaken the plant.

❦ 'Mme. Ernest Calvat'

Syns. 'Mme. Ernst Calvat', 'Pink Bourbon'
Bourbon. Schwartz, 1888.

If old-fashioned flowers and outstanding fragrance are high on your list of must-haves, this admirable Bourbon rose belongs in your garden. 'Mme. Ernest Calvat' produces plump, pink buds that open into double, medium to light rose-pink blooms that are 3 to 4 inches across. New flowers are strongly cupped; as they mature, they become almost flat, showing off their folded petals and yellow stamens. The richly perfumed blooms appear in abundance in late spring or early summer, with usually sporadic summer bloom and often another good show in fall. Semiglossy, deep green foliage is carried on thorny stems that are a rich deep purple when young. Zones 5 to 9.

HOW TO USE

'Mme. Ernest Calvat' has a tall, rather upright habit. Left unsupported, it generally grows 5 to 6 feet tall and 4 to 5 feet wide. It's a splendid sight in a cottage garden setting, or at the back of a mixed border. It also adapts to life as a 6- to 8-foot climber on a wall, fence, or pillar. The flowers are wonderful for cutting. Disease resistance is usually only moderate: take preventive measures against powdery mildew and black spot where these fungal diseases are common problems.

❦ 'Mme. Hardy'

Damask. Hardy, 1832.

'Mme. Hardy' is officially classified as a damask rose, although some experts detect traits of other roses in its form and habits. Whatever its classification, it's a splendid old rose! Pink-tinted, cream or yellow buds enclosed in ferny, leaflike sepals open to display fully double flowers that are 2½ to 3½ inches across. Cupped when new, the pleasingly perfumed blooms become flattened as they age, showing a center with incurved petals surrounding a green eye. There's only one bloom season, starting in late spring or early summer and lasting anywhere from 3 to 6 weeks, but it's definitely worth waiting for! Moderately thorny, upright to arching stems carry light green to gray-green leaves. Zones 5 to 8.

HOW TO USE

'Mme. Hardy' has an upright-spreading to somewhat sprawling habit. As a shrub, it usually grows 4 to 6 feet tall and 3 to 5 feet wide. Try it in a mixed border or cottage garden, or as an accent plant or hedge. Planted alone, it looks best with some kind of support, such as a tripod of stakes; set at 3-foot spacings for a hedge, the bushes will hold each other up. This rose also works well as a 7- to 10-foot climber trained on a wall, fence, post, or pillar. Disease resistance is generally excellent; black spot may cause a bit of leaf discoloration but seldom seriously affects the rose's health.

'Mme. Isaac Pereire'

Bourbon. Garçon, 1881.

This Bourbon isn't the easiest rose to grow well, but its fans wouldn't be without it! 'Mme. Isaac Pereire' produces rounded, reddish buds that open into large, loose rosettes filled with swirls of folded petals in a sumptuous shade of purplish pink. Sometimes the petals are in a quartered, or cross-shaped, arrangement. The 4- to 5-inch-wide blooms are held singly or in clusters, and they have an intense fragrance that some describe as being like raspberries. Expect a generous flush of flowers in mid- to late spring, usually followed by sporadic summer bloom and another good show in fall. The fall display is often the best, since some earlier blooms may be misshapen. Long, thorny canes carry semiglossy, medium to deep green leaves. Zones 6 to 9.

HOW TO USE

As a shrub, 'Mme. Isaac Pereire' has a rather open (some might say gangly) habit, generally growing 6 to 8 feet tall and 5 to 6 feet across. Happily, it adapts quite well to training as a moderate climber, about 8 to 10 feet tall; try it on a wall, fence, trellis, or pillar. Consider placing it near an outdoor seating area, such as a garden bench or a deck or patio, so that you can enjoy the delicious fragrance while you relax. If you don't take preventive measures, 'Mme. Isaac Pereire' is susceptible to both mildew and black spot, sometimes to the point where it drops its leaves in summer, but it usually recovers and produces another flush of foliage and flowers by fall.

❦'Mme. Legras de St. Germain'

Alba. Introduced in 1846.

You'll usually find 'Mme. Legras de St. Germain' listed as an alba rose, but experts suspect it has some Noisette or damask influence as well. By any classification, it's a lovely rose, with tapering, light yellow buds that emerge through ferny, leaflike structures called sepals. The elegant buds unfurl into fully double, domed to flattened rosettes that become ball-shaped as the outer petals fold back. The 2- to 4-inch-wide, clustered flowers are creamy to pure white with a touch of yellow in the center, and they have a strong, sweet scent. They appear in one splendid show, usually in late spring or early summer. Light gray-green foliage is held on long, almost thornless canes. Zones 3 to 8.

HOW TO USE

'Mme. Legras de St. Germain' is a vigorous rose, generally growing 6 to 8 feet tall and wide as a free-standing shrub. Planted in groups, it makes a handsome large screen. It also works well as a 12- to 15-foot climber, trained on a fence, arbor, or pillar. 'Mme. Legras de St. Germain' can tolerate some shade, so consider it for a site that is bright but doesn't have full sun. Disease resistance is generally good, although some black spot may appear after bloom if you don't take preventive measures.

❦'Mme. Pierre Oger'

Bourbon. Oger, 1878.

If you love delicately shaded flowers, you'll swoon over the beautiful blooms of this exquisite Bourbon rose. Rounded, red-blushed buds open to display double, deeply cupped flowers that are 2 to 3 inches across. Newly opened blooms are palest pink, and they stay that way when the weather is cloudy. But when touched by the sun, the petal edges darken to cherry pink; the stronger the sun, the more intense the color. The richly fragrant flowers first appear in mid- to late spring, with moderate re-bloom in summer and often other good show in fall. Slender, slightly thorny stems carry an abundant covering of light to medium green leaves. Zones 6 to 10.

HOW TO USE

'Mme. Pierre Oger' has a rather narrow base, with canes that arch outward toward the top, creating a vase-shaped habit. Expect a height of 4 to

6 feet and a spread of 3 to 5 feet in most areas. Enjoy it at the back of a mixed border, perhaps combined with lower-growing, pink-flowered perennials such as *Dianthus* 'Bath's Pink' to echo its pink blooms. It also adapts to training on a fence or trellis. Both mildew and black spot can occur on unprotected plants, but they generally aren't bad enough to seriously weaken the bush.

❦ 'Mme. Plantier'

Hybrid alba. Plantier, 1835.

'Mme. Plantier' is usually listed as a hybrid alba, rather than a true alba, because of certain non-alba traits that various experts attribute to damask, Noisette, and *Rosa moschata* influences. Plump, red-blushed, cream-colored buds open into very double, flattened flowers that are 2 to 4 inches across, with tightly incurved center petals surrounding a small green eye. New blooms are creamy white, normally aging to pure white, although they may show a hint of pink in cool conditions. More fragrant than most albas, the clustered flowers of 'Mme. Plantier' appear in one magnificent show, usually in mid- to late spring. Scattered blooms occasionally appear later in the season. Long, arching, nearly thornless canes carry grayish green leaves. Zones 4 to 8.

HOW TO USE

As a free-standing shrub, 'Mme. Plantier' has a spreading, mounded habit, growing anywhere from 4 to 8 feet tall and wide. (Before selecting a planting site, it's smart to find a specimen already growing in your area so that you can see what size to expect in your climate.) It's pretty enough to stand alone as a landscape accent, but it also looks great grouped into a mass planting or a hedge, or used at the back of a mixed border. 'Mme. Plantier' also adapts to life as a 10- to 20-foot climber; try training it on a wall or tall fence or let it scramble up into a tree. A spot with some protection from hot midday sun is ideal. Apart from a bit of mildew in some areas, diseases are seldom a problem.

❦ 'Mme. Zöetmans'

Damask. Marest, 1830.

Most experts classify 'Mme. Zöetmans' as a damask rose, but occasionally you'll find it grouped with the closely related gallica roses. Either way, it's a lovely addition to any rose collection. Rounded white buds lightly tinged with red open into very double, 3-inch flowers. They start out creamy pink and cupped, opening white and flat with incurved center petals surrounding a small green eye. Held in small clusters, the strongly scented flowers appear in abundance in late spring or early summer. Medium green foliage is carried on thorny stems that arch under the weight of the blooms. Zones 5 to 9.

HOW TO USE

'Mme. Zöetmans' has a compact, somewhat spreading habit, generally growing about 4 feet tall and wide. It's a super choice for growing in a large container, and it also makes a handsome hedge. Tuck it into a foundation planting, or use it in a cottage garden or mixed border, paired with other old-fashioned favorites, such as foxgloves (*Digitalis* spp.), catmints (*Nepeta* spp.), and lady's mantle *(Alchemilla mollis)*. Disease resistance is generally good, although mildew may be a problem in some areas.

❦ 'Mons. Tillier'

Syns. 'Monsieur Tillier', 'M. Tillier'
Tea. Bernaix, 1891.

The uniquely shaded blooms of 'Mons. Tillier' are a big part of this tea rose's charm, but it's more than just a novelty: it's an excellent long-flowering selection for the South. Pointed, coral red buds open into very double, broadly cupped to flat, 3-inch blooms. The inner petals tend to fold back along their length, giving them a pointed appearance. The exact color is hard to describe, because it changes depending on the weather and the age of the bloom, but it usually starts off a rather bright pink with orange tints, aging to soft orange-red and then to reddish purple. Reports of its fragrance vary from slight to strong; the scent does tend to be more noticeable in newly opened flowers. Look for blooms to appear in mid- to late spring, with good repeat well into winter in most areas. Twiggy, moderately thorny stems carry semiglossy, olive-green to dark green leaves. Zones 7 to 10.

HOW TO USE

'Mons. Tillier' has a vigorous, upright, bushy habit, growing anywhere from 3 to 6 feet tall and wide. A grouping of three or more bushes of 'Mons. Tillier' certainly makes an eye-catching landscape accent. In areas where it stays fairly compact, consider growing it in a foundation planting or near a deck or patio, where you can get up close to admire the distinctive flowers. 'Mons. Tillier' generally has excellent disease resistance.

❦ 'Moonlight'

Hybrid musk. Pemberton, 1913.

This lovely hybrid musk is an excellent choice for adding multiseason interest to just about any moderate- to warm-climate garden. Tapered, cream-colored buds unfurl into single to semidouble, flat, 2-inch blooms that open a creamy yellow color and age to white. Most gardeners appreciate this rose's moderate to strong scent, although some can detect little fragrance. The clustered flowers first appear in late spring to early summer, with moderate to good repeat through summer into fall. A generous show of small, orange-red hips also appears near the end of the season, lasting into winter. Long, arching canes carry glossy, deep green leaves. Zones 6 to 9.

HOW TO USE
Grown as a shrub, 'Moonlight' has a somewhat open, sprawling habit, growing anywhere from 4 to 8 feet tall and about as wide. If you have the room, it makes a pretty hedge or screen planting. To enjoy the long season of beautiful blooms without giving up as much garden space, use it as a 10- to 12-foot climber trained on a pillar or fence or allowed to scramble into a tree. Like other hybrid musks, 'Moonlight' can tolerate light shade. Apart from a bit of mildew in some areas, diseases usually don't bother this rose.

❦ 'Morden Centennial'

Shrub. Marshall, 1980.

Here's a hardy and handsome shrub rose that's perfectly suited to cold-climate gardens. 'Morden Centennial' produces pointed, egg-shaped, deep pink buds that open to double, broadly cupped to nearly flat flowers usually 3 to 4 inches across. Held singly or in clusters, the lightly fragrant flowers appear in abundance over a long season, from late spring or early summer well into fall. They are followed by a splendid crop of bright orange-red hips that extend the show into winter. Upright, thorny stems carry semiglossy, dark green leaves. Zones 3 to 9.

HOW TO USE

'Morden Centennial' forms a rather rounded, bushy shrub. Size ranges from 2 to 5 feet tall and wide, depending on where you live. (You might want to look for someone already growing this rose in conditions similar to yours, to find out what size you can expect.) Grow it alone as a landscape accent, or enjoy it in groups as a mass planting or handsome flowering hedge. It's also excellent for adding multiseason interest to a foundation planting or a mixed border. Disease resistance is generally good, although some black spot may develop if you don't take preventive measures.

❦ 'Mrs. B. R. Cant'

Syn. 'Mrs. Benjamin R. Cant'
Tea. Cant, 1901.

Many a southern garden is graced by the magnificent blooms of this superb tea rose. Plump, pointed, deep pink buds open to display fully double, cupped flowers that are about 4 inches across and packed with folded petals. The color is generally a light rosy pink on the tops of the petals, with a deeper shade on the undersides; in cooler temperatures, the color is more intense, reaching toward deep red. Reports on its fragrance vary widely: some rave about its outstanding perfume, whereas others can detect little or no scent. Flowering starts early—usually in midspring—and continues well into winter. Branching stems bear medium to deep green leaves. Zones 7 to 10.

HOW TO USE

'Mrs. B. R. Cant' has an upright, bushy habit. In the northern parts of its range, expect a height and spread of 3 to 5 feet; in warmer areas, 6 to 8 feet tall and wide is more common. Grow it anywhere you have the space for it: perhaps as a screen planting, or as a landscape accent. The flowers are great for cutting. Diseases are rarely a problem in most areas.

❦ 'Mrs. Dudley Cross'

Syn. 'Dudley Cross'
Tea. Paul, 1908.

Warm-climate gardeners have long had a love affair with this eye-catching and easy-to-grow tea rose. 'Mrs. Dudley Cross' offers long, tapered, light yellow buds blushed with pink, opening to reveal very double, cupped blooms that are 3 to 4 inches across. The petals are a delicate, soft yellow blushed with varying amounts of pink, depending on the age of the bloom and the growing conditions. Held in small clusters, the lightly to moderately scented flowers first appear in midspring, with good repeat continuing well into winter. Olive green to dark green, glossy foliage is held on nearly thornless canes. Zones 7 to 10.

HOW TO USE

'Mrs. Dudley Cross' forms a shrub that is somewhat open and spreading, especially when young. It fills in as it ages, generally reaching 4 to 6 feet in height and spread; long-established bushes may reach 8 feet. Plant it alone as a pretty, long-flowering landscape accent, or enjoy it in a mixed border. The long-lasting blooms are also excellent for cutting. Apart from a touch of mildew in some areas, disease resistance is usually excellent.

❦ 'Mrs. Oakley Fisher'

Hybrid tea. Cant, 1921.

You probably wouldn't guess 'Mrs. Oakley Fisher' is a hybrid tea rose by looking at its flowers: they have the simple form and delicate coloring of a dainty wild rose. Pointed, orange buds blushed lightly with red unfurl into single, flat flowers about 3 inches in diameter. The petal color ranges from pale peachy yellow to deep orange-yellow (cool weather brings out the richest color), accented in the center with a cluster of golden orange stamens. Some gardeners describe the scent as light to moderate; others rave over the strong, sweet fragrance. 'Mrs. Oakley Fisher' flowers for many months, usually starting in midspring and continuing freely until heavy frost. Small, rounded, orange hips may appear in fall. Thorny canes carry dark green, glossy leaves. Zones 6 to 10.

HOW TO USE

'Mrs. Oakley Fisher' has a branching, shrubby habit, generally growing 3 to 5 feet tall and about as wide. Its compact habit makes it a great choice for a foundation planting or for edging a deck, patio, or pathway. In a border, the peachy orange color blends beautifully with blue and purple flowers, such as those of sages (*Salvia* spp.). Disease resistance is usually good.

'Mrs. R. M. Finch'

Polyantha. Finch, 1923.

'Mrs. R. M. Finch' is a pretty polyantha with a compact growth habit, adding months of color to even small spaces. Pointed pink buds open into semidouble to double, cupped blooms about 2 inches across. New blooms are a medium rose-pink with a paler center, aging to a lighter pink overall (this happens very quickly in hot, sunny conditions). Fragrance is usually mild. The clustered blooms begin in mid- to late spring, with excellent repeat through the rest of the summer and into fall. Moderately thorny canes carry semiglossy, light green leaves. Zones 6 to 9.

HOW TO USE

'Mrs. R. M. Finch' has a dense, bushy habit, forming a compact shrub that's 2 to 4 feet tall and about as wide. A single clump makes a charming landscape accent or container plant; it also looks lovely planted in masses or as a low hedge. Add it to beds and borders for months of delicate color. This easy-care rose is seldom bothered by diseases.

'Mutabilis'

Syns. 'Tipo Ideale'; *Rosa chinensis mutabilis, R. mutabilis*
Hybrid China. Cultivated before 1894.

It's easy to identify this distinctive hybrid China rose: Just look for several different flower colors on the same bush! 'Mutabilis' produces tapered, orange-red buds that unfurl to display single, cupped to nearly flat flowers that are 2 to 3 inches across. New blooms are usually soft yellow on top (retaining the orange blush underneath), aging to peach, then pink, then deep pinkish red; all colors can appear on the bush at the same time. New flowers have a light scent; older blooms are generally not fragrant. Held in loose clusters, the flowers first appear in mid- to late spring in most areas, with dependable repeat bloom until hard frost. Long, branching canes carry glossy, dark green leaves. Zones 7 to 10.

HOW TO USE

In most areas, 'Mutabilis' forms a somewhat open, spreading shrub. In the cooler parts of its range, winter tip dieback keeps plants a fairly compact 3 to 5 feet tall and wide. Milder climates allow more abundant growth, so plants can grow 6 to 10 feet tall and wide. 'Mutabilis' looks marvelous in just about any site, grown alone as a landscape accent or grouped into a mass planting. In mixed borders, it blends beautifully with a wide range of bright and pastel companions, as well as silvery foliage. It can also adapt to life as a climber, reaching 10 to 15 feet, or even taller in very protected sites. Diseases seldom disturb this rose.

❦ 'My Sunshine'

Syn. TINshine
Miniature. Bennett, 1986.

'My Sunshine' is a great miniature rose for any spot where you'd enjoy bright, cheerful color. Small, pointed buds open into single, flat, 1-inch-wide flowers composed of nearly circular petals, each with a tiny point on the rim. They bloom in a sunny shade of yellow, further crowned with golden stamens. Held singly or in small clusters, the lightly fragrant flowers appear in abundance from late spring or early summer well into fall. Thorny stems bear an ample covering of small, medium green, semiglossy leaves. Zones 5 to 10.

HOW TO USE
'My Sunshine' has a dense, bushy habit, usually growing 18 to 22 inches tall and about as wide. Use to add a welcoming touch to a walkway or to surround a deck or patio with season-long color. 'My Sunshine' is also wonderful in beds and borders; try pairing it with bright blue flowers, such as *Veronica* 'Sunny Border Blue', for a show-stopping combination. 'My Sunshine' looks super in planters, too! Disease resistance is generally excellent.

❦ 'Nastarana'

Syns. 'Persian Musk Rose'; *Rosa moschata nastarana, R. pissartii*
Noisette. Introduced in 1879.

'Nastarana' isn't one of the best-known Noisette roses, but it's certainly a charming addition to a mild-climate garden. Pink-blushed, egg-shaped buds open to display single to semidouble, loosely ruffled flowers that are about 2 inches wide. Accented with a cluster of yellow stamens in the center, the clustered white blooms are often lightly tinged with pale pink, and they have a moderate to strong scent. The bloom season generally begins in late spring, with good repeat continuing well into fall, and even into winter in warm areas. Small, orange-red hips add extra interest in fall. Slender stems bear medium to dark green, glossy leaves. Zones 6 to 9.

HOW TO USE

'Nastarana' has a vigorous, upright habit. In the cooler parts of its range, it tends to form a compact shrub, generally growing 3 to 4 feet tall and 2 to 3 feet across. In milder areas, you could use it as a large shrub (6 to 8 feet tall and wide), or train it as a 10- to 15-foot climber. Use it to add months of flowers to the back of mixed borders, or as a screen. Disease resistance is moderate: black spot and mildew may occur if you don't take preventive measures.

❦ 'Nearly Wild'

Floribunda. Brownell, 1941.

This wonderful floribunda offers the delicate beauty of simple blooms on a compact bush that's easy to tuck into any garden. Tapering, deep pink buds unfurl into single, nearly flat flowers about 2 inches across, in a bright shade of rose-pink that pales as the blooms age. Each bloom is accented with a crown of golden stamens, along with a white eye that often extends out into the petals as they mature. Fragrance is generally mild to moderate. The clustered flowers appear in abundance starting in late spring or early summer, with nearly continuous rebloom until frost. Branching, thorny stems bear medium green, semiglossy leaves. Zones 4 to 9.

HOW TO USE

'Nearly Wild' has a low, spreading habit, forming a bushy, mounded shrub that's 2 to 4 feet tall and about as wide. A grouping of three or more makes a spectacular sight, used as a landscape accent or low hedge or in a foundation planting or mixed border. You'll often see this rose touted as disease-free, and it can be quite trouble-free in some areas, but be aware that 'Nearly Wild' can develop both black spot and powdery mildew if you don't take preventive measures where conditions are favorable for these diseases.

❦ 'Nevada'

Hybrid moyesii. Dot, 1927.

'Nevada' is classified by the American Rose Society as a hybrid moyesii, but you'll usually find it grouped with other modern shrub roses in catalogs. However you classify it, this rose is a winner if you appreciate big blooms. Egg-shaped to oval, light pink buds open into single to semidouble, saucer-shaped flowers that are 3 to 5 inches across. The flowers are usually creamy white, sometimes tinged with pink, and accented with deep golden stamens. They have little or no fragrance. Blooms appear in profusion in late spring or early summer, in clusters all along the canes. This splendid show is generally followed by sporadic to moderate rebloom in summer, with another good display in fall. Light gray-green leaves are borne on arching canes that have few thorns. Zones 5 to 9.

HOW TO USE
'Nevada' has a bushy, upright habit. Left to grow unrestrained, it will form a shrub with a height and spread of 6 to 8 feet in most areas. It makes a striking landscape accent or screen planting if you have the room. Where garden space is limited, consider training it on a fence or arbor. Removing the oldest stems each year will help keep the bush vigorous. Black spot may be a problem if you don't take preventive measures; otherwise, disease resistance is generally good.

❦ 'New Dawn'

Syns. 'Everblooming Dr. W. Van Fleet', 'The New Dawn'
Large-flowered climber. Dreer, 1930.

One of the most popular roses of all time, 'New Dawn' practically needs no introduction! But if you're not familiar with it yet, you'll quickly be won over by this large-flowered climber. Pointed, medium pink buds open into loosely double, 3-inch blooms that are creamy pink with high centers. As they age, the color fades to pale pink or nearly white (especially in strong sun), with a cupped to flat form crowned with yellow stamens. Opinions vary on its fragrance, but most agree it has at least a moderate sweet or fruity scent. Held singly or in clusters, the flowers appear in glorious profusion in late spring or early summer, usually followed by fair summer rebloom and another good show in fall. Moderately thorny stems carry medium to deep green, glossy foliage. Zones 5 to 10.

HOW TO USE
'New Dawn' has a vigorous growth habit. Left unsupported, it forms a large, mounding shrub that can reach 8 to 10 feet tall and wide; regular pruning can keep it somewhat smaller. This rose really shines when used as a 10- to 20-foot climber adorning an arbor, arch, wall, trellis, pillar, or pergola post. It also looks lovely when allowed to scramble into a tree. Disease resistance is usually excellent, although a bit of powdery mildew has been reported in some regions.

World Rose Hall of Fame 1997

'Newport Fairy'

Syn. 'Newport Rambler'
Hybrid wichurana. Gardner, 1908.

'Newport Fairy' isn't a rose for a small space: this hybrid wichurana (also listed by some as a hybrid multiflora) can easily reach 20 feet or more! If you have the room for it, you'll enjoy its show of deep pink buds that open into single, 2-inch, clustered blooms. The lightly fragrant flowers are a rich shade of rose-pink, each accented with a white eye and a cluster of yellow stamens. Expect one spectacular display for about a month in late spring or early summer; repeat bloom, if any, is sporadic. Long canes carry glossy, medium green leaves. Zones 5 to 10.

HOW TO USE
'Newport Fairy' is a fast-growing rambler, generally growing 15 to 20 feet tall, or even much larger with support. Don't expect this rose to fit a small trellis or pillar; it needs a large, very sturdy support. Train it against a large wall or fence, encourage it to ramble over an outbuilding, or let it find its way up into a sturdy tree. Disease resistance is usually good.

'Nicole'

Syn. KORicole
Floribunda. Kordes, 1985.

If you enjoy brightly colored blooms, you'll love the dramatic bicolored flowers of this fabulous floribunda. 'Nicole' produces pointed, cream-colored buds blushed with pink, unfurling to display double, 4-inch-wide, cupped rosettes that open nearly flat with yellow stamens in the center. The white petals are dramatically edged with intense magenta-pink to pinkish red when new; strong sun quickly fades the color contrast. Clustered flowers first appear in late spring or early summer, with good repeat through the rest of the growing season. Glossy, deep green foliage is carried on thorny canes. Zones 5 to 9.

HOW TO USE

'Nicole' forms a tall, upright bush that's usually 5 to 7 feet tall and 4 to 6 feet across. Enjoy it in masses as a screen planting, or at the back of a mixed border. Ideas for pretty partners include pink- and white-flowered cosmos *(Cosmos bipinnatus)*, the white daisies of boltonia *(Boltonia asteroides)*, or the silvery foliage of *Artemisia* 'Huntingdon' or *A.* 'Powis Castle'. 'Nicole' usually has good disease resistance.

❦ 'Nozomi'

Syn. 'Heideroslein Nozomi'
Climbing miniature. Onodera, 1968.

This charming selection is officially classified as a climbing miniature rose, but it really shines when left unsupported to form a ground-hugging mound. 'Nozomi' produces pointed, medium pink buds that open into single, flat flowers just 1½ inches across. New blooms are pale pink, aging to white and accented with a large crown of bright yellow stamens. Fragrance is slight, at best. The flowers bloom in clusters all along the canes in one splendid show in early summer, occasionally with scattered repeat into late summer. Long, thorny canes carry glossy, deep green leaves. Zones 5 to 9.

HOW TO USE

Trained to a support, 'Nozomi' makes a cute 3- to 5-foot climber that's ideal for a small trellis, fence, or post. Without support, it has a trailing habit, generally reaching 1 to 2 feet tall and 4 to 6 feet across. Let it weave through perennials in a bed or border or trail out of a container planting. It also looks super spilling over a low wall or cascading down a gentle slope. 'Nozomi' is seldom bothered by diseases.

❦ 'Nymphenburg'

Hybrid musk. Kordes, 1954.

The soft colors of this hybrid musk rose allow it to blend beautifully into a range of garden settings. Plump, peachy pink buds open into broadly cupped to flat, semidouble flowers that are about 3 inches across. The color varies somewhat depending on the growing conditions, but it's usually a shade of salmon pink or peach pink, with yellow toward the base of the petals and yellow stamens in the center. Held in clusters, the moderately to strongly scented flowers appear in abundance in late spring to early summer, with some repeat bloom through the rest of the season. Orange-red hips may appear in fall. Glossy, dark green foliage is held on long canes. Zones 6 to 10.

HOW TO USE

'Nymphenburg' is a vigorous rose, forming either a somewhat open, upright shrub, usually 6 to 8 feet tall and about as wide, or a 12- to 18-foot climber. Left unsupported, it makes an attractive screen planting; as a climber, it looks lovely on an arch or arbor, or against a wall or fence. The delicately shaded blooms look especially lovely against the gray color of weathered wood, or against green- or white-painted structures. 'Nymphenburg' generally has good disease resistance.

❦ 'Old Blush'

Syns. 'Common Blush China', 'Common Monthly', 'Old Pink Daily', 'Old Pink Monthly', 'Parson's Pink China'
China. Parsons, 1752.

This classic China rose goes by many names, but whatever you call it, it's a beauty! Reddish pink buds open to display loosely cupped, semidouble blooms that are about 3 inches in diameter. The new blooms are generally light pink, darkening to medium to bright pink as they age. Fragrance is on the light side. 'Old Blush' blooms generously for a long season. The display of large, loose flower clusters is usually heaviest in spring and fall, but the show in between is quite good, too, and it may continue well into winter in warm climates. Orange hips may appear among the blooms in fall. Nearly thornless stems bear glossy, medium green leaves that are evergreen south of Zone 6. Zones 6 to 10.

HOW TO USE

'Old Blush' forms an upright, somewhat open and spreading shrub. In the cooler parts of its range, expect a height and spread of 2 to 4 feet; in mild areas, 4 to 6 feet or more in height and spread is common. 'Old Blush' is a handsome landscape shrub, planted alone or in masses as an accent or as a hedge. It looks lovely in a mixed border, too. In sheltered spots, you can train it to a fence, wall, or trellis as a 6- to 10-foot climber. Disease resistance is moderate; take preventive measures against powdery mildew if this fungal disease is common in your area.

'Climbing Old Blush' is similar but can reach 10 to 25 feet in height. It's best in Zones 7 to 10.

❦ 'Olympiad'

Syns. 'Olympiode'; MACauck
Hybrid tea. McGredy, 1982.

'Olympiad' ranks among the best of the red hybrid tea roses. In fact, many of its fans consider it nearly perfect — all it lacks is great fragrance. Elegant, long buds unfurl to display double, high-centered, pure red blooms that are 4 to 5 inches across. The scent is generally slight. Usually held singly on long stems, the flowers appear freely in late spring or early summer, followed by good repeat bloom through the rest of the season. Very thorny stems bear semiglossy, medium green leaves. Zones 5 to 9.

HOW TO USE

'Olympiad' has an upright habit and tends to be a bit bushier than most hybrid tea roses. Expect a height of 4 to 6 feet and a spread of 3 to 4 feet in most areas, although it can grow taller in mild climates. This splendid red rose is a must-have for the cutting garden, but it's also lovely in beds and borders. 'Olympiad' makes a dense, thorny hedge, too. Disease resistance is generally good, but you may want to take preventive measures against black spot if this fungal disease is a serious problem where you live.

All-America Rose Selection 1984

❦ 'Orange Mothersday'

Syn. 'Orange Morsdag'
Polyantha. Grootendorst, 1956.

Orange roses aren't for everyone, but if you enjoy their warm hues, this polyantha is one of the best. Small, oval buds open into double, 1½-inch, bright orange blooms that are ball shaped at first but develop a cupped form as they open. Held in clusters, the lightly scented flowers bloom prolifically starting in late spring or early summer, with moderate repeat through the rest of the summer into fall. Lightly to moderately thorny canes carry small, glossy, deep green leaves. Zones 5 to 9.

HOW TO USE

'Orange Mothersday' has a compact, bushy habit, usually growing just 2 to 4 feet tall and about as wide. Enjoy its eye-catching color in beds, borders, and foundation plantings; it looks very nice in a container, too. Pair it with rich purples and golden-hued partners, such as violet sage (*Salvia × superba*), *Verbena* 'Homestead Purple', and sunflower heliopsis *(Heliopsis helianthoides),* for a color-packed combination! Mildew may be a problem in cooler climates; otherwise, disease resistance is generally good.

❦ 'Oranges 'n' Lemons'

Syn. MACoranlem
Shrub. McGredy, 1994.

If your taste in rose colors runs on the wild side, this shrub rose belongs in your garden! Tapered, golden buds tipped with orange open into double, 3-inch flowers that start out with high centers, opening wide to show a clump of yellow stamens. The broad, golden yellow petals are irregularly splashed and speckled with bright orange; in hot weather, the golden color may pale to light yellow. Held in small clusters, the flowers have a mild, fruity fragrance. They appear abundantly in late spring or early summer, generally with fair to good repeat through the rest of the season. Arching, moderately thorny canes carry foliage that is deep red when new and a glossy, dark green when mature. Zones 5 to 9.

HOW TO USE

'Oranges 'n' Lemons' is a tall-growing, vigorous rose, with long canes that arch out from a narrow base to create a fountainlike effect. It can grow anywhere from 4 to 10 feet tall and 3 to 8 feet wide, depending on your climate. Some gardeners rave about this rose, but others haven't had good luck with it; it's smart to talk to other rose growers in your area to find out how it has performed for them. Where it's happy, it's an amazing sight in a mixed border with other hot colors. In mild climates, 'Oranges 'n' Lemons' also makes an intriguing climber for a wall, trellis, post, or pillar. This selection is usually quite disease resistant, although black spot may be a problem if you don't take preventive measures.

❦ 'Pacesetter'

Syns. 'Pace Setter', SAVapace
Miniature. Schwartz, 1979.

This award-winning miniature has been around a while, and it remains one of the best white-flowered selections in its class. Elegant, tapered buds unfurl to display crisp white, double, 1½-inch blooms with the classic high-centered form of a hybrid tea rose. Usually produced singly on long stems, the flowers have a moderate to strong, fruity scent; they appear in late spring or early summer with good repeat through the rest of the season. Matte, dark green leaves are held on prickly stems. Zones 5 to 9.

HOW TO USE

'Pacesetter' forms an upright bush that's usually 18 to 24 inches tall and about 15 to 18 inches wide. Its long-lasting, long-stemmed blooms make it an ideal candidate for the cutting garden, but it's also a lovely addition to beds and borders, particularly when planted in groups of three or more. 'Pacesetter' generally has good disease resistance.

ARS Award of Excellence for Miniature Roses 1981

❦ 'Parade'

Large-flowered climber. Boerner, 1953.

'Parade' is a modern rose, but its cupped blooms have all the charm of an old-fashioned favorite. This large-flowered climber produces light red, egg-shaped buds that open into open-cupped to nearly flat, double flowers. The blooms are a rich rose-pink color, and each one is 3½ to 4½ inches across; grouped into clusters, they make quite a show! Most gardeners agree that the scent is at least moderate, with sweet and fruity overtones. Expect a splendid display of flowers in late spring or early summer and another in fall, with light to moderate rebloom in between. Vigorous, upright canes carry glossy, deep green foliage. Zones 5 to 9.

HOW TO USE

You'll most often see 'Parade' used as an 8- to 10-foot climber, although it can also make a large, somewhat open shrub that's normally 6 to 8 feet tall and about as wide. It's a delightful choice for adorning a pillar, fence, trellis, or archway with months of color and fragrance. Its moderate growth rate makes it particularly well suited to smaller gardens, where a more rampant rose could become a maintenance problem. Removing the older wood each year and deadheading regularly will encourage healthy growth and good rebloom. 'Parade' normally isn't bothered by diseases.

'Party Girl'

Miniature. Saville, 1979.

The delicately shaded blooms of this pretty miniature blend beautifully into any pastel color scheme. Long, pointed buds unfurl into double, high-centered flowers that are just 1 to 1½ inches across. The petals are usually a soft shade of peachy yellow, lightly blushed with pale pink; in hot climates, they tend to fade quickly to creamy white. Held singly or in clusters, the moderately fragrant flowers appear over a long season, usually starting in late spring or early summer and continuing into fall. Medium to deep green, glossy leaves are borne on branching stems. Zones 6 to 10.

HOW TO USE

'Party Girl' tends to form a compact bush that's 12 to 18 inches tall and about as wide. It makes a charming edging plant for a walkway, foundation planting, bed, or border, and it looks lovely in containers, too! Sweet alyssum *(Lobularia maritima)* makes a great companion, either in its normal white-flowered form or in purple or pink for more of a contrast; just make sure you leave space around the rose for good air circulation. Disease resistance is moderate: Powdery mildew can be a problem if you don't take preventive measures.

ARS Award of Excellence for Miniature Roses 1981; Miniature Rose Hall of Fame 1999

❦ 'Pascali'

Syn. 'Blanche Pasca'; LENip
Hybrid tea. Lens, 1963.

'Pascali' has long set the standard for white hybrid tea roses and remains the favorite of many gardeners. Tapered, creamy buds tinged with green open into double, high-centered flowers that are 3 to 4 inches across. Depending on growing conditions, the petals are snowy white to creamy white, often shading to ivory at the base, and occasionally they show a faint pink tinge. Reports of its fragrance range from light to moderate. Flowers first appear in late spring or early summer, with good rebloom through the rest of the summer and into fall. Moderately thorny canes carry semiglossy, deep green leaves. Zones 6 to 9.

HOW TO USE

Like many hybrid tea roses, 'Pascali' tends to have a rather narrow, upright habit. Height can range anywhere from 3 to 6 feet or more, with a spread of 1 to 4 feet. It's a good idea to find a bush already growing in conditions similar to yours so that you can see what size to expect in your area; otherwise, figure an average of about 4 feet by 2 feet and plan accordingly. This rose produces a steady supply of flowers for cutting, but it's also pretty in a bed or border, especially when planted in a drift of three or more to create a bushier effect. Disease resistance is normally excellent, although both black spot and powdery mildew have been reported on unprotected plants in some areas.

All-America Rose Selection 1969; World Rose Hall of Fame 1991

❦ 'Pat Austin'

Syn. AUSmum
Shrub. Austin, 1997.

The beautiful blooms of this English rose add both striking color and great fragrance to the garden. Egg-shaped, peach-orange buds blushed with red open into double, deeply cupped flowers that are 3 to 5 inches across, with large petals that are coppery orange on top and peachy yellow underneath. The clustered flowers are held on rather slender stems, so they tend to nod: a trait that some find appealing and others find annoying. Graced with a moderate to strong, fruity-rosy fragrance, the flowers first appear in late spring to early summer, with good repeat through summer into fall. Moderately thorny, arching canes bear glossy, medium to deep green foliage. Zones 5 to 9.

HOW TO USE

'Pat Austin' forms a rounded to spreading bush that's generally 3 to 5 feet tall and about as wide. It's a distinctive addition to beds and borders, where it blends beautifully with a wide range of other colors. Pair it with yellow and pinks for a soft look, or create a striking Southwest-style combination by combining it with blues and deep purples, such as lavenders and butterfly bush (perhaps *Buddleia davidii* 'Black Knight'). Disease resistance is moderate to good; take preventive measures against black spot.

✿ 'Paul Neyron'

Hybrid perpetual. Levet, 1869.

If you like your rose blooms big and bold, this hybrid perpetual is for you! Sometimes referred to as "the cabbage rose" (a term that correctly belongs to the centifolia class), 'Paul Neyron' produces oval to rounded buds that can be as big as golf balls. These open to display fully double, cupped blooms 5 to 6 inches in diameter (or even up to 7 inches, in some cases) and packed with swirls of rosy pink petals. Some describe the scent as mild, while others report it as being strong. Flowers are normally produced singly atop the stems. Expect the best show of bloom in late spring and fall, with some repeat bloom in between. Nearly thornless stems bear rich green, semiglossy leaves. Zones 5 to 8.

HOW TO USE

'Paul Neyron' generally has a strongly upright habit, reaching 4 to 6 feet tall and 3 to 4 feet wide. You'll hear conflicting reports about this rose's vigor: some claim it is a strong plant with sturdy canes, whereas others dismiss it as weak and spindly. It's a good idea to find a bush already growing in conditions similar to yours so that you can see what to expect in your area. Where it grows well, 'Paul Neyron' is a striking sight at the back of a mixed border (it looks rather like a peony in bloom!), and it makes an interesting hedge, too. Disease resistance also varies: in some gardens it is excellent, but black spot, mildew, and rust have all been reported in areas where these diseases are common, so it's smart to take preventive measures.

❦ 'Paul's Himalayan Musk Rambler'

Hybrid musk. Paul, 1916.

Definitely not a rose for a small garden, this hybrid musk needs lots of room to reach its full glory. Oval, medium pink buds open into double rosettes in a pretty shade of light pink. The moderately fragrant flowers are rather small — each is just 1½ inches across — but they're grouped into large, open, trailing clusters that create a glorious display for several weeks in early to midsummer. Long, slender, thorny canes carry light green leaves. Zones 4 to 9.

HOW TO USE

'Paul's Himalayan Musk Rambler' is unquestionably vigorous, easily scrambling to heights of 20 to 30 feet. Give this rose a very sturdy support, and a site where you will not have to resort to heavy pruning to control its size. It's happiest when allowed to clamber into a tree, but it can also make a handsome covering for an outbuilding if given some guidance. 'Paul's Himalayan Musk Rambler' is seldom seriously affected by diseases.

❦ 'Peace'

Syns. 'Gioia', 'Gloria Dei', 'Mme. A. Meilland'
Hybrid tea. Meilland, 1945.

Easily the best-selling hybrid tea to date, 'Peace' has been known and loved by generations of gardeners for its lovely color and large blooms. Plump, pink-blushed, yellow buds open to display double, 5- to 6-inch flowers that begin with high centers and open to a cupped form. You'll notice that just about every photograph of this rose looks different, because the colors can vary depending on growing conditions. Generally, the petals are soft yellow edged with pink; in cool, cloudy conditions, the blooms may appear mostly a golden yellow, while sun and heat fade the yellow and darken the pink. Fragrance is normally on the light side, though it may be more noticeable when the blooms are new. Expect a good show in late spring or early summer, with good repeat through the rest of the season. Glossy, deep green leaves are carried on moderately thorny canes. Zones 5 to 9.

HOW TO USE

'Peace' forms an upright bush, normally growing 4 to 5 feet tall and 3 to 4 feet across. Its long-lasting blooms make a favorite for the cutting garden: a single flower is enough to fill a small vase! It also makes a distinctive addition to beds and borders, looking particularly pretty with blue-flowered companions, such as catmints (*Nepeta* spp.). Disease resistance is moderate; take preventive measures against black spot and mildew if these problems are common in your area.

'Climbing Peace' (Brandy, 1950) is a beautiful rose where it's happy, reaching up to 20 feet in height. Gardeners in some areas complain of mostly leafy growth and sparse flowering, however; this selection seems to perform best in warmer climates.

All-America Rose Selection 1946; World Rose Hall of Fame 1976

❦ 'Pearl Meidiland'

Syns. 'Perle Meillandécor'; MEIplatin
Shrub. Meilland, 1989.

The next time you're looking for a low-growing, easy-care plant to fill space or cover a gentle slope, look past the traditional creeping junipers to this charming shrub rose. 'Pearl Meidiland' produces clusters of egg-shaped to oval buds that open into double, 2½-inch blooms that begin with high centers and open to a flattened form. New blooms are pale pink, aging to near white. They lack fragrance, but they make up for that by blooming in abundance over a long season: expect nearly continuous bloom from late spring to fall in most areas. Long, trailing stems are amply clad in glossy, deep green leaves. Zones 4 to 9.

HOW TO USE

'Pearl Meidiland' has a vigorous, spreading habit, forming a low mound that's only 2 to 3 feet tall but 4 to 6 feet across. It's a terrific choice for covering a slight slope, and it also looks super cascading over a low wall or out of a large planter. Disease resistance is generally quite good, although a bit of black spot may appear in some areas.

❦ 'Penelope'

Hybrid musk. Pemberton, 1924.

This hybrid musk may not be the showiest rose around, but it definitely adds a touch of elegance to any landscape. Pointed, peachy pink buds open into semi-double, cupped to flattened flowers that are 2 to 3 inches across. The new blooms are normally pale pink, aging to cream or white, and are accented with eye-catching yellow stamens. Reports of its fragrance vary from slight to strong; most gardeners agree that the scent is at least moderate. The clustered flowers appear over a long season, with a profuse display in late spring and usually again in fall, with moderate to good repeat in between. Attractive pinkish orange hips ripen among the blooms at the end of the season. Moderately thorny, branching canes bear shiny, deep green leaves that may be tinged with purple when new. Zones 6 to 10.

HOW TO USE

When left to grow at will, 'Penelope' forms a spreading, somewhat open mound that's normally 5 to 6 feet tall and about as wide. In warm areas, it may grow to 8 feet tall and wide as a shrub, or it can be trained on a pillar, trellis, or arbor. With regular pruning, however, 'Penelope' forms a much bushier, more compact plant. It's pretty enough to stand alone as an accent, but it also looks super when grown in groups, either as a mass planting or as a hedge. 'Penelope' can tolerate a bit of shade, but it may be more susceptible to mildew there; in most conditions, diseases aren't a problem.

❦ 'Perle d'Or'

Syn. 'Yellow Cécile Brünner'
Polyantha. Rambaux, 1884.

'Perle d'Or' is normally classified as a polyantha, but you'll also find it listed in some references as a China rose. By either classification, this distinctive rose is a charming addition to the garden. Small, pointed, peach pink buds produce double, 1- to 1½-inch blooms full of narrow petals that curl back to create a pompom-like form. New flowers are soft yellow to creamy peach, fading to nearly white in hot, sunny conditions. The moderately to richly fragrant, clustered flowers appear in abundance in mid- to late spring, followed by good repeat through the rest of the growing season. Nearly thornless stems carry medium green, semiglossy leaves. Zones 6 to 10.

HOW TO USE

'Perle d'Or' has an upright, bushy habit, creating a well-branched shrub that's generally 3 to 4 feet tall and about as wide, though it can reach as much as 6 to 8 feet in height and spread in the warmest parts of its range. With its soft color and pleasing fragrance, this rose is a delightful addition to a mixed border, particularly when paired with blue flowers such as catmints (*Nepeta* spp.) and sages (*Salvia* spp.). 'Perle d'Or' also looks super planted in groups of three or more as a landscape accent. Black spot may occur but usually isn't serious; otherwise, this rose is usually quite healthy.

'Peter Frankenfeld'

Hybrid tea. Kordes, 1966.

If you're looking for a hybrid tea with large, perfectly formed flowers and rich color, 'Peter Frankenfeld' may be just the rose for you. Deep reddish pink, tapered buds unfurl to display double, high-centered blooms that are 4 to 5 inches across, in a rich shade of rose-pink. The scent is mild at most, but the bush is quite generous with its flowers, starting in late spring to early summer with good to excellent repeat into fall. Medium green, semiglossy foliage is carried on moderately thorny canes. Zones 5 to 9.

HOW TO USE

'Peter Frankenfeld' has an upright, branching habit, usually growing 4 to 5 feet tall and about 3 feet across. It's a natural for the cutting garden, but it's also pretty in beds and borders, especially when planted in groups of three or more to create a drift of color. Use it to add zip to a mostly pastel planting, or pair it with bright yellows and purples for an eye-catching combination. 'Peter Frankenfeld' generally has good disease resistance.

'Petite Pink Scotch'

Shrub. Found in 1949 by Batchelor, original date unknown.

This compact shrub certainly isn't one of the showiest roses available, but it's a charming, carefree addition to just about any landscape. Tiny buds pop open to reveal double, cupped to rosette-form flowers that are just ½ to 1 inch across, filled with medium to light pink petals that fade quickly to near white in strong sun. The clustered blooms have little or no fragrance, and the flowering season lasts for just a few weeks, starting in mid- to late spring. Very prickly, slender, trailing canes carry an ample covering of tiny, glossy, bright green leaves that may be evergreen in mild winters. The handsome form and foliage of this rose make it look great even when not in bloom. Zones 5 to 9.

HOW TO USE

'Petite Pink Scotch' forms a dense mound that grows 2 to 4 feet tall and 3 to 5 feet across. Let it cascade over a low wall or out of a raised bed, or use it as a groundcover on a gentle slope. It also makes a cute compact, informal hedge. Deadheading after bloom makes the bush look tidier but can be time-consuming; it's easiest to wait until the petals have thoroughly dried and brush them off with a gloved hand or a broom. If you're looking for a pretty but nonfussy rose for a low-maintenance area, definitely give this one some thought; it seldom needs pruning and is rarely bothered by disease problems.

❦ 'Phyllis Bide'

Climbing polyantha. Bide, 1923.

'Phyllis Bide' is classified by the American Rose Society as a climbing polyantha, but you may also find it listed in other references and catalogs as a multiflora rambler. By any name, this charming climber is a lovely sight during its long bloom season. Its pointed, yellow buds unfurl into small, semidouble, loosely cupped blooms that are about 2 inches across, starting in soft yellow and aging to cream lightly touched with peach or pink. Held in large, loose clusters, the lightly fragrant flowers first appear in late spring to early summer, with good repeat through the rest of the growing season. Arching, branching stems bear glossy, medium green leaves. Zones 6 to 9.

HOW TO USE

'Phyllis Bide' is a rather vigorous, upright rose, usually growing 6 to 10 feet tall as a climber. It's a delight for decorating a wall, fence, trellis, or pillar with months of bloom. With pruning, this climbing polyantha also adapts to life as a shrub that's about 6 feet tall and wide. 'Phyllis Bide' usually isn't seriously bothered by diseases.

❦ 'Pierre de Ronsard'

Syns. 'Eden', 'Eden Climber', 'Eden Rose 88', 'Grimpant Pierre de Ronsard'; MElviolin
Large-flowered climber. Meilland, 1987.

Officially known as 'Pierre de Ronsard', this rose in the Romantica Series is widely sold in the United States as 'Eden Climber'. Whatever you call it, you'll love its fabulous, old-fashioned flowers! Plump, egg-shaped, cream-colored buds tinged with pink or red open into 3-inch-wide, double, deeply cupped blooms that are creamy white blushed with pink. The flowers look as though they should be richly fragrant, but they generally have little scent. The show usually starts in early summer, with at least some repeat bloom well into fall. Moderately to lightly thorny stems bear glossy, rich green leaves. Zones 5 to 9.

HOW TO USE
'Pierre de Ronsard' is a moderately vigorous climber, normally growing 8 to 10 feet tall with support. Enjoy its opulent blooms on a wall, fence, trellis, pillar, or post. You could also grow this rose as a large shrub (about 6 feet tall and wide) at the back of a border, or as a specimen or screen. Diseases usually aren't a major problem.

❦ 'Pierrine'

Syn. MICpie
Miniature. Williams, 1988.

This cute miniature rose is a real charmer in both the garden and arrangements. Small, pointed buds open into classic hybrid tea-type blooms — double, with high centers — but each flower is just 1½ inches across. The color is normally in the medium pink range, but cool weather may intensify the hue to a deeper coral pink. Scent is slight at best. Held singly, the flowers appear in a generous show in early summer, with good repeat through the rest of the summer into fall. You may also see small orange hips on the bush in fall. Thorny stems carry medium green, semiglossy foliage. Zones 6 to 9.

HOW TO USE
'Pierrine' has an upright habit, forming a bushy plant that is generally 1 to 2 feet tall and about as wide. Its long-lasting flowers make it a splendid choice for the garden as well as for cutting. Enjoy it in beds, borders, and

foundation plantings as a color accent, or as an edging for a path or walk-way. 'Pierrine' looks great in containers, too. In pots or in the garden, a low carpet of sweet alyssum (Lobularia maritima) makes a pretty and fra-grant companion. Disease resistance is generally good.

❦ 'Pink Meidiland'

Syns. 'Schloss Heidegg'; MEIpoque
Shrub. Meilland, 1984.

This easy-care shrub rose will provide month after month of landscape interest. Pointed, red buds open to display single, saucer-shaped flowers that are 2 to 2½ inches across. The clustered blooms are bright pink with a distinct white eye around a crown of bright yellow stamens. The fra-grance is mild, at best. Look for a prolific flush of flowers in late spring or early summer, followed by moderate to good rebloom until frost. A crop of small, reddish orange hips extends the show well into winter. Semiglossy, medium green foliage is held on branching stems. Zones 5 to 9.

HOW TO USE
'Pink Meidiland' has an upright, bushy habit, forming a relatively com-pact shrub that generally grows 2 to 4 feet tall and about as wide. It looks super planted in groups of three or more, used alone as a landscape ac-cent, or combined with perennials and other plants in a mixed border. Set fairly close (2 to 3 feet apart), it also makes a nice informal hedge. 'Pink Meidiland' may develop some black spot if you don't take preventive measures, but otherwise disease problems usually aren't serious.

❦ 'Pink Parfait'

Grandiflora. Swim, 1960.

This lovely grandiflora has been around for many years, and with good reason: its delicately shaded blooms add a touch of class to any planting. Egg-shaped to tapered, reddish pink buds unfurl into double flowers that are 3½ to 4 inches across, starting with high centers and opening to a cupped form. The clustered blooms are various shades of pink or peachy pink, usually creamier in the center and relatively paler overall in hot weather. The fragrance is generally light, and either sweet or fruity. 'Pink Parfait' provides a generous display of flowers in late spring to early sum-mer, with good repeat through the rest of the season. Lightly thorny stems carry semiglossy, medium green leaves. Zones 5 to 9.

HOW TO USE

'Pink Parfait' forms an upright, shrubby bush that's generally 3 to 4 feet tall and 2 to 3 feet across. Enjoy its changing colors in a bed or border, paired with companions such as soft yellow lady's mantle *(Alchemilla mollis)* and purple-blue balloon flower *(Platycodon grandiflorus).* Don't forget to include a bush of 'Pink Parfait' in your cutting garden to have a supply of flowers to admire indoors. A site with a bit of afternoon shade will help keep the colors somewhat richer. 'Pink Parfait' normally doesn't have serious disease problems.

All-America Rose Selection 1961

❦ 'Playboy'

Syn. 'Cheerio'
Floribunda. Cocker, 1976.

Handsome in leaf and bold in bloom, this fiery floribunda is definitely one you can't overlook! Pointed, orange-red buds open into single, broadly cupped flowers that are about 3½ inches across. Centered with golden stamens, the bright blooms are a glowing combination of orange-yellow shaded with scarlet around the edge of each wavy petal. The clustered flowers usually have only a light, sweet scent, but they're produced in abundance in late spring or early summer with quick repeat through the rest of the summer into fall. Well-branched, moderately thorny canes carry very shiny, deep green leaves that make the bush look great even when it's not flowering. Zones 5 to 9.

HOW TO USE

'Playboy' has a bushy, upright habit, normally growing 3 to 4 feet tall and about as wide, though it can reach up to 6 feet in some areas. Not for the color cautious, this showy rose is a stunning sight in beds and borders that feature other hot-colored plants, such as cannas, dahlias, yellow and orange cosmos *(Cosmos sulphureus),* and annual sages, including *Salvia coccinea* and *S. splendens.* For a dramatic landscape accent, try it as a hedge or in a mass planting, or use it to light up a collection of evergreens in a foundation planting. 'Playboy' usually isn't seriously bothered by diseases.

❦ 'Playgirl'

Syn. MORplag
Floribunda. Moore, 1986.

There's nothing demure about the hot pink blooms of this dazzling floribunda. Its pointed buds open to reveal single, saucer-shaped, 3-inch-wide
blooms that are a strong, bright pink accented with a crown of yellow stamens. Held singly or in small clusters, the flowers generally have little
scent, but they're produced freely over a long period, from late spring or
early summer well into fall. Semiglossy, medium green leaves are held on
lightly thorny canes. Zones 5 to 9.

HOW TO USE
'Playgirl' forms a bushy, upright, relatively compact shrub, generally
growing 3 to 4 feet tall and about as wide. It adds months of eye-catching
color to beds and borders. Use it to add zip to a mostly pastel planting, or
pair it with other bright flowers for an exciting display. If you're really ad-
venturous, consider combining it with the yellow-orange-scarlet blooms
of 'Playboy'! 'Playgirl' also makes a stunning low hedge, and it looks great
in large containers, too. Disease resistance is generally quite good.

❦ 'Playtime'

Syn. MORplati
Floribunda. Moore, 1989.

'Playtime' provides an amazing display of brilliant blooms for months of
knock-your-socks-off color. Produced singly or in small clusters, the
pointed buds of this floribunda open into single, nearly flat flowers that
are about 3 inches in diameter, in a vibrant shade of reddish orange accented with golden stamens in the center. The fragrance is usually mild at
best, but 'Playtime' makes up for that lack by blooming generously from
late spring or early summer well into fall. Rounded, orange-red hips extend the show into winter. Thorny stems carry glossy, dark green leaves.
Zones 5 to 9.

HOW TO USE
'Playtime' has an upright, bushy habit, forming a compact shrub that's
normally 2 to 3 feet tall and about as wide. Enjoy it in beds, borders and
foundation plantings combined with equally dramatic colors, such as

yellow-orange sunflower heliopsis *(Heliopsis helianthoides)* and scarlet Maltese cross *(Lychnis chalcedonica).* If that's a little too wild for your taste, try surrounding it with purple-leaved plants, such as purple fountain grass *(Pennisetum setaceum* 'Rubrum') and one or more of the many purple heucheras. Diseases usually aren't a serious problem.

❦ 'Polka'

Syns. 'Lord Byron', 'Polka 91', 'Scented Dawn'; MEItosier
Large-flowered climber. Meilland, 1996.

This climber in the Romantica Series combines the charm of an old-fashioned flower with the long flowering season of a modern rose. Pointed, peachy orange buds swirl open to reveal fully double, saucer-shaped, soft peach blooms about 3½ inches across, packed with slightly wavy petals. Held singly or in clusters, the flowers generally have a delightful fragrance. They appear in glorious profusion in late spring, with good repeat through the rest of the growing season. Thorny canes carry semiglossy, medium green leaves. Zones 5 to 9.

HOW TO USE

'Polka' has an upright habit. It's often used as a 6- to 12-foot climber, but with pruning, it can also adapt to life as a shrub that's 4 to 6 feet tall and wide. 'Polka' adds a long season of interest to the garden when trained on a pillar or against a wall or fence, or sited in the back of a mixed border paired with other soft colors. This rose appears to have excellent disease resistance.

❦ 'Poulsen's Pearl'

Floribunda. Poulsen, 1949.

'Poulsen's Pearl' is a pretty little floribunda that adds a touch of wild-rose charm to any garden. Pointed buds open to display single, saucer-shaped to nearly flat flowers that are 2½ to 3 inches across, in a soft shade of pink accented with a crown of reddish stamens. Fragrance is light to moderate. Held in clusters, the flowers first appear in late spring or early summer, with reliable repeat bloom through the rest of the summer and into fall. Sturdy, moderately thorny stems carry light to medium green, semiglossy leaves. Zones 5 to 9.

HOW   TO   USE

'Poulsen's Pearl' forms an upright, bushy, relatively compact shrub, generally growing 2½ to 3½ feet tall and about as wide. Enjoy its beauty in beds, borders, and foundation plantings; it looks particularly good planted in groups of three or more to create a drift of color. Try it in a cottage garden setting with other single-flowered roses, mixed with perennials, annuals, herbs, and bulbs. Diseases rarely bother 'Poulsen's Pearl'.

✿ 'Prairie Princess'

Shrub. Buck, 1972.

Cold-climate gardeners take note: this lovely shrub rose was bred and selected by Dr. Griffith Buck at Iowa State University for its outstanding hardiness, as well as its disease resistance. Egg-shaped, coral pink buds open into semidouble, 3-inch blooms that are a soft shade of orange-pink, touched with white at the center and accented with creamy yellow stamens. New blooms have a high center, opening to a broadly cupped form. Held singly or in small clusters, the slightly scented blooms appear in abundance starting in late spring, followed by regular flushes of flowers through the rest of the growing season. Orange-red hips extend the season of interest into winter. Semiglossy, medium green leaves are carried on thorny stems. Zones 3 to 9.

HOW   TO   USE

'Prairie Princess' has an upright, bushy habit. It's most commonly grown as a shrub, reaching 5 to 6 in height and 4 to 5 feet in spread. Enjoy it planted alone or in a mass planting as a landscape accent, or as a long-blooming hedge. It also adapts to training as a 6-foot climber if given support, such as a wall, fence, trellis, or post. Diseases generally don't cause serious problems.

✿ 'Priscilla Burton'

Syn. MACrat
Floribunda. McGredy, 1978.

The colors of this charming floribunda vary so widely, you'll rarely see two pictures — or even two actual blooms — that look exactly alike. Long, pointed buds open into cupped, semidouble blooms about 3 inches across, in shades of deep pink or red with a white center and lighter pink to silvery markings on the petals. Reports on its fragrance range from slight to strong. The clustered flowers first appear in late spring to early summer, with good repeat through the rest of the summer into fall. Thorny stems bear shiny, deep green leaves. Zones 5 to 9.

HOW TO USE

'Priscilla Burton' has an upright habit but can vary in size from 2 to 6 feet tall and 2 to 4 feet across, depending on the climate and on whether it is grafted or growing on its own roots. It's smart to find someone in your area who is already growing this rose to find out what size to expect before you choose a planting site. This rose's changeable color makes an interesting accent in a bed or border. It looks particularly pretty with silver-leaved companions, such as artemisias and lamb's ears *(Stachys byzantina)*. Black spot may be a problem if you don't take preventive measures; otherwise, disease resistance is generally good.

❦ 'Pristine'

Syn. JACpico
Hybrid tea. Warriner, 1978.

This hybrid tea is a favorite with many gardeners for its elegantly formed and delicately shaded blooms. Tapered, white buds tinged with red unfurl to display double, high-centered flowers up to 6 inches across. The white to cream petals are blushed with light to medium pink. Normally held singly, the flowers open quickly, displaying a cluster of orange-yellow stamens in the center. Fragrance is usually light to moderate. Flowers first appear in late spring or early summer, with good rebloom through the rest of the season. Thick, wickedly thorny canes carry large, deep green, glossy foliage. Zones 5 to 9.

HOW TO USE

'Pristine' has a tall, rather spreading habit, growing anywhere from 4 to 7 feet tall and 3 to 6 feet wide. In some areas, this vigorous rose can even be sprawling; pruning to inward-facing buds helps encourage more upright growth. Before you choose a planting site, try to find someone in your area who is already growing this rose to find out what to expect in your conditions. Enjoy the beautiful blooms at the back of a mixed border, perhaps paired with pink-flowered companions to echo the pink blush in the petals. 'Pristine' can be prone to black spot if you don't take preventive measures; otherwise, disease resistance is generally good.

❦ 'Prosperity'

Hybrid musk. Pemberton, 1919.

'Prosperity' can add a touch of elegance to any garden, but this hybrid musk looks particularly pretty in lightly shaded areas, where its color remains richest. Small, pointed, pale pink buds open into semidouble to double, 2-inch rosettes that are creamy white with a hint of yellow at the base of the petals and golden stamens in the center. Newly opened blooms may be tinged with pink, especially in cool weather. Held in large clusters, the flowers have a moderate, sweet scent. The bloom display begins in mid- to late spring in most areas, usually with good repeat through the rest of the season; in some areas, though, it tends to produce a prolific display in spring and fall and take a rest in summer. Orange-red hips extend the show into winter. Moderately thorny, arching stems bear medium to deep green, glossy leaves. Zones 6 to 9.

HOW TO USE

Left on its own, 'Prosperity' produces a rather vase-shaped shrub, generally growing 4 to 5 feet tall and 4 to 7 feet wide. Regular pruning can encourage bushier, more compact growth. Either way, it's a beautiful sight at the back of a bed or border, or as a hedge. 'Prosperity' also responds to training as a climber, growing up to 8 to 10 feet tall given the support of a wall, fence, pillar, or arbor. It may develop a touch of mildew in shady conditions; otherwise, 'Prosperity' seldom has serious disease problems.

❦ 'Prospero'

Syn. AUSpero
Shrub. Austin, 1983.

The deeply hued blooms of this English rose are a stunning sight, in a color that's matched by few other modern roses. Plump, deep red buds open into very double, slightly domed to flattened rosettes that are 3 to 4 inches across, packed with folded petals that start out deep red and age to deep purple. Graced with a moderate to strong old-rose fragrance, the flowers first appear in late spring or early summer, with moderate to good repeat through the rest of the summer and into fall. Thorny canes carry matte, deep green leaves. Zones 5 to 10.

HOW TO USE

'Prospero' has a compact, upright-spreading habit, generally growing 2 to 4 feet tall and about as wide. It's a great choice for adding antique-rose charm to a small garden, where there isn't room for a larger-growing rose. The deep color of the blooms looks splendid in beds and borders when combined with lighter flowers or with silvery foliage, such as that of pinks (*Dianthus* spp.) or lamb's ears *(Stachys byzantina).* Disease resistance is moderate; powdery mildew or rust may develop if you don't take preventive measures.

'Queen Elizabeth'

Syns. 'Queen of England', 'The Queen Elizabeth Rose'
Grandiflora. Lammerts, 1954.

The first member of the grandiflora class, this adaptable, vigorous rose has been around for many years and is still widely available. Long, tapered buds unfurl to display double, high-centered to cupped, clear pink blooms that are about 4 inches across. Held singly or in clusters, the flowers normally have little or no fragrance. They appear in separate flushes from late spring or early summer through the rest of the growing season. Long, sturdy canes carry shiny, deep green leaves. Zones 5 to 9.

HOW TO USE

'Queen Elizabeth' produces a very vigorous, tall, narrow bush, growing 5 to 8 feet or more in height and just 2½ to 3½ feet across. It's a pretty sight at the back of a mixed border, behind tall perennials and moderate-sized shrubs. It makes an interesting tall hedge, too, and the long-lasting, long-stemmed blooms are excellent for cutting. 'Queen Elizabeth' generally has good disease resistance, but it's smart to take preventive measures against black spot.

'Climbing Queen Elizabeth' (Whisler, 1957) offers the same elegant, pink flowers — though sometimes much less generously — along 10- to 20-foot-long canes.

All-America Rose Selection 1955; World Rose Hall of Fame 1979

❀ 'Rainbow's End'

Syn. SAValife
Miniature. Saville, 1984.

This distinctive miniature is definitely an eye-catching addition to any landscape. Small, pointed buds unfurl to display double, high-centered blooms up to 2 inches across, with medium to deep yellow petals that have scarlet to hot pink edges, aging to white heavily flushed with scarlet or pink. The color contrast is most distinct in cool, sunny weather; on cloudy days, the flowers may be mostly yellow. Scent is slight at best. Usually produced in clusters, the flowers bloom abundantly for months, from late spring to frost. Well-branched, moderately thorny stems bear deep green, glossy leaves. Zones 5 to 9.

HOW TO USE

'Rainbow's End' has a bushy, compact habit, generally growing 1 to 2 feet tall and about as wide. It's an attention getter wherever you plant it: in a bed or border, as an edging for a path or walkway, or around a deck or patio. It looks super in containers, too. Disease resistance is generally good, but black spot may be a problem if you don't take preventive measures.

'Climbing Rainbow's End' (SAVaclend; Saville/O'Brien, 1998) offers the same multicolored blooms on long canes that can reach to 6 to 12 feet or more in height.

ARS Award of Excellence for Miniature Roses 1986

❀ 'Red Cascade'

Syn. MOORcap
Climbing miniature. Moore, 1976.

It may be classified as a climbing miniature, but don't let that fool you: this rose can fill quite a bit of space! Tiny, pointed buds pop open to reveal semidouble or double, ½- to 1-inch, blood red blooms that are cupped at first, opening to more of a saucer shape. Fragrance is usually mild at best. 'Red Cascade' produces a generous display of long-lasting, clustered flowers. The show generally starts in late spring, with excellent repeat until frost. Very thorny, trailing canes bear glossy, deep green foliage. Zones 5 to 9.

HOW TO USE

Though officially classified as a climber, this vigorous rose adapts to a variety of uses. Left unsupported, 'Red Cascade' forms a spreading mound that's about 3 feet tall and 5 to 10 feet in diameter. Let it trail down a slope or spill over a retaining wall. Trained against a support, such as a large trellis, pillar, or post, it can grow anywhere from 6 to 18 feet tall (expect the greater height in warm climates). Young plants look charming trailing out of windowboxes or hanging baskets, but be prepared to move them to a permanent spot after a year or two: they get large quickly. 'Red Cascade' also looks marvelous planted next to another red climber, such as once-blooming 'American Pillar'. Both mildew and black spot can mar the foliage some years, but most gardeners report moderate to good disease resistance.

ARS Award of Excellence for Miniature Roses 1976

❦ 'Red Ribbons'

Syns. 'Chilterns', 'Fiery Sunsation', 'Roselina'; KORtemma
Shrub. Kordes, 1998.

If you're looking for a low-growing, groundcover-type rose, this bright shrub belongs on your list of roses to consider. Deep red, egg-shaped buds open into semidouble, cupped to flat blooms that are 2 to 3 inches across, in a brilliant shade of red accented with a crown of golden stamens. Held in large clusters, the slightly scented flowers open quickly, but they appear in abundance from late spring or early summer into fall. Glossy, deep green foliage is held on moderately thorny stems. Zones 5 to 9.

HOW TO USE

'Red Ribbons' has a low, mound-forming habit, growing just 2 to 2½ feet tall but spreading 4 to 7 feet in diameter. It's well suited to covering a gentle slope or filling a low-maintenance area with months of bloom. Try planting it atop a low wall and letting it spill over the edge for a sheet of eye-catching color. Black spot has been reported in some areas, but otherwise disease resistance is usually quite good.

✿ 'Regensberg'

Syns. 'Buffalo Bill'; MACyoumis
Floribunda. McGredy, 1979.

One of a group of "handpainted" roses introduced by Sam McGredy, this charming floribunda offers delicately shaded blooms that are each marked slightly differently. 'Regensberg' produces light pink, egg-shaped buds that open into semidouble to double, cupped to flat flowers that are about 4½ inches across. The coloring varies depending on weather conditions and the age of the bloom, but the petals are generally rosy pink on top, often edged and/or streaked with white, with a white eye; the undersides of the petals are ivory to white. The color contrast of the petal markings tends to be most distinct on new blooms, especially in cool weather. Reports of its fragrance range from slight to strong. Held in small but abundant clusters, the flowers first appear in late spring to early summer, with good repeat bloom until fall. Slightly thorny stems bear shiny, deep green leaves. Zones 5 to 8.

HOW TO USE
'Regensberg' forms a compact, spreading shrub that's usually 18 to 30 inches tall and 2 to 3 feet across. It's a lovely sight in a bed or border, particularly when planted in a group of three or more to create a mass of color. It also works well as an edging for a walkway, as a border for a deck or patio, and in containers. Disease resistance is normally excellent.

✿ 'Reine des Violettes'

Syn. 'Queen of the Violets'
Hybrid perpetual. Millet-Malet, 1860.

This hybrid perpetual is a classic, prized by generations of gardeners for its unique color and intense fragrance. Plump buds open to reveal fully double, 3- to 5-inch flowers that have a flattened rosette form with a cluster of short, tightly incurved petals in the center. The flower color varies somewhat but is usually violet-red to rosy purple at first, aging to a soft purple; cool weather tends to bring out the richest hues. Held singly or in small clusters, the individual blooms aren't long lasting, but they are glorious when the bush is in full flower. The show is usually best in late spring to early summer, with good repeat through the rest of the season in some areas and only sparse rebloom in others. Matte, grayish green leaves are carried on nearly thornless stems. Zones 5 to 9.

HOW TO USE

'Reine des Violettes' has a somewhat bushy, upright habit. As a shrub, it can range from 5 to 8 feet tall and 3 to 6 feet wide, although hard pruning during the dormant season can encourage more compact growth. 'Reine des Violettes' also adapts to training as an 8- to 12-foot climber on a wall, trellis, or pillar. If you don't take preventive measures, black spot can be a problem in some areas, but the bush usually recovers, particularly when kept vigorous with good soil care and regular watering.

❦ 'Rêve d'Or'

Noisette. Ducher, 1869.

'Rêve d'Or' is a Noisette rose that adds a touch of elegance to warm-climate gardens. Peach-colored, egg-shaped buds often tinged with red open into semidouble to double, loosely ruffled blooms that are 3 to 4 inches across. The yellow flowers are flushed with peach when new (particularly in cool conditions), fading to a soft butter yellow. Held singly or in small clusters, the delightfully fragrant blooms appear in abundance in mid- to late spring, with moderate to good repeat in summer and often another good flush in fall. Slender, branching canes carry semiglossy, dark green leaves. Some gardeners report that the stems are almost thornless, but others describe their bushes as having plenty of thorns. Zones 7 to 10.

HOW TO USE

'Rêve d'Or' is a vigorous grower that is normally trained as a 10- to 18-foot climber on a wall, tall pillar, trellis, arbor, or gazebo. Left unsupported, it can make a very large shrub, about 8 to 10 feet tall and 6 to 8 feet across. Disease resistance is generally good, although you may see some black spot or a touch of mildew if you don't take preventive measures.

❦ 'Rio Samba'

Syn. JACrite
Hybrid tea. Warriner, 1991.

The multihued blooms of this handsome hybrid tea aren't for everyone, but they are undeniably eye-catching. Tapered yellow buds blushed with scarlet spiral open into double, high-centered, 3- to 5-inch flowers. The yellow petals are edged with varying amounts of orange, red, or magenta, so each flower is different. Cooler conditions seem to bring out the richest hues; in very hot weather, blooms may be all yellow or quickly fade to pale yellow or cream with a pink blush. The slightly scented flowers may be held singly or in small clusters on long stems. Moderately thorny canes bear matte, medium to deep green leaves. Zones 5 to 10.

HOW TO USE

'Rio Samba' has an upright, somewhat rounded habit. It normally grows rather large, reaching anywhere from 5 to 8 feet tall and about as wide. Enjoy a single bush as an accent, or plant several together for a striking landscape accent. The colorful, long-stemmed blooms make 'Rio Samba' a good choice for the cutting garden, too. Disease resistance is generally good in most areas.

All-America Rose Selection 1993

❦ 'Rise 'n' Shine'

Syns. 'Golden Meillandina', 'Golden Sunblaze'
Miniature. Moore, 1977.

The cheerful color and elegant flower form of this popular miniature make it a favorite with gardeners and exhibitors alike. Tapered, golden buds unfurl to reveal double, high-centered blooms about 1½ inches across, in a clear medium yellow. The petals usually hold their color well but may fade to near ivory in strong sun. As they mature, the edges often roll back to create a point at the tip of each petal, giving the fully open bloom a starry or dahlia-like form. Held singly or in clusters, the mildly fragrant flowers first appear in late spring, and the bush is rarely out of bloom through the rest of the growing season. Medium green, semiglossy leaves are carried on fairly smooth stems. Zones 5 to 10.

HOW TO USE

'Rise 'n' Shine' has a bushy, upright habit, usually growing 1 to 2 feet tall and about as wide. It's hard to think of a bad way to use this marvelous mini! Enjoy it in beds, borders and foundation plantings, or use it to edge a path or a deck or patio. It's charming in containers and also provides ample blooms for small indoor arrangements. Try it in a hot-color planting with reds and oranges, or use it to perk up a planting of pastel pinks and blues. Disease resistance is moderate to good; black spot can be a problem if you don't take preventive measures.

ARS Award of Excellence for Miniature Roses 1978; Miniature Rose Hall of Fame 1999

❦ 'Robin Hood'

Syn. 'Robin des Bois'
Hybrid musk. Pemberton, 1927.

One of brightest of the hybrid musk roses, 'Robin Hood' offers a handsome show of cheerful color for months at a time. Small, pointed buds open into semidouble, slightly cupped blooms that are just ½ to 1 inch across. The individual flowers are tiny, but they are certainly showy, in an eye-catching shade of cherry red to reddish pink accented with a white eye and a crown of yellow stamens. Held in large, elongated clusters, the flowers have little or no scent, but they make up for that by blooming freely from late spring to frost. Tiny red hips extend the interest into winter. Moderately thorny, arching stems carry small, dark green leaves. Zones 6 to 10.

HOW TO USE

'Robin Hood' forms a dense, somewhat mounded shrub, growing anywhere from 4 to 7 feet tall and about as wide. Before you choose a planting site, try to find someone who's already growing this rose in your area so that you can find out what size to expect in your conditions. 'Robin Hood' is handsome enough to grow by itself as a landscape accent, but it also looks pretty in beds and borders, or used as a hedge. It can tolerate some light shade. Disease resistance is generally good.

❦ 'Robusta'

Syns. 'Kordes' Rose Robusta'; KORgosa
Shrub. Kordes, 1979.

It's hard to beat this splendid shrub rose, which combines the sturdy constitution of its *Rosa rugosa* parent with the glossy foliage and rich color of more modern roses. Sharply pointed buds open into single, cupped to saucer-shaped blooms that are about 2½ inches across. The glowing red petals are sometimes touched with white at the base, and they're accented with a crown of golden stamens. Fragrance is light at best. The single or clustered flowers appear in abundance over a long season, from late spring or early summer well into fall. Rounded, reddish hips extend the show into winter. Stout, thorny canes carry shiny, deep green leaves. Zones 4 to 8.

HOW TO USE

'Robusta' forms a bushy, upright shrub that grows 5 to 8 feet tall and 4 to 6 feet across. Planted alone, it makes a handsome landscape specimen or a stunning addition to a foundation planting; in groups, it's outstanding for providing knock-your-socks-off color as a mass planting or dense hedge. Disease resistance is usually moderate to good; it's smart to take preventive measures against powdery mildew and black spot.

❧ *Rosa banksiae*

Syns. *R. banksiana;* Banksian Rose, Banks' Rose, Lady Banks' Rose
Species. Cultivated since 1796.

Definitely not for the small property, this vigorous species rose offers a spectacular spring show in warm-climate gardens that can accommodate its rampant growth habit. There are actually four different forms, varying by flower color and flower form. *R. banksiae normalis* is considered to be the "wild" form, with single white flowers. *R. banksiae banksiae* (also known as 'Banksiae Alba', *R. banksiae alba, R. banksiae alba-plena,* White Banksia, or White Lady Banks' Rose) offers exceptionally fragrant, double white flowers. *R. banksiae lutea* (*R. banksiae lutea-plena,* Yellow Lady Banks' Rose) is the most commonly grown form, with double yellow flowers that are only slightly fragrant. *R. banksiae lutescens* has single light yellow blooms. All four have small, oval buds that open to clustered, 1-inch-wide, rosette-form flowers, usually blooming in early or midspring to late spring. Slender, thornless canes carry semievergreen to evergreen, shiny, dark green leaves with narrow leaflets. Zones 8 to 10.

HOW TO USE

All four forms of this rose have a vigorous, rambling habit, so they're usually used as 20- to 30-foot climbers. They need a sturdy support, such as a well-built pergola or arbor; they also like to scramble into trees. They are rarely bothered by diseases.

❦ *Rosa eglanteria*

Syns. *R. rubiginosa;* Eglantine, Sweet Brier Rose, Sweetbriar
Species. Cultivated before 1551.

Beloved by gardeners for hundreds of years, this fragrant, nonfussy
species rose still deserves a place in modern landscapes. Prickly-looking
buds open into single, flat blooms that are 1 to 2 inches across, in a clear
medium pink, with a pale pink to near white eye crowned with yellow
stamens. Held singly or in small clusters, the moderately fragrant flowers
appear just once a season, for a few weeks in late spring to early summer.
An abundant crop of slightly bristly, scarlet, oval hips adds interest from
late summer into winter. Arching, thorny canes carry dark green foliage
that has an apple-like fragrance, particularly noticeable after a rain or
during humid weather, or when the leaves are cut or rubbed. Zones
4 to 9.

HOW TO USE

R. eglanteria is a vigorous grower, forming a vase-shaped to spreading
shrub that's usually 6 to 10 feet tall and about as wide. Use it at the back of
a mixed border to add fragrance and multiseason interest; it's a natural
choice for cottage gardens, too. It also makes a charming informal hedge
or screen. Given support, it can adapt to life as a 10- to 15-foot climber.
Take preventive measures against black spot in areas where this fungal
disease is a problem; otherwise, disease resistance is generally good.

❦ *Rosa gallica officinalis*

Syns. 'Officinalis'; *R. x centifolia provincialis, R. gallica maxima, R.
gallica plena, R. officinalis, R. provincialis;* Apothecary's Rose, Double French Rose, Red Rose of Lancaster, Rose of Provins
Species. Cultivated before 1600.

This classic rose has been cultivated for centuries for use in medicines
and perfume. But this species isn't just practical: it's very pretty, too, offering several seasons of interest on a relatively compact bush. The show
starts in late spring to early summer, with three to four weeks of bloom.
The semidouble flowers are a rich, deep reddish pink; they start out
cupped and open almost flat, up to 4 inches across. The fresh blooms are
moderately fragrant; the dried petals are heavily scented. In fall, this rose
offers another showy display, this time of abundant, rounded to oval, orange-red hips. Throughout the growing season, rough, dark green leaves

with a grayish cast are carried on upright stems. The canes have bristles but few true thorns. Zones 3 to 10.

HOW TO USE

R. gallica officinalis forms a rounded bush that's usually 3 to 4 feet tall and wide. When grown on its own roots (not grafted), it can spread by suckers. The compact plants are excellent for small properties, in beds and borders, herb gardens, and cottage-garden plantings. This versatile rose also makes a great low, dense hedge. It is resistant to black spot but may get some mildew, particularly in fall.

    R. gallica versicolor (also known as *R. gallica rosa mundi, R. gallica variegata, R. mundi,* and 'Rosa Mundi') has irregular white striping on the reddish pink petals; otherwise, it is similar to *R. gallica officinalis.*

❧ *Rosa glauca*

Syns. *R. ferruginea, R. rubrifolia;* Red-leaved Rose
Species. Cultivated before 1830.

Most roses are prized for their flowers, but this species rose is grown primarily for its handsome foliage. Small, pointed buds pop open to reveal single, flat flowers about 1 inch across, in a medium to bright pink with a white eye crowned by yellow stamens. Scent is slight at best. The blooms are usually produced in small clusters, and they're held close to the canes. The flowering season is short — just a few weeks in late spring to early summer — but an abundant crop of oblong, red hips ripens in late summer and often lasts on the bush until the following spring. The most distinctive feature, though, is the foliage, which is usually blue-green with purplish veins and a light purplish blush over all. Sun brings out more of the purple or coppery tones, while leaves in shade are mostly blue-green. The leaves turn yellow or orange in fall. They are held on dark, arching, almost thornless stems. Zones 2 to 8.

HOW TO USE

R. glauca forms an upright, somewhat open, vase-shaped shrub. Its normal size in the garden is in the range of 6 to 9 feet tall and 5 to 8 feet wide, although established bushes left unpruned can reach 15 feet or more over time. Planted alone or at the back of a mixed border, *R. glauca* makes a wonderful accent with four-season interest. It tends to produce suckers, making it a good choice for creating a large, multiseason hedge or screen. This rose appreciates a bit of afternoon shade in hot climates and tolerates partial shade elsewhere. Disease resistance is generally good, although some areas report problems with leaf spots.

❧ *Rosa hugonis*

Syns. *R. xanthina;* Father Hugo Rose, Father Hugo's Rose, Golden Rose of China
Species. Cultivated since 1899.

One of the earliest roses to bloom in spring, this pretty species roses also offers interest in other seasons. Pointed buds open into single, cupped- or saucer-shaped flowers about 2 inches across, with slightly crumpled-looking, lemon yellow petals. They have little or no fragrance. Held singly on short stems, the blooms are produced close to the canes for several weeks, starting in early to midspring. Small, rounded, red hips appear among the leaves in late summer. Slender, prickly canes carry fernlike blue-green foliage that turns orange-bronze to deep red in fall. Zones 4 to 8.

HOW TO USE
R. hugonis has an upright, arching habit, growing anywhere from 4 to 9 feet tall and 4 to 7 feet across. It looks lovely in a mixed border, especially when paired with blue-flowered companions such as catmints (*Nepeta* spp.) or *Geranium* 'Johnson's Blue'. Be aware that this rose can spread by suckers; this trait makes it useful as an informal hedge or screen. *R. hugonis* is rarely bothered by diseases.

❧ 'Rosa Mundi' See *Rosa gallica officinalis* (*R. gallica versicolor*)

❧ 'Rosarium Uetersen'

Syns. 'Netersen', 'Rosarium Netersen', 'Rosarium Ueteresen'; KORtersen
Large-flowered climber. Kordes, 1977.

It may take a little searching to find this large-flowered climber, but it is worth the effort for these gorgeous, old-fashioned flowers. Red, egg-shaped buds open into very double, broad, flat blooms packed with deep coral pink petals. Individual 3- to 4-inch flowers are held in tight clusters, and they have a light to moderate, sweet or fruity fragrance. They appear in abundance in late spring or early summer, with moderate rebloom through the rest of the growing season. Shiny, medium green foliage is carried on upright, thorny stems. Zone 4 to 9.

HOW TO USE
'Rosarium Uetersen' (pronounced something like *row-SAIR-ee-um OOT-er-sen*) is most often used as an 8- to 12-foot climber. Enjoy its exquisite flowers at eye level by training it against a wall or fence, or on an arbor or pillar. Left unsupported, this rose will form a shrub that's 6 to 8 feet tall and 4 to 6 feet across — a handsome landscape accent if you have the room! 'Rosarium Uetersen' is generally quite disease resistant.

❧ *Rosa roxburghii*

Syns. *R. microphylla, R. roxburghii plena;* Burr Rose, Chestnut Rose, Chinquapin Rose
Species. Cultivated before 1814.

This species rose gets one of its common names, chestnut rose, from the likeness between its prickle-encased fruits and those of the chestnut tree. Its plump buds, which are also covered with prickles, open into double rosettes that can range in size from 2 to 4 inches in diameter. Usually borne singly on short stems, the blooms are deep pink in the center and lighter pink on the outside. Reports on the fragrance vary from slight to strong. Expect a good display of flowers in mid- to late spring. Repeat bloom is generally best in warm areas, especially when the plants are deadheaded; elsewhere, rebloom tends to be sporadic. Warm-climate gardeners also tend to see the best fruit set, in the form of prickly, rounded, green to orange hips. Small, medium green leaves with many leaflets are carried on arching, thorny canes that have peeling bark when older. Zones 6 to 9.

HOW TO USE
R. roxburghii produces a bushy, mounding shrub that can grow anywhere from 3 to 10 feet tall and 4 to 15 feet across, depending on climate. Pruning can help keep the bush more compact, as can planting in light shade. It looks great in shrub borders and in mixed borders; be aware that it spreads by suckers, though. Disease resistance is generally excellent.

R. roxburghii normalis is the once-blooming, "wild" form of this rose, with single, light pink flowers. It is often more vigorous than the double-flowered form.

❧ *Rosa rugosa*

Syns. Beach Rose, Hedgehog Rose, Japanese Rose, Kiska Rose, Rugosa Rose, Tomato Rose
Species. Cultivated before 1799.

If you're looking for a sturdy, reliable rose that will provide lots of interest but need little care, this species could be a great choice for you! Long, tapered buds produced singly or in clusters open into single, saucer-shaped blooms that are 3 to 4 inches across, usually in shades of purplish pink or white accented with cream-colored stamens. Opinions on the fragrance vary, but most gardeners can detect at least a moderate scent. In many areas, this is one of the first roses to start blooming (in mid- to late spring) and the last to stop; in fact, the late-season flowers often open next to the large, rounded, red fruits that have developed from earlier blooms. Sturdy, very prickly canes carry deeply veined, glossy, dark green leaves that turn bright yellow, orange, or red in fall. Zones 2 to 9.

HOW TO USE

R. rugosa forms a dense rounded shrub that can grow anywhere from 4 to 12 feet tall and about as wide. Look for a bush already growing in your area to see what size to expect in your conditions. If you want good rose-hip production, set out at least two seed-grown plants, or two different cultivars, for cross-pollination. It's perfect for creating a dense hedge or screen, because it spreads by suckering. In the Deep South, this species seems to grow best when grafted onto the roots of 'Fortuniana'. *R. rugosa* plants are sensitive to many sprays and to overfertilization, so it's best to leave them alone. These tough roses can tolerate some shade, as well as difficult sites such as seaside gardens and plantings along streets and parking lots. Disease resistance is generally excellent.

R. rugosa alba has clear white, single flowers. *R. rugosa rubra* is a vigorous form with bright magenta-purple, single blooms.

❧ *Rosa sericea pteracantha*

Syns. *R. omeiensis pteracantha;* Wingthorn Rose
Species. Cultivated since 1890.

Many gardeners consider thorns to be a nuisance — particularly at pruning time — but here's a species you'll grow *for* its beautiful thorns! Small buds open into single, flat, white flowers about 2 inches across, with little or no fragrance. Held in loose clusters on stems at least 2 years old, the blooms appear for just a few weeks (mid- to late spring in most areas), followed by small, oval, orange-red hips later in the season. Fine-textured, gray-green leaves are held on the arching stems. The real attraction of this rose, though, is the large, broad, blood red thorns that appear on the first-year stems; after their first season, the thorns turn brown and aren't especially attractive. Zones 5 to 9.

HOW TO USE

R. sericea pteracantha has a narrow, upright to vase-shaped habit, reaching 8 to 12 feet tall and 6 to 8 feet wide if left unpruned. To get the best display of colorful thorns, though, it's best to prune the bushes hard or even cut all the growth down to the ground in late winter. This rose makes an interesting accent planted alone or in a mixed border. It can tolerate light shade and is seldom bothered by serious disease problems.

❧ *Rosa setigera*

Syns. *R. fenestrata, R. trifoliata;* Prairie Rose
Species. Cultivated since 1810.

This pretty North American native rose tends to grow rather large, but its simple flowers give it a dainty effect during its summer bloom display. *R. setigera* produces small clusters of bright pink buds, which open to reveal single, flat, 2- to 3-inch-wide flowers that have deep to light pink petals crowned with golden stamens. Some gardeners can't detect any scent at all, but others describe this rose as having a strong, sweet perfume. Bloom time varies from mid- to late summer, depending on where you live, and is followed by a display of small, red, rounded hips. Long canes with moderately thorny canes carry matte, dark green leaves (each with three leaflets) that turn reddish in fall. Zones 4 to 9.

HOW TO USE

R. setigera is a vigorous grower, normally forming a large, sprawling shrub that can grow anywhere from 5 to 20 or more feet tall and about as wide. That makes it too large for most properties, but fortunately, it also adapts to training as a 15- to 30-foot climber. Give it the support of a large fence, arbor, or gazebo, or let it scramble up into trees. *R. setigera* has good disease resistance.

❦ *Rosa spinosissima*

Syns. *R. illinoensis, R. pimpinellifolia;* Burnet Rose, Scotch Rose
Species. Cultivated before 1600.

As you may guess from its name, *R. spinosissima* is amply armed with very spiny stems, but you may not know that it's also a very charming and adaptable species rose. Small buds open into single, flat, 1- to 2-inch flowers, usually with cream-colored to white petals surrounding golden yellow stamens. Produced singly along the canes in mid- to late spring, the blooms generally have a light, sweet scent. Rounded, purplish black hips ripen in late summer. Thorny and bristly canes bear small, gray-green leaves. Zones 3 to 8.

HOW TO USE

R. spinosissima forms an arching or mounding, suckering bush that may grow 2 to 6 feet tall and 4 to 7 feet across; expect the greatest size in rich soil. Its spiny nature makes it a natural choice for an informal hedge. It also adapts to container growing, but make sure you site it where the thorns won't snag passersby. This rose tolerates poor soil and light shade and is seldom bothered by diseases.

❦ *Rosa virginiana*

Syns. *R. lucida;* Virginia Rose
Species. Cultivated before 1807.

The suckering habit of this native North American rose makes it unsuitable for a small garden, but if you have the space, it's a lovely choice for multiseason interest. Pointed buds generally produced in clusters open to reveal single, flat, 2-inch-wide flowers with clear pink petals crowned by bright yellow stamens. Fragrance can range from slight to strong, because of seedling variation. Bloom time also varies, depending on where you live, but it usually lasts for several weeks in early to midsummer. Shiny, red, cherry-sized fruits ripen in late summer to fall and last well into winter. Often red tinged in spring, the foliage is shiny and light green in the summer; in fall, it may turn purple, red, orange, or yellow. The arching canes vary in their thorniness, again because of the natural variation in seed-grown plants. Zones 3 to 8.

HOW TO USE

R. virginiana is a fast-growing rose with a bushy, upright habit. Height is 5 to 7 feet and the spread of a single bush is 3 to 4 feet, but this rose produces lots of suckers, so it can form a dense thicket over time. That makes it useful as a broad screen or mass planting, especially in sites where most other roses don't thrive, such as lightly shaded areas or seaside gardens. Disease resistance is generally excellent.

❦ *Rosa wichurana*

Syns. *R. bracteata, R. luciae, R. mokanensis, R. taquetii*; Memorial Rose
Species. Cultivated since 1891.

This glossy-leaved species rose is the ancestor of many of today's best-loved roses, but it's also worth growing in its own right if you have the space. Small, clustered buds open into single, flat flowers up to 2 inches across, with white petals and golden stamens. Fragrance is generally at least moderate; some describe it as sweet, and others say it is fruity. It is one of the later roses to bloom, generally flowering in mid- to late summer, followed by small, orange-red, egg-shaped hips. Long, flexible, thorny canes carry glossy, deep green, semievergreen to evergreen leaves. Zones 5 to 9.

HOW TO USE

Left unsupported, *R. wichurana* tends to form a spreading mound up to 6 feet tall. Its stems tend to root wherever they touch the ground, so one bush can easily spread to 20 feet wide over time. It looks super sprawling down a slope. It also likes to scramble up into shrubs and trees, where it can climb 10 to 20 feet in height. Diseases rarely bother this rose.

❦ 'Rose de Rescht'

Portland. Reintroduced in 1940s.

With its many-petaled flowers, intense fragrance, and compact growth habit, this Portland is a marvelous addition to an existing old-rose collection — or a great choice to start one. Plump, deep reddish pink buds held in small clusters open into very full, domed rosettes that are 2 to 3 inches across. The color is somewhat variable, depending on the weather, but is generally an intense reddish pink with purplish tints. The flowers are graced with a strong old-rose fragrance. Expect a splendid show in late spring or early summer, usually with additional flushes of repeat bloom through the rest of the summer and into fall. Thorny stems are amply clad in matte, dark green foliage. Zones 5 to 8.

HOW TO USE

'Rose de Rescht' forms a bushy, domed mound that's just 3 to 4 feet tall and wide. This compact size makes it an excellent choice for small gardens, but it also deserves a place in larger gardens as well as in beds, borders, foundation plantings, and even large containers. It looks particularly pretty with silver-leaved companions, such as artemisias and lamb's ears *(Stachys byzantina)*. Black spot, mildew, and rust have all been reported. These diseases generally aren't serious enough to permanently weaken the bush, but it's still wise to consider taking preventive measures.

❦ 'Rose du Roi'

Syn. 'Lee's Crimson Perpetual'
Portland. Lelieur, 1815.

This richly perfumed Portland is a parent of many of the earliest hybrid perpetual roses. Rounded, red buds open to reveal double, flattened rosettes that are 3 to 4 inches across, with tightly incurved center petals. Bright red, often with some purple shading, the flowers have a strong old-rose fragrance. They appear in abundance in early summer, with moderate to good repeat into fall. Thorny stems bear matte, dark green leaves. Zones 6 to 9.

HOW TO USE

'Rose du Roi' has a low, somewhat spreading habit, growing 3 to 4 feet tall and about as wide. It's ideal for a mixed border or cottage garden setting, and it makes a charming compact, informal hedge. It's also attractive in a large planter. Both powdery mildew and black spot have been reported, so take preventive measures if these diseases are common in your area.

❦ 'Roseraie de l'Hay'

Hybrid rugosa. Cochet-Cochet, 1901.

One of the most popular hybrid rugosa roses, 'Roseraie de l'Hay' is a great choice for adding multiseason interest to any landscape. Long, pointed buds unfurl to reveal semidouble to double, loosely ruffled blooms that are 3 to 4 inches across, with reddish purple to magenta-purple petals. As they mature, the flowers open flat to reveal light yellow stamens. Fragrance is generally intense, with spicy or spicy-sweet overtones. Flowering starts with an excellent display in late spring, with moderate to excellent repeat continuing into fall. Don't expect a good display of hips from this selection, though. Sturdy, prickly stems carry deeply veined, rich green leaves that turn yellow or orange-yellow in fall. Zones 3 to 8.

HOW TO USE

'Roseraie de l'Hay' produces a rounded bush that's normally 5 to 8 feet tall and about as wide. Its dense form and thorny stems make it a natural for hedges; it's also wonderful planted in masses to screen an unpleasant view, or used at the back of a large border. This sturdy rose can tolerate the tough conditions of seaside gardens and exposed sites. Disease resistance is generally quite good.

❦ 'Royal Sunset'

Large-flowered climber. Morey, 1960.

This large-flowered climber has been around for more than forty years, and with good reason; few other selections come close its distinctive color. Pointed, orange buds open into semidouble to double, high-centered, 4- to 5-inch flowers that open to a cupped form, aging through shades of peach to peachy pink. Most gardeners rave about the intense, fruity fragrance, but a few describe the scent as only mild to moderate. Held singly or in small clusters, the blooms appear on both new and old stems, so expect a generous display from late spring or early summer well into fall. Thorny, reddish canes carry shiny, dark green leaves. Zones 6 to 10.

HOW TO USE

You'll most often see 'Royal Sunset' used as an 8- to 15-foot climber. It's lovely trained on an arch or arbor, or against a fence or large trellis. With regular pruning, this rose also adapts to life as a 6- to 8-foot-tall and wide shrub, making an eye-catching accent at the back of a mixed border. Blue- and yellow-flowered partners make especially pretty companions. Black spot may cause some leaf damage if you don't take preventive measures in humid areas; otherwise, disease resistance is generally excellent.

❦ 'Rugosa Magnifica'

Hybrid rugosa. Van Fleet, 1905.

It may not be as widely available as many other hybrid rugosa roses, but 'Rugosa Magnifica' is certainly worth searching for. Tapered buds unfurl to reveal loosely double, nearly flat flowers that are 3 to 4 inches across, with magenta-red petals accented by a crown of yellow stamens. The fragrance is on the spicy side and ranges from moderate to strong. 'Rugosa Magnifica' blooms abundantly in late spring or early summer, with good repeat through the rest of the season until frost. Large, showy, orange hips add interest well into winter. Thorny stems bear deeply veined, medium green leaves. Zones 4 to 8.

HOW TO USE

'Rugosa Magnifica' has a bushy, rather spreading habit, growing 4 to 5 feet tall and about as wide. It makes a handsome multiseason landscape accent, either planted alone or set out in groups as a screen or hedge. Its ruffled blooms and wonderful perfume also make it an excellent addition to a cottage-style garden. Disease resistance is generally excellent.

❦ 'Russelliana'

Syns. 'Old Spanish Rose', 'Russell's Cottage Rose', 'Scarlet Grevillea', 'Souvenir de la Bataille de Marengo'
Hybrid multiflora. Introduced before 1837.

In the past, this sturdy hybrid multiflora was often used as the rootstock for grafted roses, and it's still a fairly common sight in cemeteries and on older properties. Plump buds open into fully double, flat flowers about 3 inches in diameter. The clustered blooms are an intense pinkish red color, sometimes marked with white; as they age, they fade to light purplish pink. Graced with a moderate to strong old-rose perfume, the flowers usually appear only once a season, in mid- to late spring or early to mid-summer, depending on where you live. Look for large, rounded, orange-red hips to ripen in late summer to fall. Long, very thorny canes carry deeply veined, dark gray-green foliage. Zones 5 to 9.

HOW TO USE

Without support, 'Russelliana' grows as a mounded shrub that's 6 to 12 feet tall and wide. It may be too large for many gardens, but it makes a handsome landscape accent if you have the space for it. This rose also works well as a climber when trained on a sturdy structure or allowed to scramble up into trees, where it can grow 10 to 20 feet tall. Mildew may appear in some areas, but normally 'Russelliana' has excellent disease resistance.

᭥ 'Salet'

Moss. Lacharme, 1854.

'Salet' may not have as much of the "mossy" outgrowth its relatives are known for, but it's one of the most reliably repeat-blooming of the moss class. Lightly mossed, rounded buds open into very double, broadly cupped to flat flowers that are 2½ to 3½ inches in diameter. Each ruffled bloom is composed of irregular swirls of fairly narrow petals surrounding a loose "button" of incurved center petals. The color is generally medium rose-pink aging to lighter pink, with the richest hues in cool weather. Graced with a strong, rather sweet scent, the flowers appear in abundance in late spring or early summer, usually followed by two or more additional flushes of bloom in late summer or fall. Zones 5 to 8.

HOW TO USE

'Salet' forms a bushy, upright shrub that grows 4 to 5 feet tall and 3 to 4 feet across. Its informal, perfumed blooms add old-fashioned charm to a mixed border, and it makes an interesting hedge, too. 'Salet' is also a great addition to a cottage-garden setting, or to a collection of other antique roses. Disease resistance is generally moderate to good, but take preventive measures against black spot and powdery mildew in areas where these fungal diseases are common.

❦ 'Sally Holmes'

Shrub. Holmes, 1976.

'Sally Holmes' is classified by the American Rose Society as a shrub, but many catalogs still list it with the hybrid musk roses. Either way, it's a splendid choice for almost any garden. Pointed, coral pink to peach-colored buds open into single, flat, 4-inch flowers held in large clusters. The petals are creamy to pure white, with a light blush of pink or peach in cool conditions, and are accented by a crown of yellow stamens. Fragrance is only light to moderate, but you'll hardly notice that lack when you see the splendid display of flowers in late spring or early summer, followed by good repeat bloom through the rest of the season in most areas. Deep green, glossy leaves are carried on moderately thorny, arching canes. Zones 5 to 9.

HOW TO USE

In the cooler parts of its range, 'Sally Holmes' generally grows as an upright, bushy shrub that's 4 to 6 feet tall and about as wide. In milder climates, it can grow much larger, reaching to 10 feet tall and wide as a shrub or 10 to 15 feet tall as a climber. Try to find a bush already growing in your area so that you can see what size to expect in your conditions before you select a planting site. Enjoy it as a shrub at the back of a border or as a hedge, or train it as a climber on a wall, fence, trellis, pillar, or pergola post. This wonderful rose can tolerate slight shade. A bit of black spot may develop in some areas, but 'Sally Holmes' is normally quite disease resistant.

❦ 'Sarah Van Fleet'

Hybrid rugosa. Van Fleet, 1926.

'Sarah Van Fleet' may lack the showy hips of its hybrid rugosa relatives, but it certainly isn't stingy with its blooms! Tapered, reddish pink buds open to display semidouble to double, cupped to nearly flat, 3½-inch flowers with medium rose-pink petals and yellow stamens. The clustered blooms are blessed with a strong, spicy-sweet perfume, and they appear over a long season: from late spring to frost. Very thorny canes carry deeply veined, medium green, glossy leaves. Zones 5 to 9.

HOW TO USE

'Sarah Van Fleet' has an upright, bushy habit, growing anywhere from 5 to 8 feet tall and 4 to 6 feet across. It's great for planting at the back of a mixed border to add months of color and fragrance. It also makes a handsome and effective hedge or barrier — few intruders will attempt to push through those thorny stems! 'Sarah Van Fleet' is slightly less cold hardy than most rugosa roses but is better adapted to heat, making it a good choice for warm-climate gardens. Rust, black spot, and mildew have all been reported, but in most areas, disease resistance is moderate to good.

ꝏ 'Scabrosa'

Syns. 'Rugosa Superba', 'Superba'; *Rosa rugosa scabrosa*
Hybrid rugosa. Harkness, 1950.

Take all of the great qualities of *Rosa rugosa* — beautiful flowers, pleasing fragrance, long bloom season, handsome hips, and great fall color — put them on a more robust bush, and you have one of the best hybrid rugosas available today. Pointed, bright pink buds open into single, saucer-shaped to flat flowers about 5 inches across, with bright magenta-pink, slightly crinkled petals surrounding a crown of creamy yellow stamens. Some says the fragrance is slight, whereas others describe it as moderate to strong and spicy-sweet. Held singly or in clusters, the flowers first appear in late spring, with nearly continuous rebloom through the rest of the growing season. A generous display of large, plump, orange-red hips continues the show well into winter. Very thorny canes carry glossy, bright green leaves that turn reddish or golden in fall. Zones 3 to 8.

HOW TO USE

'Scabrosa' has a bushy, rather rounded habit. Some gardeners report that it stays rather compact — 3 to 4 feet tall and wide — but most find that 'Scabrosa' makes a large shrub, growing 5 to 7 feet tall and wide. Enjoy it as a multiseason mass planting or screen, or as an informal hedge. Diseases rarely bother 'Scabrosa'.

❦ 'Scarlet Meidiland'

Syns. 'Scarlet Meillandécor'; MEIkrotal
Shrub. Meilland, 1987.

If you're searching for a low-growing rose with high color impact, give this shrub rose a second look. Short, pointed buds open into double, cupped, 1- to 2-inch blooms with brilliant red petals and golden stamens. The clustered flowers don't have any fragrance, but they make up for that lack by producing masses of bloom in late spring or early summer, followed by moderate repeat through the rest of the growing season. Bright red hips ripen in late summer to fall and extend the show into winter. Trailing, thorny stems bear glossy, deep green leaves. Zones 4 to 9.

HOW TO USE

'Scarlet Meidiland' forms a spreading mound that's 2 to 4 feet tall and 5 to 7 feet or more in width. Use it to add multiseason interest to a large-scale mixed planting, or grow it in groups of three or more for a low-maintenance mass planting. It also looks handsome planted at the top of a low wall or slope and allowed to cascade over the side. Disease resistance is generally good, although black spot has been reported in some areas.

❦ 'Scentimental'

Syn. WEKplapep
Floribunda. Carruth, 1997.

Even gardeners who normally don't like striped blooms are excited by the dramatic flowers of this eye-catching floribunda. Large, egg-shaped buds open into double, high-centered to cupped blooms that are about 4½ inches across, with cream to white petals that are randomly striped and splashed with varying amounts of pink and red. Moderate to cool temperatures seem to bring out the most distinctive color contrast. The clustered flowers usually have a moderate to strong, spicy-sweet fragrance. Individual blooms tend to last only a day or two, but they appear in abundance starting in late spring or early summer, followed by additional flushes in summer and fall. Matte, medium to dark green leaves are carried on moderately thorny canes. Zones 5 to 9.

HOW TO USE

'Scentimental' forms an upright, somewhat rounded shrub that's usually 3 to 4 feet tall and 2 to 3 feet across, although it can grow 5 to 6 feet tall in favorable climates. It's a lovely addition to a bed or border, particularly when planted in groups of three or more bushes to create a drift of peppermint-swirled blooms. Highlight the flowers by giving them an all-green background, such as an underplanting of parsley and a backdrop of evergreens, or pair them with white flowers, such as a carpet of sweet alyssum *(Lobularia maritima)*. Disease resistance is generally good, although black spot can appear if you don't take preventive measures.

All-America Rose Selection 1997

✿ 'Scentsational'

Syns. SAVamor, SAVascent
Miniature. Saville, 1995.

Disappointed in the lack of fragrance in many miniature roses? Then you definitely need to give 'Scentsational' a try! Elegant, tapered buds unfurl to reveal double, hybrid tea–form flowers about 2 inches across, with pinkish lavender petals that may be tipped with deeper pink. Golden stamens are visible when the flowers are fully open. Held singly or in small clusters, the richly perfumed blooms first appear in late spring, with good repeat bloom through the rest of the growing season. Lightly thorny canes carry red-tinged new leaves that turn a semiglossy, medium green as they age. Zones 6 to 10.

HOW TO USE

'Scentsational' has an upright to somewhat spreading habit, generally growing 18 to 30 inches tall and 15 to 24 inches across. It's pretty in a bed or border, and it's a lovely addition to a cutting garden for small arrangements. To enjoy it to its fullest, site it in a raised bed or plant it in containers on a deck or patio so that you can easily enjoy the fragrance. Take preventive measures against black spot if you live where this disease is a common problem; otherwise, expect good disease resistance.

✿ 'Schneekoppe'

Syn. 'Snow Pavement'
Hybrid rugosa. Baum, 1984.

You're equally likely to find this hybrid rugosa listed as 'Schneekoppe' or 'Snow Pavement'; by either name, it's a wonderful choice for adding multiseason interest to a small garden. Pointed, light pink buds open to semi-double, broadly cupped, 3½-inch blooms with yellow stamens and white petals that are blushed with light pink or palest purple. Graced with a moderate to strong, spicy-sweet scent, the clustered blooms first appear in late spring or early summer, with good repeat through the rest of the summer and up to heavy frost. Orange-red hips begin to ripen in late summer and continue to add interest well into winter. Thorny canes carry deeply veined, bright to deep green foliage with good fall color. Zones 3 to 8.

HOW TO USE

'Schneekoppe' has a low-growing, bushy habit, growing just 3 to 4 feet tall and wide. Set out in groups of three or more, it makes an attractive mass planting, low hedge, or edging. Or tuck individual bushes into beds, borders, and foundation plantings to add months of color from the flowers and fruits. Diseases usually don't bother 'Schneekoppe'.

'Rotesmeer' ('Purple Pavement'; Baum, 1986) is similar but has deep magenta-pink flowers. You may also see it listed as 'Rotes Meer', but that name properly belongs to another rose.

🌿 'Sea Foam'

Shrub. Schwartz, 1964.

The American Rose Society classifies 'Sea Foam' as a shrub rose, but this charming rose actually grows as either a climber or as a ground cover, depending on how you train it. Pink-blushed, pointed buds open to display double, 2½-inch rosettes that are white to cream colored to palest pink, depending on weather conditions. (Cool conditions seem to bring out more of the pink tints.) The clustered flowers don't have much fragrance, but they make up for that lack by appearing in glorious abundance in midspring, followed by excellent repeat bloom through the rest of the growing season. Long, trailing, thorny canes bear glossy, deep green leaves. Zones 4 to 9.

HOW TO USE

Left unsupported, 'Sea Foam' forms a handsome, spreading mound that's 2 to 4 feet tall and 3 to 8 feet or more across. Allow it to cascade down a slope or spill over a low wall, or grow it in groups of three or more to create an eye-catching mass planting. Given the support of a fence or pillar,

'Sea Foam' can reach 8 to 12 feet in height. Black spot can be a problem in some areas; otherwise, disease resistance is usually excellent.

🦋'Secret'

Syn. HILaroma
Hybrid tea. Tracy, 1992.

Anyone who says that modern roses lack fragrance hasn't stopped to smell this powerfully perfumed hybrid tea rose! Long, tapered buds spiral open to reveal double, high-centered flowers that are 4 to 6 inches across, with ivory to palest pink petals blushed with pink around the edges. Usually held singly on long stems, the flowers are graced with an exceptional spicy-sweet-fruity fragrance, and they appear over a long season — from late spring or early summer with generous repeat into fall. Moderately thorny, well-branched canes carry semiglossy, medium to deep green foliage. Zones 5 to 9.

HOW TO USE
'Secret' has a bushy, upright habit, growing 3 to 5 feet tall and 2 to 3 feet across. It's a must-have for the cutting garden: one bloom can scent an entire room! 'Secret' also is beautiful in beds and borders, particularly when planted in groups of three or more to create a bushier effect. Wet weather can lead to spotting on the petals, and black spot can be a problem if you don't take preventive measures; otherwise, disease resistance is generally good.

All-America Rose Selection 1994

🦋'Sexy Rexy'

Syns. 'Heckenzauber'; MACrexy
Floribunda. McGredy, 1984.

What an attention-grabbing name for such a demure pink floribunda! Pointed, deep pink buds open to reveal very double, cupped to rosette-like, medium to light pink blooms that are about 3 inches in diameter. The scent is only mild, but you can hardly complain about that when you see the generous clusters of flowers that appear repeatedly over a long season from late spring or early summer well into fall. Thorny, well-branched stems carry glossy, light to medium green leaves. Zones 5 to 9.

HOW TO USE

'Sexy Rexy' forms an upright to rounded bush that generally grows 3 to 5 feet tall and about as wide. This handsome, free-flowering selection fits easily into many parts of the landscape, including beds, borders, foundation plantings, and containers. Combine it with white- or pastel-colored companions for a soft look, or create more drama by pairing it with deep purple foliage: perhaps a backdrop of purple smoke bush (such as *Cotinus coggygria* 'Royal Purple') or an underplanting of a purple-leaved heuchera such as 'Plum Pudding'. With its abundance of blooms produced on strong, straight stems, 'Sexy Rexy' is also a wonderful addition to a cutting garden. Regular deadheading helps promote the best rebloom. Disease resistance is normally very good, but it can be prone to black spot if you don't take preventive measures.

🌿 'Sharifa Asma'

Syn. AUSreef
Shrub. Austin, 1995.

The delicately shaded flowers and compact habit of this English rose may catch your eye, but it's the fragrance that will win your heart. Plump, pink buds blushed with red open into very double, cupped blooms that expand into 3- to 4-inch rosettes. Each flower is full of swirled, soft pink petals touched with yellow at the base; as they age, the outer petals often fade to ivory, especially in hot weather. The richly perfumed, clustered blooms first appear in a generous display in late spring or early summer, followed by additional flushes of flowers through the rest of the growing season. Somewhat arching, thorny stems carry dark green, semiglossy leaves. Zones 5 to 9.

HOW TO USE

'Sharifa Asma' has an upright, bushy habit, normally growing 3 to 5 feet tall and 3 to 4 feet across. It's marvelous in a bed, border, or cottage garden, especially when paired with soft-colored companions such as *Dianthus* 'Bath's Pink', catmints (*Nepeta* spp.), and lavenders, or with silvery foliage such as southernwood *(Artemisia abrotanum)* and lamb's ears *(Stachys byzantina)*. Both black spot and powdery mildew can be a problem if you don't take preventive measures, but in most areas, this rose shows good to excellent disease resistance.

❦ 'Sheila's Perfume'

Syn. HARsherry
Floribunda. Sheridan, 1982.

Beautiful blooms and wonderful perfume: two great reasons to try this delightful floribunda. Egg-shaped, yellow buds blushed with pink unfurl to display semidouble to double, high-centered blooms about 3½ inches across. The edges of each yellow petal are brushed with varying amounts of deep pink to cherry red, with the most distinct contrast in cool conditions. Held singly or in clusters, the flowers are normally quite fragrant, although some gardeners describe the scent as slight to moderate. Expect the show to start in late spring or early summer, with good repeat bloom through the rest of the summer and into fall. Upright, thorny stems bear shiny, deep green leaves. Zones 5 to 10.

HOW TO USE

'Sheila's Perfume' produces a bushy, rounded to somewhat spreading shrub that's 2 to 4 feet tall and 2 to 3 feet wide. Enjoy it in beds, borders, foundation plantings, and large containers. It is striking when planted in groups of three or more as a mass or hedge. Don't forget to include one in your cutting garden, as well! 'Sheila's Perfume' generally has good disease resistance.

❦ 'Showbiz'

Syns. 'Bernhard Daneke Rose', 'Ingrid Weibull'; TANweieke
Floribunda. Tantau, 1983.

This compact floribunda may be short in stature, but it's big on floral impact! Pointed, deep red buds open into semidouble to double, broadly cupped, 3-inch blooms composed of brilliant scarlet petals surrounding a crown of golden stamens. Held in large clusters, the long-lasting flowers have little or no fragrance, but they appear in abundance. Expect a splendid show in late spring to early summer and again in fall, with good repeat bloom in between. Deep green, glossy leaves are borne on thorny stems. Zones 5 to 9.

HOW TO USE

'Showbiz' forms a low, rounded bush that's normally 2 to 4 feet tall and 2 to 3 feet across. Its compact habit makes it easy to tuck into beds, borders, foundation plantings, and even containers. Create a dramatic display by combining it with other eye-catching flowers, such as orange narrow-leaved zinnias (*Zinnia angustifolia* 'Profusion Orange') or a compact Mexican sunflower (*Tithonia rotundifolia* 'Fiesta del Sol'), along with green-flowered tobacco plant (*Nicotiana* 'Lime Green'). A few gardeners report problems with black spot, but most find this rose to be quite healthy and trouble-free.

All-America Rose Selection 1985

❦ 'Silver Jubilee'

Hybrid tea. Cocker, 1978.

If the softly shaded blooms of this hybrid tea catch your eye, you're not alone: it's a favorite with many gardeners, and with flower arrangers, too! Tapered, reddish pink buds unfurl to display double, high-centered blooms that are normally 3 to 4 inches across, although they can be larger if you pinch out the center bud in each cluster. The flowers are a complex blend of peach and pink, with darker shades on the undersides of the petals. The scent is slight. 'Silver Jubilee' blooms abundantly starting in late spring to early summer, with good repeat bloom through the rest of the growing season. Thorny canes bear glossy, medium green leaves. Zones 5 to 9.

HOW TO USE
'Silver Jubilee' produces an upright bush that's generally 3 to 4 feet tall and 2 to 3 feet across. It puts on a glorious display in a bed or border, particularly when planted in groups of three or more to create a drift of color. It also makes an attractive, compact, informal hedge. Include at least one in your cutting garden, as well. 'Silver Jubilee' normally isn't seriously bothered by diseases.

❦ 'Simplex'

Miniature. Moore, 1961.

The simple flowers of this miniature rose offer the dainty charm of a wild rose on a relatively petite plant. Pointed, peach-colored buds pop open to reveal single, flat flowers just 1 to 1½ inches across. Five white petals that are tinged with pink in cool conditions surround a crown of showy golden stamens. The clustered blooms don't offer much in the way of fragrance, but they compensate for that lack by flowering freely from late spring to fall. Well-branched stems bear glossy, medium green foliage. Zones 6 to 10.

HOW TO USE

'Simplex' has a bushy, mounded habit, growing just 12 to 18 inches tall and about as wide. This mini is marvelous as an edging plant for a path or walkway, or around a deck or patio. It also looks great in groups of three or more in a bed, border, or foundation planting. Tuck a few into containers, too, so that it's easier to admire the delicate blooms. 'Simplex' generally exhibits excellent disease resistance.

✸ 'Simplicity'

Syn. JACink
Floribunda. Warriner, 1978.

'Simplicity' is officially classified as a floribunda, but you'll often see it sold as a "hedge rose," based on its suggested use in the landscape. Long, pointed buds open into semidouble, loosely cupped flowers that are 3 to 4 inches across, with medium to light pink petals surrounding a crown of yellow stamens. Fragrance is minimal at best, but the bush normally blooms abundantly from late spring or early summer into fall. Lightly thorny stems bear dark green, semiglossy leaves. Zones 5 to 9.

HOW TO USE

'Simplicity' has a very upright bushy habit, normally growing 4 to 6 feet tall and 2½ to 4 feet across. It's perhaps not the best choice for a high-visibility area, such as along a path or near the house; there are many other roses with more shapely blooms and fragrance to boot. Where this rose really can shine, however, is out in the landscape: next to a fence, for instance, or along the back of a border, where you can enjoy the colorful effect from a distance. Set it out in groups of three or more to get the best effect. Disease resistance is generally good, but take preventive measures against black spot if this problem is common in your area.

Several other colors are available in this series, including 'Purple Simplicity' (reddish magenta), 'Red Simplicity' (scarlet), 'White Simplicity' (white), and 'Yellow Simplicity' (golden yellow). Apart from the color, all are similar to the original.

❦ 'Singin' in the Rain'

Syns. 'Love's Spring', 'Spek's Centennial'; MACivy
Floribunda. McGredy, 1994.

If you're looking for something different than the usual red, pink, and white roses, consider trying the sunset-shaded blooms of this intriguing floribunda. Pointed buds open into double, high-centered blooms that are 2 to 3 inches across. The colors can vary quite a bit, depending on the weather, but are somewhere between soft copper and pink to peachy gold and coppery orange. The blooms usually have a moderate sweet or musky scent, and they appear from late spring or early summer with good repeat bloom into fall. Lightly to moderately thorny, well-branched canes carry glossy, deep green foliage. Zones 5 to 10.

HOW TO USE

'Singin' in the Rain' forms a bushy, rather rounded shrub that's 3 to 6 feet tall and about as wide. Its unique coloring adds a touch of interest to beds and borders, particularly when paired with yellows or with purples and blues. Its long-stemmed blooms make it a great choice for a cutting garden, too. Gardeners in warm climates appreciate the way the flowers hold their form even in hot weather. 'Singin' in the Rain' generally offers very good disease resistance.

All-America Rose Selection 1995

❦ 'Sir Thomas Lipton'

Hybrid rugosa. Van Fleet, 1900.

This hybrid rugosa may be too vigorous for most small gardens, but if you're looking for an easy-care rose to create a dense, thorny, barrier planting, 'Sir Thomas Lipton' could be a good option for you. Pointed buds open into semidouble to double, cupped flowers about 3½ inches across, with creamy white petals and yellow stamens. Held singly or in clusters, the intensely perfumed blooms create a splendid display in mid- to late spring, followed by sporadic rebloom through the rest of the summer. (Deadheading can help encourage better repeat flowering.) Very thorny stems carry dark green, semiglossy leaves with attractive fall color. Zones 4 to 8.

HOW TO USE

'Sir Thomas Lipton' forms a bushy, upright to spreading shrub. It can range in size from 4 to 8 feet tall, with a similar spread. Before you choose a planting site, try to find an established bush growing in conditions similar to yours to see what size you can expect. This rugged rose makes a handsome hedge or screen with multiseason interest, especially in difficult sites with less than ideal soil, or in seaside gardens. Black spot has been reported in some areas, but disease resistance is generally good overall.

❦ 'Snow Bride'

Syn. 'Snowbride'
Miniature. Jolly, 1982.

Long a favorite with exhibitors, this charming miniature is also a pretty addition to the garden. Small, pointed, ivory buds open into double blooms that look like perfect hybrid tea flowers scaled down to just 1½ to 2½ inches across. Usually produced singly, the mildly fragrant flowers are cream-colored to white, often with a light yellow tint near the center. They begin blooming in late spring, with good repeat bloom through the rest of the growing season. Branching stems bear semiglossy, medium to dark green leaves. Zones 5 to 10.

HOW TO USE

'Snow Bride' has a bushy, upright habit, forming a compact bush that's 1 to 2 feet tall and 10 to 18 inches across. Its long-lasting, beautifully formed blooms make it a great choice for a cutting garden, but it's also cute in beds, borders, and containers. Try it with an underplanting of sweet alyssum (*Lobularia maritima*) to echo the rose's white flowers while adding fragrance. 'Snow Bride' can be prone to powdery mildew if you don't take preventive measures; otherwise, disease resistance is generally good.

ARS Award of Excellence for Miniature Roses 1983

❦'Snow Carpet'

Syns. 'Blanche Neige'; MACcarpe
Miniature. McGredy, 1980.

'Snow Carpet' is classified by the American Rose Society as a miniature, but you'll most often see it sold as a ground-cover rose, due to its low, spreading habit. Tiny, pointed buds pop open to reveal very double, white pompon-shaped blooms that are just ¾ inch across. Their scent is slight at best, but they appear over a long period, generally from late spring or early summer well into fall. Slender, trailing stems carry semiglossy, light to medium green leaves. Zones 5 to 10.

HOW TO USE

'Snow Carpet' forms a low, sprawling mound that's just 6 to 12 inches tall but 2 to 4 feet across. This spreading habit makes it ideal for covering quite a bit of space. Use it in groups of three or more as a ground cover in a low-maintenance area, allow it cascade down a slope, or site it to spill over a low wall. 'Snow Carpet' can be a little too vigorous for delicate companions, but if you choose equally sturdy partners such as daylilies (*Hemerocallis* spp.), catmints (*Nepeta* spp.), and sages (*Salvia* spp.), it looks great weaving among other plants in a mixed border. Disease resistance is generally good.

❦'Snow Pavement' See 'Schneekoppe'

❦'Sombreuil'

Climbing tea. Robert, 1850.

There seems to be some confusion about the true identity of the rose currently sold under this name as a climbing tea; some suggest it is actually a more modern climber correctly known as 'Colonial White', or perhaps another rose altogether. Whatever the correct name, the commonly available 'Sombreuil' (pronounced something like *som-BRAY*) is a lovely garden rose. Short, ivory buds lightly tinged with pink (particularly in cool weather) open into very double, flat, petal-packed rosettes that are usually 3½ to 4½ inches in diameter. The tightly clustered flowers are pure white to creamy white, with a hint of palest pink or peach in the center in some conditions. Most gardeners describe the scent as strong, with somewhat spicy-fruity tones, though there are some who claim their plants have only mild fragrance. Expect a superb show of flowers in mid- to late spring and often again in fall. In between, bloom may be sporadic, but there are almost always at least a few flowers. Long, sturdy, thorny canes carry dark green, semiglossy leaves. Zones 6 to 10.

HOW TO USE

You'll most often see 'Sombreuil' used as an 8- to 15-foot climber. It's a delight trained on a post or against an arch, arbor, wall, fence, or trellis. If you have the room, you could also let 'Sombreuil' grow as a large, mounded shrub that can reach about 8 feet tall and wide over time. It may develop a bit of black spot if you don't take preventive measures, but otherwise 'Sombreuil' is seldom seriously bothered by diseases.

🌹 'Souvenir de la Malmaison'

Syn. 'Queen of Beauty and Fragrance'
Bourbon. Béluze, 1843.

While it does have a few drawbacks, this beautiful Bourbon is a favorite with many old-rose appreciators. Rounded, pink buds open into very double, 4- to 5-inch flowers that start out deeply cupped and open to a flat form, with many folded, pale pink petals that fade to creamy white as they age. Held singly or in clusters, the blooms release an intense, spicy-sweet perfume. Flowering begins in mid- to late spring; repeat bloom is generous in some areas and sporadic in others. (This rose is a favorite of many southern gardeners because it blooms well in the heat that tends to discourage hybrid teas from flowering.) Thorny stems bear glossy, medium to dark green foliage. Zones 6 to 9.

HOW TO USE

'Souvenir de la Malmaison' has a bushy, somewhat spreading habit. In most areas, it will grow 2 to 4 feet tall and about as wide, although some gardeners report bushes growing as much as 6 feet in height and spread. Rainy or humid weather can cause the outer petals of the buds to brown and shrink, preventing the flower from opening properly, a condition called balling. In warm, dry conditions, though, this rose is a lovely sight in beds, borders, and cottage gardens, particularly when planted in groups of three or more. It also makes a handsome hedge, and the blooms are great for cutting. Disease resistance is generally only moderate: black spot, powdery mildew, and rust can all be problems if you don't take preventive measures.

'Climbing Souvenir de la Malmaison' (Bennett, 1893) grows 8 to 12 feet tall; repeat bloom is variable.

ᴡ 'Sparrieshoop'

Shrub. Kordes, 1953.

The cheery flowers of this free-blooming shrub rose look just like gigantic apple blossoms, and they're pleasingly perfumed as well. Long, pointed buds open to reveal single, saucer-shaped to nearly flat flowers that are about 4 inches in diameter, with medium to light pink petals surrounding a light yellow to white eye and a crown of golden stamens. Held in large clusters, the blooms are generally graced with a moderate to strong scent, particularly noticeable in warm weather. Flowering starts with a superb display in mid- to late spring, followed by moderate to good repeat bloom until frost. Medium to deep green, glossy leaves are borne on arching, thorny stems. Zones 5 to 9.

HOW TO USE

Grown as a free-standing shrub, 'Sparrieshoop' has a bushy, rather mounded habit. Expect a height and spread of 4 to 5 feet in cool areas; in warmer areas, it can grow 6 to 10 feet tall and wide. Enjoy it alone as a landscape accent or pair it with perennials and other plants in a mixed border. 'Sparrieshoop' also looks great planted in groups as a mass, screen, or hedge. Trained on a support, it forms a 6- to 10-foot climber; try it on a trellis or along a fence. Apart from a touch of mildew in some areas, diseases usually don't seriously bother 'Sparrieshoop'.

ᴡ 'Spice Twice'

Syn. JACable
Hybrid tea. Zary, 1998.

Even gardeners who normally don't like orange roses are finding this handsome hybrid tea quite appealing. Pointed, cream buds blushed with pink or peach unfurl to reveal double, high-centered blooms that are 5 to 6 inches across, with coral-orange petals backed with creamy peach. The clustered flowers generally have a light, spicy scent. The bloom season begins in late spring to early summer, with moderate to good repeat through the rest of the summer into fall. Moderately thorny canes bear semiglossy, deep green leaves. Zones 5 to 10.

HOW TO USE

'Spice Twice' has an upright habit, growing anywhere from 4 to 7 feet tall and 2 to 4 feet wide. In beds and borders, it looks best planted in groups of three or more to create a bushier effect. The long-stemmed blooms make 'Spice Twice' a good choice for cutting as well. This rose normally offers very good disease resistance.

'Stanwell Perpetual'

Hybrid spinosissima. Lee, 1838.

Whether you're new to antique roses or have long enjoyed them in your garden, this hybrid spinosissima is a wonderful addition to your collection. Produced singly on short stems, the pointed, light pink buds open into double, flat, loose rosettes that are 3 to 4 inches across. Pale pink petals that age to white surround golden stamens visible only when the flower is fully expanded. While a few gardeners claim they detect only a slight scent, most describe the fragrance as strong and sweet. Expect a bountiful show of bloom in mid- to late spring; repeat flowering can range from sporadic to generous and continues until frost. Thorny, arching canes carry small, grayish green leaves that may be mottled with purple spots. Zones 4 to 8.

HOW TO USE

'Stanwell Perpetual' tends to form a somewhat irregular, spreading mound that's 3 to 5 feet tall and wide in the cooler parts of its range and 6 to 8 feet tall and wide in warmer climates. It can look charming in beds and borders, but be aware that it can produce many suckers when grown on its own roots (not grafted). This trait is actually a bonus if you use 'Stanwell Perpetual' to create an informal hedge or mass planting, or to cover a slope. It also looks good cascading out of a container or over a low wall. Diseases rarely bother this rose.

❦ 'Starina'

Syns. MEIgabi, MEIgali
Miniature. Meilland, 1965.

This eye-catching miniature has long been one of the most popular of its class, and with good reason: it's hard to beat the bright color and beautifully formed flowers. Tapered, orange buds unfurl to reveal double, high-centered, 2-inch flowers with a classic hybrid tea form, in a glowing shade of scarlet touched with orange or yellow at the base of the petals. Held singly or in clusters, the blooms have little or no scent, but they make up for that by appearing in abundance from late spring or early summer until heavy frost. Branching stems carry glossy, medium to deep green leaves. Zones 5 to 9.

HOW TO USE

'Starina' has a compact, bushy habit, growing 1 to 2 feet tall and about as wide. This versatile mini looks great in beds, borders, and foundation plantings, particularly when grown in groups of three or more to create a drift of color. Enjoy it as an edging for a path or walkway, or tuck it into containers. Add some to your cutting garden too; the bright blooms are super for small arrangements. 'Starina' generally offers good disease resistance.

Miniature Rose Hall of Fame 1999

❦ 'St. Patrick'

Syns. 'Limelight', 'Saint Patrick'; WEKamanda
Hybrid tea. Strickland, 1996.

Cool-climate gardeners may be disappointed in the color and lack of hardiness, but in the warm climates it favors, this remarkable hybrid tea has many fans. Pointed, chartreuse buds unfurl to reveal double, high-centered to rather cupped blooms that are 4 to 5 inches in diameter. In cool conditions, the flowers tend to be a rich golden yellow; heat normally brings out more of the greenish tint this rose is known for. You may also notice more greenish color in the late-season flowers. Usually produced singly, the slightly scented blooms begin in late spring to early summer, with quick repeat blooms through the rest of the growing season. Moderately thorny canes carry matte, grayish green leaves. Zones 6 to 10.

HOW TO USE

'St. Patrick' has an upright, bushy habit, growing 3 to 5 feet tall and 2 to 4 feet wide. Its long-stemmed, long-lasting, slow-to-open blooms make it practically a must-have for the cutting garden, but it also can look pretty in beds and borders. 'St. Patrick' normally offers moderate to good disease resistance.

All-America Rose Selection 1996

❦'Sun Flare'

Syns. 'Sunflare'; JACjem
Floribunda. Warriner, 1981.

A descendant of the equally excellent floribunda 'Sunsprite', 'Sun Flare' is a spectacular addition to any landscape. Clustered, pointed buds open into double, 4-inch blooms with clear, medium yellow petals surrounding a crown of orange-gold stamens. Newly opened flowers have a high center, but they develop a loosely ruffled to nearly flat form as they age. Opinions vary on the fragrance: some say it is slight at best, while others claim it has an exceptional, licorice-like scent; most say the perfume is at least moderate. 'Sun Flare' produces a profuse flush of bloom in late spring to early summer, with generous repeat through the rest of the growing season. Thorny canes bear shiny, deep green foliage. Zones 5 to 10.

HOW TO USE

'Sun Flare' has a bushy, somewhat spreading habit. It generally grows 2 to 4 feet tall and about as wide, though long-established bushes can get larger. It's a winner in beds, borders, and foundation plantings, adding months of bright, easy-care color. 'Sun Flare' is especially nice grown in containers or raised beds, particularly near a bench, deck, patio, or other sitting area, so that you can enjoy the fragrance as well as the cheerful flowers. This rose may develop a touch of black spot if you don't take preventive measures, but otherwise it's normally quite disease resistant.

'Climbing Sun Flare' (BURyellow; Burks, 1989) is usually offered under the name 'Yellow Blaze'; it generally grows 10 to 14 feet in height.

All-America Rose Selection 1983

❦ 'Sun Sprinkles'

Syn. JAChal
Miniature. Walden, 1999.

The colorful, beautifully formed blooms of this award-winning miniature rose add months of interest to gardens of all sizes. Pointed, oval buds
open into double, deep yellow blooms, with the high-centered form of
hybrid tea roses scaled down to just 2 or 3 inches across. 'Sun Sprinkles' is
often described as having a moderate, spicy fragrance, but some gardeners say they detect little or no scent. Produced singly or in small clusters,
the flowers appear in abundance in late spring or early summer, usually
with good repeat bloom into fall. Moderately thorny canes carry glossy,
deep green leaves. Zones 5 to 10.

HOW TO USE

'Sun Sprinkles' has an upright, somewhat rounded habit. It generally
grows 18 to 24 inches tall and wide, but it may reach 3 feet tall and wide
over time. The profusion of glowing yellow blooms makes 'Sun Sprinkles'
a winner for brightening up beds, borders, foundation plantings, and
containers. It complements many color schemes, holding its own against
red and orange flowers and perking up pastel pink, lavender, and white
plantings. Disease resistance seems to be good in most areas.

*All-America Rose Selection 2001; ARS Award of Excellence for
Miniature Roses 2001*

❦ 'Sunsprite'

Syns. 'Friesia'; KORresia
Floribunda. Kordes, 1977.

'Sunsprite' is considered by many to be the best yellow-flowered floribunda, and some go so far as to describe it as one of the top-ten roses of
all time! Egg-shaped to oval, golden buds open to display double, loosely
ruffled, saucer-shaped to flat flowers about 3 inches across. The bright
yellow blooms are produced in clusters and offer an intense perfume that
some liken to that of licorice, while others say it is sweet or spicy-sweet.
Individual blooms open quickly, but they're produced in abundance over
a long season, from late spring or early summer until frost. Moderately
thorny canes carry shiny, deep green leaves. Zones 5 to 10.

HOW TO USE

'Sunsprite' produces an upright bush that generally grows 2 to 3 feet tall and about as wide, through it can reach 4 to 5 feet tall and 3 to 4 feet wide in some areas. It's splendid in beds, borders, and foundation plantings, particularly when paired with purple or blue-flowered companions, such as balloon flower *(Platycodon grandiflorus),* bellflowers (*Campanula* spp.), or edging lobelia *(Lobelia erinus).* 'Sunsprite' also looks great when grown in groups of three or more to create a mass planting, hedge, or an edging for a path, patio, or deck. Disease resistance is generally excellent, but some areas may see a touch of rust or black spot.

James Alexander Gamble Fragrance Award 1979

☙ 'Sweet Chariot'

Syns. 'Insolite'; MORchari
Miniature. Moore, 1984.

This exceptional miniature is a must-have if you enjoy growing fragrant flowers. Oval, magenta to pink buds open into double, 1-inch blooms that start with a pompon-like form and mature to nearly flat to display golden stamens. The flowers are normally in shades of purple and pink, though some nearly white blooms may appear in the same cluster. The individual flowers are small, but they're graced with a surprisingly strong old-rose scent that can carry for some distance. Expect an abundance of bloom beginning in late spring to early summer, with excellent repeat bloom through the rest of the summer and into fall. Trailing, moderately thorny stems bear tiny, matte, medium green leaves. Zones 5 to 10.

HOW TO USE

'Sweet Chariot' forms a rounded to somewhat sprawling mound that's 1 to 3 feet tall and about as wide. It's often recommended for a hanging basket, but it also shows off its cascading habit well when grown in a planter, at the edge of a raised bed, or atop a low wall — wherever you'll be around to enjoy the wonderful fragrance. It looks good in beds and borders, too, especially when grown in groups of three or more. Disease resistance is generally good.

❦ 'Sweet Revenge'

Syn. TINrevenge
Miniature. Bennett, 1996.

The unusual cantaloupe color of this pretty miniature makes it a striking addition to the garden. Tapered, orange buds open into double, high-centered blooms that look like hybrid tea flowers scaled down to just 1½ inches across, with a soft peachy orange center and deeper orange outer petals. Borne singly or in small clusters on long stems, the lightly fragrant flowers first appear in late spring to early summer, with good repeat through the rest of the growing season. Dark green, semiglossy leaves are carried on slender stems with few but long and sharp thorns. Zones 6 to 10.

HOW TO USE

'Sweet Revenge' has a bushy, upright to slightly spreading habit, usually reaching 2 to 3 feet tall and about as wide. Enjoy it in beds, borders, and foundation plantings. It looks particularly striking combined with purple-leaved companions, such as purple basil (perhaps 'Purple Ruffles' or 'Red Rubin') or a dark-leaved heuchera ('Plum Pudding' and 'Chocolate Ruffles' are just two of the many available). 'Sweet Revenge' generally isn't bothered by diseases.

❦ 'Taboo'

Syns. 'Barkarole', 'Grand Chateau'; TANelorak
Hybrid tea. Evers & Tantau, 1993.

While it's definitely not a truly black rose, this magnificent hybrid tea is about the closest thing you can get. Pointed, nearly black buds open into double, high-centered blooms usually 3 to 4 inches across, with broad, velvety petals. Usually produced singly on long stems, the flowers are a glowing medium to deep red in the center and deep maroon to near black on the outer edges. Opinions differ regarding the fragrance — mild, moderate, or strong — and it can vary even on the same bush, perhaps as a result of weather conditions or the age of the bloom. Expect good rebloom from late spring or early summer until fall. Moderately thorny stems bear glossy, deep green leaves. Zones 5 to 9.

HOW TO USE

'Taboo' has an upright habit, usually growing 4 to 6 feet tall and 2 to 3 feet across. The flowers are fabulous, but the form of the bush often leaves something to be desired: it tends to produce somewhat lopsided growth. Planting in groups of three or more can help create a bushier effect in a bed or border. It's practically a must-have for a cutting garden, as well, where the growth habit won't matter. 'Taboo' generally has good disease resistance, but powdery mildew can be a problem if you don't take preventive measures.

🌹 'Tamora'

Syn. AUStamora
Shrub. Austin, 1983.

This superb English rose is a great choice for warm-climate gardeners looking for full-bodied flowers on a compact bush. Plump, red-blushed peach buds open to display very double, cupped to rosette-like flowers usually 3 to 4 inches in diameter. The rich, peach-colored petals are tinted with varying amounts of pink and honey gold. The fragrance is generally described as strong and myrrhlike; many find it pleasing but others find it somewhat unpleasant. It's a good idea to take a test sniff before you buy to make your own evaluation. Flowering starts in late spring to early summer, with good to excellent repeat bloom through the rest of the growing season. Semiglossy, dark green leaves are carried on thorny canes. Zones 5 to 10.

HOW TO USE

'Tamora' produces a somewhat spreading bush that's 2 to 4 feet tall and about as wide. Its compact size makes it an excellent choice for a bed or border, where it looks wonderful with a variety of partners. Try pairing it with purple sage (*Salvia officinalis* 'Purpurascens') or a purple-leaved heuchera. Yellow or purple flowers also make handsome companions. 'Tamora' usually isn't seriously bothered by diseases.

✿ 'Tausendschön'

Syn. 'Thousand Beauties'
Hybrid multiflora. Schmidt, 1906.

Why should you consider growing this once-blooming hybrid multiflora when there are many repeat-flowering climbers to choose from? Its nearly thornless stems make training a snap, and the short but splendid bloom display is definitely worth waiting for! Pointed, pink buds open into double, cupped to saucer-shaped, ruffled blooms about 3 inches across. New flowers are medium to deep rose-pink with a white eye, aging to creamy pink and then white. They're held in large clusters that can contain all three colors at one time. The slightly scented blooms appear in one glorious display per year, lasting several weeks in late spring or early summer. Glossy, rich green leaves are carried on canes that have few or no thorns. Zones 4 to 9.

HOW TO USE
You'll most often see 'Tausendschön' trained as a climber, where it can grow 8 to 12 feet tall. It's a good choice for an arbor or arch in a high-traffic area, where a thornier rose could snag passersby. It also shows off well on a pillar. Consider combining it with a clematis to provide interest later in the season as well. You could also let 'Tausendschön' grow unsupported to form a sprawling ground cover. Powdery mildew can be a slight problem in some areas; otherwise, expect good disease resistance.

✿ 'The Dark Lady'

Syn. AUSbloom
Shrub. Austin, 1994.

It usually takes cool temperatures to bring out the deep color that this rose's name refers to, but even in warmer temperatures, 'The Dark Lady' is a beautiful sight. Plump but pointed, dark red buds open to display very double, 3- to 5-inch flowers that are cupped to nearly rounded with a loose central "button." Each bloom is full of swirled petals that are most often a rich magenta-pink, although they can be a luxurious deep red during the cooler days of fall. Usually held in small clusters, the flowers are graced with a moderate to strong perfume, which some liken to an old-rose scent and others say is sweet or spicy. Branching, moderately thorny stems bear matte, deep green leaves. Zones 5 to 10.

HOW TO USE

'The Dark Lady' produces a bushy, spreading shrub that's usually 3 to 5 feet tall and 4 to 6 feet across. Enjoy it in beds and borders, where it looks particularly pretty combined with silver-leaved partners, such as Artemisia 'Powis Castle' or southernwood (A. abrotanum). To get the full effect of the flowers, though, try to site 'The Dark Lady' on a gentle slope or in a raised bed. The heavy flowers tend to nod a bit, and they may weigh down the main canes, so siting the bush on rising ground will let you admire them more easily. Intense summer sun can cause the flowers to "burn" (discolor), so choose a site with light afternoon shade if you live in a warm climate. Disease resistance is generally good, although powdery mildew may appear if you don't take preventive measures.

🌱 'The Fairy'

Syns. 'Fairy', 'Feerie'
Polyantha. Bentall, 1932.

It's difficult to say enough good things abut this charming little polyantha! It has just about everything you could want in a rose, with the exception of fragrance. But when you consider its compact habit, abundant blooms, and excellent disease resistance, the lack of scent seems a small price to pay. 'The Fairy' produces rounded, dark pink buds that open to ruffled, cupped rosettes that are just 1 to 1½ inches in diameter, in a light rosy pink that ages to near white in strong sun. The individual blooms may be small, but they're held in large clusters that make quite a show. Flowering usually begins in early summer (a bit earlier in warm climates, a little later in cool areas) and continues freely through the rest of the summer into fall. Trailing, very thorny stems carry an abundant covering of small, shiny, bright green leaves. Zones 4 to 9.

HOW TO USE

'The Fairy' has a low, spreading habit, generally just 2 to 3 feet in height but stretching 3 to 6 feet in width. Its low growth and long flowering season make it a splendid choice for a mixed border; it also looks great in masses as a landscape accent or a low hedge. Use it to edge a deck or patio or to add months of easy-care color to a foundation planting. Its arching stems also show off to advantage when planted atop a low wall, on a gentle slope, or in a container. This excellent rose rarely has disease problems, and it can even tolerate a bit of shade.

❦ 'The Herbalist'

Syns. 'Herbalist'; AUSsemi
Shrub. Austin, 1994.

This charming shrub rose may not have the petal-packed blooms produced by many other English roses, but it has a simple beauty all its own. 'The Herbalist' produces tapered, deep pink buds that open to reveal semidouble, saucer-shaped flowers that are each 2 to 2½ inches across, with a cluster of showy golden stamens in the center. New blooms are deep rose-pink, gradually turning light rose-pink as they age. Blooms of all color stages are visible at any given time during the flowering season. They have little fragrance, but they're produced in abundance starting in late spring or early summer, with good repeat continuing into fall. Moderately thorny stems bear semiglossy, medium green leaves. Zones 5 to 9.

HOW TO USE

'The Herbalist' has a bushy, rather spreading habit, creating a tidy shrub that's generally 3 to 4 feet tall and about as wide. Tuck it into a cottage garden, or enjoy it in a mixed border. It blends beautifully with perennials and herbs, particularly those with white, pink, blue, or yellow flowers, as well as with silver- or purple-leaved plants. It also makes a charming informal hedge. 'The Herbalist' generally has good disease resistance.

❦ 'The Prince'

Syn. AUSvelvet
Shrub. Austin, 1993.

Opinions on the garden value of this English rose vary widely, but most agree that it's worth growing if only for the richly hued blooms. Plump, rounded, maroon buds open into very double, deeply cupped to rosette-form, 3-inch flowers filled with folded petals. New blooms tend to be magenta-red in the heat of summer, developing the best deep red color in fall: as they age, they darken to deep purple. Some gardeners report the fragrance is light to moderate, while others rave about the intoxicating perfume. Expect the first flush of bloom in late spring or early summer, with additional flushes through the rest of the growing season. Thorny stems carry deep green, slightly glossy foliage. Zones 5 to 9.

HOW TO USE

'The Prince' forms a compact, rather upright bush, growing 2 to 3 feet tall and wide in cooler climates and 3 to 4 feet tall and wide in warmer areas. Strong, hot sun can cause the petals to "burn" (discolor), so a little afternoon shade is desirable in southern gardens. 'The Prince' looks great in beds and borders, especially when paired with silvery-leaved plants. It also makes a handsome container plant or a handsome low hedge. Disease resistance is generally moderate; black spot, mildew, and rust can all be a problem if you don't take preventive measures.

✿ 'Thérèse Bugnet'

Hybrid rugosa. Bugnet, 1950.

This easy-care, free-flowering hybrid rugosa has found a home in gardens across the country, but it's a special favorite of cold-climate gardeners for its excellent cold tolerance. 'Thérèse Bugnet' (pronounced *tair-EZ boon-YAY*) produces long, reddish pink buds that open into semidouble to double, saucer-shaped, ruffled flowers about 4 inches across. New blooms are medium to deep rosy pink, softening to a medium to light lilac-pink as they age. Held in small clusters, the flowers usually have a moderate to strong, spicy scent, although there are a few gardeners who can't detect much fragrance at all. Expect a glorious bloom display in late spring or early summer, followed by sporadic to good repeat bloom in summer and often another flush in fall. Some red hips may appear in fall. Narrow grayish green leaves turn purplish or reddish (or sometimes yellow-orange) in fall; they're carried on arching stems that are thorny at the base and smooth on the upper half. Zones 2 to 8.

HOW TO USE

'Thérèse Bugnet' forms an upright, rounded or vase-shaped shrub that's 5 to 7 feet tall and 4 to 7 feet wide. It makes a great informal hedge or screen. It's also beautiful at the back of a border, but be aware that own-root (nongrafted) plants tend to spread by suckers. Disease resistance is generally good, but mildew can be problem if you don't take preventive measures.

❦ 'Tiffany'

Hybrid tea. Lindquist, 1954.

This classic hybrid tea has been around for half a century and it's still a favorite with many gardeners, thanks to its beautiful blooms and exceptional fragrance. Long, pointed, deep pink buds unfurl to reveal double, high-centered, 4- to 5-inch flowers with rosy pink petals that are touched with yellow at the base. Held singly or in clusters on long stems, the blooms exude a rich perfume that some say is fruity and others describe as old rose. Flowers appear freely over a long season, from late spring or early summer into fall. Thorny canes carry semiglossy, deep green leaves. Zones 4 to 9.

HOW TO USE

'Tiffany' forms an upright bush that's 3 to 5 feet tall and 2 to 4 feet across. Enjoy its elegant flowers in beds and borders, especially in areas where you can get close enough to sniff the superb fragrance. It's also a good choice for the cutting garden. Disease resistance is generally good, but it's wise to take preventive measures against powdery mildew.

All-America Rose Selection 1955; James Alexander Gamble Fragrance Medal 1962

❦ 'Touch of Class'

Syns. 'Marachal Le Clerc', 'Maréchal le Clerc'; KRIcarlo
Hybrid tea. Kriloff, 1984.

Exhibitors have prized this hybrid tea's exquisitely formed flowers for years, and now gardeners are beginning to appreciate it too. Elegant, tapered, reddish coral buds unfurl to display double, high-centered flowers that are 4 to 5½ inches across, with creamy pink petals that are brushed with coral, particularly around the outer edges. The scent is normally slight at best. Mostly held singly on long stems, the flowers appear in a generous flush in late spring or early summer, followed by good to excellent rebloom through the rest of summer and into fall. Moderately thorny canes carry deep green, semiglossy leaves. Zones 5 to 10.

HOW TO USE

'Touch of Class' has a bushy, upright habit, usually growing 4 to 6 feet tall and 3 to 4 feet across. It's a must-have for the cutting garden, where it provides a wealth of beautiful blooms for bouquets and arrangements. It can also look good in beds and borders, particularly when grown in groups of three or more to produce a drift of color. Disease resistance is generally good, but take preventive measures against powdery mildew if this fungal disease is a common problem in your area.

All-America Rose Selection 1986

❦ 'Toulouse Lautrec'

Syn. MEIrevolt
Hybrid tea. Meilland, 1992.

'Toulouse Lautrec' is officially classified as a hybrid tea, but when you see the full, ruffled blooms of this rose in the Romantica Series, you may just mistake it for an old garden rose. Tapered buds open into fully double, saucer-shaped to nearly flat flowers that are 3 to 4 inches in diameter. New blooms are a clear lemon-yellow; as they spread out to reveal the greenish yellow center, the outer petals age to creamy yellow. Most gardeners say the scent is moderate to strong, and some liken the fragrance to that of lemons. Usually held singly, the flowers first appear in late spring to early summer, with moderate to good repeat through the rest of the growing season. Thorny canes carry medium green, semiglossy to glossy leaves. Zones 4 to 9.

HOW TO USE

'Toulouse Lautrec' forms an upright to rounded bush, growing anywhere from 3 to 6 feet tall and about as wide. It's a beautiful addition to beds and borders, where it blends well with a variety of other colors. For a charming contrast, combine it with blue- or purple-flowered plants, such as balloon flowers *(Platycodon grandiflorus)* or mealy-cup sage *(Salvia farinacea),* or with purple-leaved companions. It also looks great with the blue-green foliage and greenish yellow flowers of rue *(Ruta graveolens).* 'Toulouse Lautrec' generally has good disease resistance.

❦ 'Tournament of Roses'

Syns. 'Berkeley', 'Poesie'; JACient
Grandiflora. Warriner, 1988.

This free-flowering grandiflora is an excellent addition to just about any landscape. Held singly or in clusters, the pointed, deep pink buds open into double, high-centered blooms that are about 4 inches across. The color ranges from coral pink to salmon pink, usually with deeper-colored centers and petal backs and lighter shades on the outer petals. There is little or no fragrance. 'Tournament of Roses' flowers generously from late spring or early summer into fall. Thorny canes carry semiglossy to glossy, dark green foliage. Zones 5 to 9.

HOW TO USE

'Tournament of Roses' forms an upright, shrubby bush that's usually 4 to 5 feet tall and 3 to 4 feet across, through it can be as compact as 2 feet or as tall as 6 feet, depending on where it's growing. Enjoy it in beds and borders, as a free-flowering hedge, or in a mass planting for a handsome landscape accent. The long-stemmed, long-lasting blooms also make this rose a great candidate for the cutting garden. Disease resistance is generally good.

All-America Rose Selection 1989

❦ 'Tradescant'

Syn. AUSdir
Shrub. Austin, 1994.

If you love deeply hued, petal-packed blooms, this handsome English rose is worth a look! Clusters of plump, maroon buds develop into very double, 2½- to 3½-inch blooms. They start out cupped and open into nearly flat rosettes filled with folded, deep burgundy red to purple-red petals. The fragrance ranges from moderate to strong; most describe it as sweet, though some liken it to an old-rose perfume. Flowering starts in late spring or early summer and continues with good repeat into fall. Moderately thorny, arching canes carry semiglossy, medium green leaves. Zones 5 to 9.

HOW TO USE

'Tradescant' forms a spreading shrub that can vary widely in size. In the cooler parts of its range, it tends to stay fairly compact, generally growing 3 to 5 feet tall and about as wide. In warm climates, though, it can get much larger: 6 to 8 feet tall as a shrub or 8 to 10 feet tall when trained on a pillar or fence. Used as a shrub, it's stunning near the middle or at the back of a border; combine it with pink or white flowers (perhaps the snowy blooms of 'Iceberg' rose), silvery foliage such as that of *Artemisia* 'Powis Castle', or the bright green blooms of *Nicotiana langsdorfii* or *N. alata* 'Lime Green'. Disease resistance is mostly moderate; both black spot and rust can occur if you don't take preventive measures.

❦ 'Tropicana'

Syns. 'Super Star'; TANorstar
Hybrid tea. Tantau, 1960.

You either like it or you don't — very few gardeners are on the fence regarding this top-selling hybrid tea! Large, tapered, orange buds spiral open to reveal double, 4- to 5-inch flowers that start out with high centers and develop into a cupped form. Some refer to the color as shocking orange or neon orange, while others more kindly describe it as coral-tinted orange. Reports also vary regarding its fragrance: most agree it is rather fruity, but the intensity can range from slight to strong. It's definitely a good idea to find a bush of 'Tropicana' in bloom before you buy so that you can judge the color and scent for yourself. Held singly or in clusters, the flowers begin blooming in late spring or early summer, with good repeat through the rest of the season. Moderately thorny canes carry glossy, deep green leaves. Zones 5 to 9.

HOW TO USE

'Tropicana' forms a tall, upright bush that's normally 4 to 6 feet tall and 2 to 3 feet across. The overall outline is often somewhat uneven, so in a bed or border, consider planting it in groups of three or more to create a more even, bushy effect. 'Tropicana' really shines in the cutting garden, where it will produce a generous amount of long-lasting flowers on long, straight stems. In some areas, this rose is healthy and vigorous, but it can be quite susceptible to black spot or mildew in others, so consider taking preventive measures against these diseases.

All-America Rose Selection 1963

❧ 'Trumpeter'

Syn. MACtrum
Floribunda. McGredy, 1977.

Looking for knock-your-socks-off color on a compact, trouble-free rose?
This fabulous floribunda belongs on your list of roses to consider! Oval
buds open to display double, ruffled-looking, cupped blooms that are 2½
to 3½ inches across, with blazing scarlet petals. Held singly or in clusters,
the long-lasting flowers have little fragrance, but they appear in abundance for months, from late spring or early summer well into fall. Moderately thorny, well-branched canes carry shiny, medium to deep green
foliage. Zones 5 to 10.

HOW TO USE

'Trumpeter' has a compact, bushy habit, usually growing 2 to 4 feet tall
and about as wide. Use it to add zip to beds and borders, or grow it in
groups of three or more as a mass planting to create a can't-miss landscape accent. This versatile rose can also adapt to life in a large container.
'Trumpeter' generally offers excellent disease resistance.

❧ 'Tuscany'

Syn. 'The Old Velvet Rose'
Hybrid gallica. Introduced sometime before 1867.

The velvety flowers of this hybrid gallica have earned it a place in gardens
for hundreds of years, and it's still a lovely sight during its relatively short
but still stunning bloom season. Plump buds open into semidouble,
loosely cupped to nearly flat flowers that are about 3½ inches across. The
petals can vary in color from deep red to deep purple and sometimes
even deep magenta, forming a rich contrast to the crown of showy golden
stamens. Some gardeners can detect only a mild fragrance, while others
praise the moderate to strong scent. 'Tuscany' flowers for several weeks,
usually starting in early summer, followed by orange hips that ripen in
fall. Matte, medium green leaves are carried on bristly stems that bear few
true thorns. Zones 4 to 8.

HOW TO USE

'Tuscany' forms a rather rounded shrub, generally growing 3 to 5 feet tall
and about as wide. It's excellent as an informal, compact hedge, and it can

adapt to life in a large container. It also looks lovely in a border or cottage garden setting, but be aware that it can produce many suckers unless you start with a grafted bush and keep the graft union above the soil line when you plant. Black spot may be a slight problem in some areas; otherwise, 'Tuscany' usually isn't seriously bothered by disease.

'Tuscany Superb' (also known as 'Superb Tuscan' or 'Superb Tuscany') is likely a seedling of 'Tuscany'. They are similar, but 'Tuscany Superb' tends to be somewhat more vigorous, with larger leaves and more petals, which somewhat hide the golden stamens. Many feel this selection is superior to the original, but others prefer the more distinct color contrast in the flowers of 'Tuscany'.

'Ultimate Pleasure'

Syn. TINpleasure
Miniature. Bennett, 1999.

This aptly named miniature rose is indeed a pleasure, both in the garden and in small arrangements. Tiny, tapered buds spiral open to reveal double, high-centered blooms like perfect hybrid tea flowers scaled down to just 1 inch across, with light pink petals that are a slightly darker shade on the undersides. Held singly or in small clusters, the lightly to moderately fragrant flowers first appear in late spring to early summer, followed by good repeat bloom through the rest of the summer and into fall. Moderately thorny stems bear medium green, semiglossy leaves. Zones 5 to 10.

HOW TO USE

'Ultimate Pleasure' has a vigorous, upright habit. The bush is rather larger than you might expect from a mini: it can easily reach 2 to 3 feet tall and about as wide. It's a charming addition to any flower bed or border, and it looks lovely in a foundation planting or a large container. Combine it with soft yellows and blues or lavender for a delicate effect (silvery foliage makes a great partner, too), or enjoy it as a complement to red and white flowers. Try it in front of hybrid tea roses to hide the "bare ankles" of the taller bushes. 'Ultimate Pleasure' usually offers excellent disease resistance.

❦ 'Vanity'

Hybrid musk. Pemberton, 1920.

Most hybrid musk roses tend to bloom in delicate pastel shades, but not 'Vanity'; it can make quite a spectacle of itself! Pointed, reddish pink buds open into single to semidouble, flat flowers that are 3 to 3½ inches in diameter, with bright rose-pink petals accented with a white eye and crowned with yellow stamens. The clustered blooms are graced with a delightful, moderate to strong, rather sweet perfume. Flowering starts in late spring, followed by nearly continuous rebloom through the rest of the growing season. Large orange hips ripen among the flowers in fall and persist into winter. Strong, arching canes are somewhat sparsely clad in glossy, deep green foliage. Zones 5 to 9.

HOW TO USE

'Vanity' is a vigorous rose that adapts well to life as either a shrub or a climber. As a free-standing shrub, it can grow anywhere from 4 to 8 feet tall and wide, with a loose, somewhat sprawling form. Planting 'Vanity' in groups of three or more produces a more even, bushy clump that makes a handsome landscape accent or back-of-the-border display. If your space is somewhat limited, try training it onto a pillar or against a fence. Like other hybrid musks, this one can tolerate light shade. The flowers are delightful for cutting. 'Vanity' generally has good to excellent disease resistance.

❦ 'Variegata di Bologna'

Bourbon. Bonfiglio, 1909.

The spectacularly striped, fragrant flowers of this distinctive Bourbon rose make it a favorite with many gardeners — and many non-gardeners, as well! Plump, rounded buds open to reveal fully double, cupped to nearly rounded blooms that are 3 to 4 inches across, with creamy white to palest pink petals dramatically streaked with purplish red. The clustered flowers carry a moderate to rich scent. Expect a splendid display of blooms for several weeks, starting in late spring or early summer. In some areas in some years, you may also see a few later flowers. Upright-arching stems bear matte, light green leaves. Zones 5 to 9.

HOW TO USE

Left unsupported, 'Variegata di Bologna' forms a somewhat sprawling shrub that is generally 5 to 8 feet tall and wide. It also makes an interesting 8- to 10-foot climber; try it on a pillar or against a fence or trellis. Light shade can encourage the best color contrast in the flowers, especially in warm climates. In humid or rainy weather, the flowers may not open properly, a condition called balling; black spot and powdery mildew may also attack if you don't take preventive measures. Lovers of this rose feel it's worth giving some extra attention to soil care and disease control in return for the splendid flowers.

❦ 'Veilchenblau'

Syns. 'Blue Rambler', 'Blue Rosalie', 'Violet Blue'
Hybrid multiflora. Schmidt, 1909.

Though not a truly blue rose, this hybrid multiflora does offer a beautiful display of unusually colored blooms. Small, reddish purple buds open into semidouble, cupped to flat flowers that are 1 to 2 inches across. They are usually violet-purple when new, aging through various shades of lavender-purple, and they're accented with a white eye and yellow stamens. The fragrance is usually moderate to strong, and most gardeners describe it as being fruity. In most areas of the country, 'Veilchenblau' produces just one splendid show a year, starting in late spring or early summer and lasting for several weeks. Arching, nearly thornless canes carry deep green leaves. Zones 5 to 9.

HOW TO USE

'Veilchenblau' is a vigorous rose that's most often used as a climber, normally growing 10 to 20 feet in height. Its smooth stems make it a pleasure to train on a pillar or arch or against a wall, fence, or trellis, especially in sites where a thorny rose could snag people who pass by. It also looks wonderful scrambling up into a tree. 'Veilchenblau' tends to produce the best-colored blooms in light shade. Powdery mildew can be a problem if you don't take preventive measures; otherwise, disease resistance is generally good.

❧ 'Veterans' Honor'

Syns. 'City of Newcastle Bicentennary', 'Five-Roses Rose', 'Lady in Red'; JACopper
Hybrid tea. Zary, 1999.

This stunning hybrid tea hasn't been around for long, but it's already winning the praise of gardeners around the country. Elegant, tapered buds spiral open to reveal very large, double, high-centered blooms that are 5 to 6 inches across, with thick, velvety, blood-red petals. Most agree that the fragrance is only slight to moderate, although some gardeners describe it as strong; the scent is often likened to that of raspberries. Normally produced singly on long stems, the long-lasting flowers first appear in late spring to early summer, with good repeat bloom through the rest of the growing season. Semiglossy, deep green leaves are borne on moderately thorny canes. Zones 5 to 9.

HOW TO USE

'Veterans' Honor' forms a tall, upright bush, generally growing 4 to 5 feet tall and 2 to 3 feet across. It's suitable for the middle to back of a bed or border, where it pairs handsomely with pink and white flowers, or with silvery foliage. It looks particularly good planted in groups of three or more to create a drift of eye-catching color. Include at least one bush in your cutting garden so that you'll have plenty of flowers to bring indoors without denuding your garden display. Powdery mildew may be a problem if you don't take preventive measures; otherwise, 'Veterans' Honor' seems quite disease resistant.

❧ 'Voodoo'

Syn. AROmiclea
Hybrid tea. Christensen, 1984.

The sunset-shaded flowers of this handsome hybrid tea are a true delight! Large, pointed, golden orange buds open into double, high-centered blooms that are 4 to 6 inches in diameter. The petals are shaded with coral pink, peach, and yellow and are blushed with scarlet where touched by the sun. Most gardeners agree that the scent is moderate to strong, with sweet and/or fruity tones. Usually held singly on long stems, the flowers begin blooming in late spring to early summer, followed by good repeat bloom through the rest of the summer into fall. Thorny canes carry glossy, deep green leaves. Zones 5 to 10.

HOW TO USE

'Voodoo' forms a tall, upright bush, generally growing 4 to 6 feet tall and 2 to 3 feet across. Enjoy the intricately shaded blooms in beds and borders. The bushes look particularly good when grown in groups of three or more. Long-stemmed 'Voodoo' blooms are well suited for cutting, too. Disease resistance is normally good to excellent, although a bit of black spot may appear if you don't take preventive measures.

All-America Rose Selection 1986

❧ 'White Pet'

Syn. 'Little White Pet'
Polyantha. Henderson, 1879.

This compact charmer is actually a sport of a large hybrid sempervirens rose, but it's classified by the American Rose Society as a polyantha because it shares many of the traits of that class. Tiny, pointed, pink buds pop open to reveal double, 1-inch, pompon- to rosette-form flowers. The white blossoms may retain a light pink tinge on the outer petals, particularly in cool weather. Graced with a moderate to strong scent that some describe as musk and others describe as sweet, the large bloom clusters appear freely from late spring to frost. Arching to trailing stems carry glossy, deep green leaves. Zones 5 to 9.

HOW TO USE

'White Pet' forms a low, spreading mound that's 1 to 3 feet tall and about as wide. Its compact growth makes it an excellent choice for a container or a small garden, but it also has a lot to offer larger spaces, particularly when planted in groups of three or more. Enjoy its splendid display in beds, borders, and foundation plantings, or try it as a low hedge or edging around a deck or patio. Diseases generally don't bother 'White Pet'.

❧ 'William Baffin'

Hybrid kordesii. Svejda, 1983.

A pretty, care-free shrub or climber ideally suited to cold-climate gardens, this hybrid kordesii is part of the Canadian Explorer Series, a group of roses selected for their hardiness and disease resistance. Egg-shaped, dark pink buds open into semidouble to double, cupped to saucer-shaped blooms that are 3 to 4 inches across. Deep pink petals that may be marked with white are accented by a white eye and crowned with golden stamens. The scent is mild at best. 'William Baffin' blooms generously over a long season. Held in large clusters, the flowers appear in an impressive show that starts anytime from late spring to midsummer, depending on where you live. Expect sporadic to moderate rebloom after that, followed by another generous bloom display in fall. Upright to arching, thorny canes carry glossy, medium green leaves. Zones 3 to 9.

HOW TO USE

'William Baffin' can grow either as a large shrub or as a climber. Left unsupported, it can grow 5 to 8 feet tall and wide; it looks superb planted in masses as a landscape accent or as a hedge. The strong, thorny stems can make training a challenge, but it's worth the effort if you're looking for a hardy, nearly carefree, 8- to 12-foot climber for a cool climate. 'William Baffin' is rarely bothered by diseases.

'William Lobb'

Syn. 'Old Velvet Moss'
Moss. Laffay, 1855.

The beautifully shaded blooms of this moss rose have made it a favorite with gardeners for nearly 150 years, and it's still a lovely rose to grow if you have the space. Heavily mossed buds (they look like they're covered with many soft bristles) open into double, cupped blooms that are 3 to 4 inches across, with a crown of golden stamens in the center. The petals are usually a deep wine purple at first, with a lighter purplish pink on the undersides; they age through various shades of soft purple. The flowers release a moderate to strong old-rose perfume. (The "moss" is also fragrant, releasing a pine-like scent when you brush it.) 'William Lobb' produces one superb show of blooms, usually in late spring or early summer. Very thorny, arching canes carry matte, medium green leaves. Zones 4 to 9.

HOW TO USE

'William Lobb' normally produces a rather open, upright to spreading shrub that's 6 to 8 feet tall and 5 to 7 feet across. It does benefit from support, however, particularly during the bloom season. Try training it as an 8- to 12-foot climber on a fence, arbor, trellis or pillar; just make sure you wear sturdy leather gloves to protect your hands. Powdery mildew may be a problem if you don't take preventive measures; otherwise, 'William Lobb' normally has good disease resistance..

❦ 'Will Scarlet'

Hybrid musk. Hilling, 1948.

'Will Scarlet' is definitely brighter than most hybrid musks, adding months of eye-catching color from its flowers and fruits. Pointed, red buds open to display semidouble, cupped to nearly flat flowers that are 2 to 3 inches in diameter with a crown of golden stamens. The petals may appear scarlet in some conditions, but usually they are more on the cherry-red side, aging lighter. The slightly scented, clustered blooms appear in abundance in late spring to early summer, with excellent repeat continuing well into fall. Glossy, orange-red hips extend the season of interest into winter. Long, arching, thorny canes carry glossy, medium to deep green leaves. Zones 6 to 9.

HOW TO USE

Left unsupported, 'Will Scarlet' produces a large, bushy shrub that ranges in size from 5 to 8 feet tall and 4 to 7 feet across. Enjoy it as a landscape accent or as a large screen or informal hedge. It also adapts to training as a 10- to 12-foot climber; enjoy it on a fence, arbor, or large trellis. A touch of powdery mildew or black spot may appear if you don't take preventive measures; otherwise, diseases usually don't seriously bother 'Will Scarlet'.

❦ 'Winsome'

Syn. SAVawin
Miniature. Saville, 1984.

'Winsome' is a wonderful choice for adding cheerful color to your garden. This miniature rose produces small, pointed, reddish buds that open into double, high-centered blooms that are 1 to 1½ inches across, with purplish pink petals tinged with red, especially in cool weather. Yellow stamens are visible when the flowers are fully open. Fragrance is variable but usually slight. Held singly or in clusters, the flowers first appear in late spring, with generous repeat bloom through the rest of the growing season. Dark green, semiglossy leaves are carried on nearly smooth canes. Zones 5 to 9.

HOW TO USE

'Winsome' grows as a rounded bush that's normally 18 to 24 inches tall and about as wide, though it can get up to 3 feet tall and wide in very warm areas. Use it to add zip to pastel plantings in beds and borders, or enjoy it as an eye-catching edging along a path or around a deck or patio. It also grows well in containers. Disease resistance is generally good, although some black spot may occur if you don't take preventive measures.

ARS Award of Excellence for Miniature Roses 1985

✻ 'X-Rated'

Syn. TINx
Miniature. Bennett, 1993.

The demurely blushed blooms of this sweet miniature rose belie the reputation you might expect from its name! Tiny buds tinged with pink open to reveal double, high-centered blooms about 1½ inches across. The creamy white petals are lightly brushed with pink, coral, or salmon, especially on the outermost edges of the flower. (You'll notice the most distinct color contrast when the weather is cool.) Reports on its fragrance range from slight to strong. Usually borne singly on relatively long stems, the flowers normally first appear in late spring, with good repeat bloom through the rest of the growing season. Zones 5 to 10.

HOW TO USE

'X-Rated' forms a somewhat spreading bush that's usually 18 to 24 inches tall and about as wide. Enjoy its elegant blooms in beds, borders, foundation plantings, and containers, or as an edging around a deck or patio. 'X-Rated' can be susceptible to powdery mildew if you don't take preventive measures; otherwise, disease resistance is generally good.

✻ 'Yantai'

Syn. TINtai
Mini-flora. Bennett, 1989.

Now reclassified as a mini-flora, 'Yantai' still often appears in catalog descriptions as a miniature rose. Either way, it's worth seeking out if you enjoy softly shaded flowers. Small, egg-shaped buds unfurl slowly to reveal double, high-centered blooms up to 2 inches across, with light yellow petals that shade to deeper yellow at their base. Cool weather seems to intensify the colors a bit, while strong sun can pale them to near white. You may also notice a light blush of pink or peach near the tips of the petals, particularly in cool weather. The long-lasting flowers have a light to moderate, fruity fragrance, and they appear in abundance over a long season, from late spring into fall. Moderately thorny stems bear semiglossy, medium green leaves. Zones 5 to 10.

HOW TO USE
'Yantai' has a relatively tall, bushy, spreading habit, generally growing 18 to 30 inches tall and about as wide. Its soft colors blend beautifully with a wide range of companions in beds, borders, and containers. Try it with an underplanting of a white- or pink-flowered sweet alyssum (such as *Lobularia maritima* 'Carpet of Snow' or 'Rosie O'Day'), or create a handsome contrast by growing it with purple-blue balloon flower *(Platycodon grandiflorus)* or the soft purple leaves of purple sage *(Salvia officinalis* 'Purpurascens'). 'Yantai' is seldom bothered by diseases.

❦ 'Yolande d'Aragon'

Portland. Vibert, 1843.

The American Rose Society classifies 'Yolande d'Aragon' as a Portland, but you're likely to find it grouped with the hybrid perpetual roses in catalogs. By any name, however, this rose is indeed sweet, with plump, reddish pink buds that open into very double blooms about 3½ inches across. Filled with swirled petals that can range in color from rose-pink to purplish pink, the blooms form shallow, broad, flat-topped cups. The delightfully fragrant, clustered flowers appear in abundance in late spring to early summer, followed by sporadic to good repeat into fall. Very thorny canes carry matte to slightly glossy, medium green leaves. Zones 5 to 9.

HOW TO USE
'Yolande d'Aragon' forms an upright, moderate-size shrub that's usually 4 to 6 feet tall and 3 to 4 feet across. Use it to add a long season of interest to a mixed border or cottage garden setting. It looks especially lovely paired with silvery foliage, such as that of southernwood *(Artemisia abrotanum)* or the pink-and-white-flowered form of rose campion

(*Lychnis coronaria* 'Angel Blush'). You could also train 'Yolande d'Aragon' against a fence or trellis. Disease resistance is generally good, although both black spot and powdery mildew can appear if you don't take preventive measures.

'Yves Piaget'

Syns. 'Queen Adelaide', 'The Royal Brompton Rose'; MEIvildo
Hybrid tea. Meilland, 1985.

Large, full flowers give this hybrid tea rose in the Romantica Series a decidedly old-fashioned appearance. Plump, pointed, reddish buds open to reveal nearly rounded to deeply cupped, fully double blooms up to 6 inches across. Each exquisite flower is packed with wavy-edged petals that are normally a rich, deep pink, though they may show a lilac tinge in some conditions. Creamy stamens are visible in fully open flowers. Held on long, straight stems, the blooms are graced with a moderate to strong scent that's often described as sweet. Flowering starts in late spring to early summer, with good repeat bloom through the rest of the growing season. Medium to dark green, semiglossy leaves are carried on canes that bear few thorns. Zones 5 to 9.

HOW TO USE

'Yves Piaget' produces an upright bush that's generally 3 to 5 feet tall and 2½ to 4 feet wide. Use it to add a touch of old-fashioned charm to beds and borders, or site it near a bench, deck, patio, or other sitting area where you can enjoy the sight and scent of the gorgeous blooms. Disease resistance is good in most areas, but mildew may occur in particularly cool, damp conditions.

'Zéphirine Drouhin'

Bourbon. Bizot, 1868.

This beautiful Bourbon rose is one of the best-known climbers, and little wonder: its smooth stems, bright blooms, and pleasing fragrance make it a favorite with many gardeners. Long, pointed buds open into semidouble to double, loosely cupped flowers that are 3 to 4 inches across; raspberry sherbet–pink petals are touched with white at the base and accented with a crown of yellow stamens. Held singly or in clusters, the flowers have a moderate to intense, old-rose to somewhat fruity fragrance. 'Zéphirine Drouhin' generally produces a good flush of bloom in late spring or early summer and, in warm areas, another in fall; you may see occasional blooms in summer, depending on your climate. (Be aware that it may take several years for this rose to get established and bloom well.) Semiglossy, medium green leaves are carried on long canes that bear few or no thorns. Zones 6 to 9.

HOW TO USE

You'll most often see 'Zéphirine Drouhin' used as a climber. In the cooler parts of its range, it's normally about 8 feet tall; in warmer areas, it can stretch up to 15 feet in height. The smooth stems make it a pleasure to train on an arbor, arch, pillar, fence, or trellis — any structure where it can receive good air circulation around the leaves. Disease resistance is only moderate in most areas; rust, black spot, and powdery mildew may occur if you don't take preventive measures.

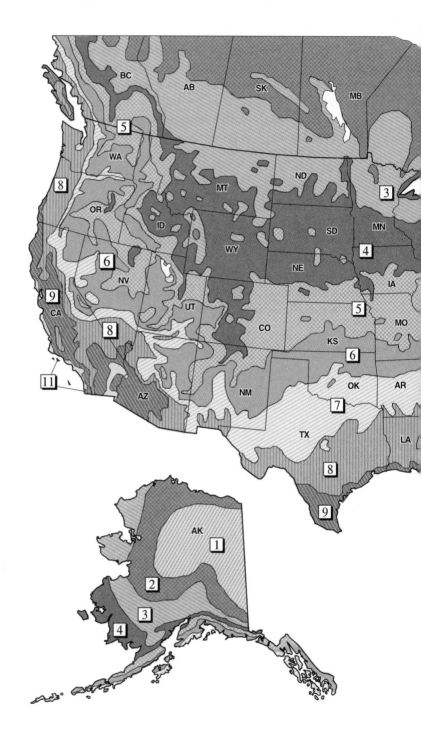

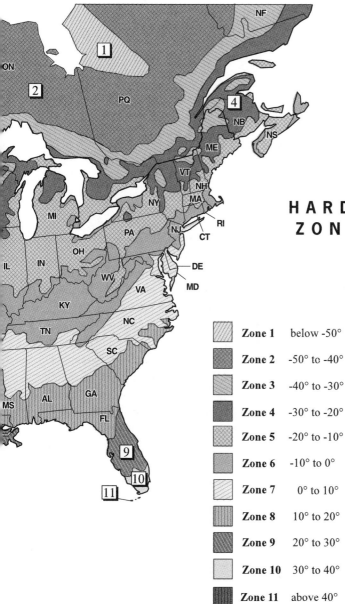

HARDINESS ZONE MAP

	Zone 1	below -50°
Zone 2	-50° to -40°
Zone 3	-40° to -30°
Zone 4	-30° to -20°
Zone 5	-20° to -10°
Zone 6	-10° to 0°
Zone 7	0° to 10°
Zone 8	10° to 20°
Zone 9	20° to 30°
Zone 10	30° to 40°
Zone 11	above 40°

✿ Photo Credits

RICH BAER: 18, 25, 27 top inset, 27 bottom, 28 bottom, 29 bottom, 29 bottom inset, 32 top, 33 top, 34 bottom, 37 bottom, 38 top, 38 bottom, 41 bottom, 45 top, 46 bottom, 50 top, 50 bottom, 60 bottom, 61 top, 73 top, 76 top, 80 top, 82 bottom, 88 bottom, 94 top, 95 top, 98 top, 99 bottom, 102 top, 104 top, 105 bottom, 109 top, 110 bottom, 111 top, 112 bottom, 113 bottom, 114 top, 115 bottom, 117 bottom, 118 bottom, 120 bottom, 121 bottom, 124 bottom, 125 top, 125 bottom, 131 top, 134 top, 134 bottom, 135 bottom, 139 top, 142 bottom, 143 top, 144 top, 147 bottom, 149 top, 154 top, 155 top, 155 bottom, 156 top, 157 bottom, 158 top, 163 bottom, 165 top, 166 top, 166 bottom, 167 top, 167 bottom, 170 bottom, 172 top, 173 top, 174 top, 177 bottom, 179 top, 180 top, 180 bottom, 184 top, 185 bottom, 186 top, 186 bottom, 189 bottom, 192 top, 195 bottom, 197 top, 197 bottom, 202 bottom, 206 top, 209 top, 215 top, 215 bottom, 216 top

THOMAS ELTZROTH: 14, 26 top, 27 bottom inset, 60 top, 106 bottom, 110 top, 117 top, 130 bottom, 137 bottom, 148 top, 153 top, 161 bottom, 181 top, 213 top

DEREK FELL: 26 bottom, 28 top, 29 top, 31 bottom, 35 top, 43 bottom, 44 bottom, 52 top left, 52 bottom, 55 bottom, 132 bottom, 140 bottom, 171 top, 175 top, 175 bottom, 202 top, 204 top, 206 bottom, 207 top, 211 bottom

MARGE GARFIELD: 29 top inset, 31 top, 51 bottom, 70 top

P. A. HARING: 12, 27 top, 30 top, 32 bottom, 33 bottom, 34 top, 35 bottom, 36 top, 36 bottom, 37 top, 39 top, 39 bottom, 40 top, 40 bottom, 41 top, 42 top, 42 bottom, 43 top, 44 top, 47 bottom, 48 top, 48 bottom, 49 top, 49 bottom, 51 top, 52 top right, 53 top, 53 bottom, 55 top, 56 top, 56 bottom, 57 top, 57 bottom, 58 top, 58 bottom, 59 top, 59 bottom, 62 top, 62 bottom, 63 bottom, 64 top, 64 bottom, 65 top, 65 bottom, 66 top,

66 bottom, 67 top, 67 bottom, 68 top, 68 bottom, 69 top, 69 bottom, 71 top, 71 bottom, 72 top, 72 bottom, 74 top, 74 bottom, 75 top, 75 bottom, 76 bottom, 77 top, 77 bottom, 78 bottom, 79 top, 79 bottom, 80 bottom, 81 top, 81 bottom, 82 top, 83 top, 83 bottom, 84 top, 84 bottom, 85 top, 85 bottom, 86 top, 86 bottom, 87 top, 87 bottom, 88 top, 89 top, 89 bottom, 90 bottom, 91 top, 91 bottom, 92 top, 92 bottom, 93 top, 93 bottom, 94 bottom, 95 bottom, 96 top, 96 bottom, 97 top, 97 bottom, 98 bottom, 99 top, 100 top, 100 bottom, 101 top, 101 bottom, 102 bottom, 103 top, 104 bottom, 105 top, 106 top, 107 top, 107 bottom, 108 top, 108 bottom, 109 bottom, 111 bottom, 112 top, 113 top, 114 bottom, 115 top, 116 top, 116 bottom, 118 top, 119 top, 119 bottom, 120 top, 122 top, 122 bottom, 123 top, 126 top, 126 bottom, 127 top, 127 bottom, 128 top, 128 bottom, 129 top, 129 bottom, 130 top, 131 bottom, 132 top, 133 top, 133 bottom, 135 top, 136 top, 136 bottom, 137 top, 138 top, 138 bottom, 139 bottom, 140 top, 141 top, 141 bottom, 142 top, 143 bottom, 145 top, 145 bottom, 146 top, 147 top, 148 bottom, 149 bottom, 150 top, 152 top, 152 bottom, 153 bottom, 154 bottom, 156 bottom, 157 top, 158 bottom, 159 bottom, 160 top, 160 bottom, 161 top, 162 top, 162 bottom, 163 top, 164 top, 164 bottom, 165 bottom, 168 top, 168 bottom, 169 top, 169 bottom, 170 top, 171 bottom, 173 bottom, 174 bottom, 176 top, 176 bottom, 177 top, 178 bottom, 181 bottom, 182 top, 182 bottom, 183 top, 183 bottom, 184 bottom, 185 top, 187 bottom, 188 top, 188 bottom, 189 top, 190 top, 190 bottom, 191 top, 191 bottom, 192 bottom, 193 top, 193 bottom, 194 top, 194 bottom, 195 top, 196 top, 198 bottom, 200 top, 201 top, 201 bottom, 203 top, 203 bottom, 204 bottom, 205 top, 205 bottom, 207 bottom, 208 top, 208 bottom, 209 bottom, 210 top, 210 bottom, 212 top, 212 bottom, 213 bottom, 214 top, 216 bottom, 217

SAXON HOLT: 30 bottom, 61 bottom, 179 bottom

STEVE JONES: 73 bottom, 90 top, 103 bottom, 144 bottom, 146 bottom, 196 bottom, 211 top

MIKE LOWE: 46 top, 54 top, 63 top, 70 bottom, 123 bottom, 124 top, 151 top, 159 top, 172 bottom, 178 top, 200 bottom

CHARLES MANN: ii–iii, vi–1

S. MCKESSAR AND C. TWEET OF WWW.JUSTOURPIC-TURES.COM: 45 bottom, 47 top, 54 bottom, 150 bottom, 151 bottom

NANCY ONDRA: 8, 10, 21, 78 top, 121 top, 214 bottom

TINY PETALS NURSERY: 187 top, 198 top, 199 top, 199 bottom

❧ Acknowledgments

Special thanks to Marilyn Wellan for sharing her vast experience and knowledge in her review of the Encyclopedia of Roses entries, to Sue O'Brien of Tiny Petals Nursery in her review of the miniature rose entries, and to Baxter Williams in his review of the plant list. Thanks also to Dr. Tommy Cairns and Peter Haring for answering my questions and sharing their opinions. I also owe a great big "thank you" to all of the participants in the Roses Forum (http://forums.gardenweb.com/forums/roses/) for being so generous in sharing their expertise on all aspects of growing and enjoying roses. You folks are the greatest! Last but not least, my love to Mom and Dad, and to my Sheltie companions, Guinevere and Princess.

ℜ Index

Page numbers in italics refer to illustrations.